THE HINDU TEMPLE

THE HINDU TEMPLE

Stella Kramrisch

Photographs by

Raymond Burnier

VOLUME TWO

MOTILAL BANARSIDASS PUBLISHERS
PRIVATE LIMITED • DELHI

First published by the University of Calcutta, 1946
Reprint: Delhi, 1976, 1980, 1986, 1991, 1996

ISBN: 81-208-0224-1 (Vol. II)
ISBN: 81-208-0222-5 (Set)

Also available at:

MOTILAL BANARSIDASS

41 U.A., Bungalow Road, Jawahar Nagar, Delhi 110 007
120 Royapettah High Road, Mylapore, Madras 600 004
16 St. Mark's Road, Bangalore 560 001
Ashok Rajpath, Patna 800 004
Chowk, Varanasi 221 001

PRINTED IN INDIA
BY JAINENDRA PRAKASH JAIN AT SHRI JAINENDRA PRESS,
A-45 NARAINA, PHASE I, NEW DELHI 110 028
AND PUBLISHED BY NARENDRA PRAKASH JAIN FOR
MOTILAL BANARSIDASS PUBLISHERS PRIVATE LIMITED,
BUNGALOW ROAD, DELHI 110 007

CONTENTS

VOLUME I

VOLUME II

CONTENTS

VIII

THE IMAGES OF THE TEMPLE

प्रकृतिर्विकृतिस्तस्य रूपेण परमात्मनः ।
अलक्ष्यं तस्य तद्रूपं प्रकृतिस्सा प्रकीर्तिता ॥
साकारा विकृतिर्ज्ञेया तस्य सर्वं जगत्स्मृतम् ।
पूजाध्यानादिकं कर्तुं साकारस्यैव शक्यते ॥

"The Supreme Spirit has two states of Form: the [one, the] Nature of the World (prakṛti) and [the other,] its transformation as appearance (vikṛti). Prakṛti is His invisible form. Vikṛti is the aspect (ākāra) in which He pervades the Universe. Worship and meditation can be performed in relation to His aspect (sākāra) only."

'Viṣṇudharmottara', III. ch. XLVI. 2-3.

अनामरूपिण्यचिन्त्ये चिन्त्ये वै विश्वरूपिणि ।
चिन्त्याऽचिन्त्यात्मिके देवि नारायणि नमोऽस्तुते ॥

"Nameless and Formless Thou art, O Thou Unknowable. All forms of the universe are Thine; thus Thou art known. Known and Unknowable, Goddess Nārāyaṇī, Obeisance."

'Devīmāhātmya', XI, 'Nārāyaṇīstuti'.

VIII

THE IMAGES OF THE TEMPLE

POSITION AND PROPORTION OF THE IMAGES OF THE GODS

The Hindu temple is a monument, whose outer surface consists of sculptures. The Maṇḍapas, the various halls, preceding the Prāsāda itself in which is contained the innermost sanctuary, the Garbhagṛha, are architecture in the accepted meaning. The Prāsāda itself however is almost completely a solid mass but for the Garbhagṛha, which is a small, dark, cubical chamber even in the largest temples. But for the main image or imageless symbol enshrined within, the walls of the Garbhagṛha, as a rule, are plain. The carvings cease at its door; there they confront the devotee for the last time as he approaches the innermost sanctuary; he may not himself, as in the temples of South India proceed further, the officiating priest performing the rites for him.

Thus when going to the temple (abhigamana) with speech, body and mind centred on the divinity whose presence is installed in the image or symbol, the devotee becomes part of the architecture of the Maṇḍapa whose interior he traverses, in which he also may pause and gaze at the images that confront him; images which are carved on the pillars, the capitals and on the ceiling; guiding him onwards to the main image or symbol in the Garbhagṛha, or upward to the dome and its central point.

While approaching (abhigamana) the innermost sanctuary and passing through the halls in front of it, the Bhakta is within the sacred architecture; together with the images he is enclosed in a dim, soothing atmosphere caressing the eye after the fierce light of the day outside. The atmosphere of the Maṇḍapa is charged not only with the scent of flowers, burning oil lamps, and the incense coming from the sanctuary, but is tense with the impact of the pillars and carvings.

This closeness of the carved images and the worshipper in one space is brought to its maximum in the inner ambulatory which, in the larger temples (sāndhāra), surrounds the Garbhagṛha. The rite of circumambulation (pradakṣiṇa) is more a communion by movement with the images stationed on the walls than a visual recognition of their identity and the perfection of their workmanship.

The rite of circumambulation however is also performed outside the temple, whether there be an enclosed inner ambulatory (sāndhāra) or not (nirandhāra). It is then that the Prāsāda is beheld in its full effect imparting a total exposition of its meaning.[1]

"The body (ākṛti) of the temple is Prakṛti" ('Agnipurāṇa', LXI. 25), it is in the likeness of the primordial substance of the manifested world, has its aim and purpose beyond it and is supported by it.

Viewed from the outside, the Prāsāda is a monument on whose multi-buttressed walls are displayed the images; above the walls and in continuation of the buttresses rises the superstructure whose sloping walls lead towards a point, the apex of the finial. The finial is raised above the body itself of the Prāsāda, placed as it is on the crown of the temple ('āmalaka', or 'harmya', the latter in South Indian temples).

The main display of the figure sculptures is on the perpendicular walls. (Pls. I, III, XLIII, LXXI). The temple has no façade; it faces the four directions. Its walls however are not four surfaces meeting at right angles. Each wall projects with a number of offsets, the main pier being in the centre. The buttresses vary in thickness; in the majority of temples built throughout India (except in the South) the offsets are moreover frequently superimposed resulting in a stepped, cross-shaped plan. Whereas the plain walls of the dark Garbhagṛha form a square in plan, the carved walls of the exterior of the temple, exposed to the light of the sun, the moon and the stars, form an indented plan. The plan of the centre of the temple, the square, is translated by its walls into a perimeter of variedly stepped and indented design which even may be 'star shaped'. The outside of the Prāsāda far from exhibiting carved surfaces only, itself has volume. It consists of the piers of varying thickness whose front and side walls have images and carvings; recesses, narrow vertical chases and steps hold shaded space, or darkness. The volume of the wall space of a Hindu temple forms a unity of relations in height, breadth and depth; in it are integrated space volumes. The texture of the walls is not only that of the stone of which they are built or of the plaster with which they may be overlaid; these lend a particular quality of the surface only to the closely built texture of the buttresses and offsets and their intervals which form space volumes and rhythms of graded light and darkness.

In this texture, the carved figures belong to the body of the wall and also to the spaces between, inasmuch as their own volume projects into the intervals; the carved figures, moreover, reach even further into space or else they are also more deeply part of the wall than are the outer or main surfaces of any offset. Niches are sunk in the main buttresses; there the chief images are placed, the Pārśva-

[1] Pradakṣiṇa in a Śaiva temple, is not performed by going round and round the temple as in temples of other gods, but from the Bull to Caṇḍa (whose image is stationed to the west of the Northern 'door' ; Ī.P. III. XII. 59) and back to Nandin, thence to the Somasūtra, the water chute, and back again to Nandin, thence to Caṇḍa and from there again to the Bull.

"Vṛṣaṃ caṇḍaṃ vṛṣaṃ caiva
Somasūtraṃ punarvṛṣaṃ
Caṇḍaṃ ca somasūtraṃ ca
Punaścaṇḍam punarvṛṣam".

Looking up from the Somasūtra, the devotee worships the flag on the Śikhara (I.A. IX. p. 149 ; re. Somasūtra or Praṇāla, see Part V, note 107 ; both the terms are used here to indicate the channel (aṃbumārga) and the chute.

devatās, the main aspects of the divinity whose image or symbol is enshrined in the Garbhagṛha. Placed within the body of the wall, within a niche or "massive door" (ghanadvāra) as it is called, on the co-ordinates of the Prāsāda these main images are nearer to their centre which is also that of the entire monument, the temple. The surrounding images (āvaraṇa-devatās) are however more exposed; carved, as they sometimes are, almost completely in the round, they are yet of one piece of stone with the surfaces in ressault and remain connected with them by the strut-like extensions of their modelled limbs at angles not meant for view.

The carved figures on the surface of the temple are thus at different distances from the centre. They are part of it, not only ritually and iconographically but also in their position in space. They appear projected from the centre through the thickness of the wall or they are embedded in it as it steps forth. The entire volume of buttresses and interspaces, the whole monument, is dynamically in a state of movement; its stages are marked by the relative depth of the surface "en ressault". A movement more powerful than that of any single figure propels, as it were, from the centre each single figure together with the wall to its position on the perimeter. The paradoxical name of the niche, Ghanadvāra, which means "massive door" expresses the coming forth of the image from and through the massive wall.

A movement from the centre propels, as it were, the walls of the temple with their interstices and carvings. The perimeter of the temple thus generally has the shape of a cross with recessed angles. From each of its walls or piers with their offsets, carved images project further into space. This ultimate progression too is embodied in the volume of the walls, bound as they are, in the horizontal, by bands of mouldings above and below the rows of images so that the single figures on their socles are held within space-zones parallel to the wall and in depth equal to the projecting bands of mouldings. This closely enmeshed dynamic mass, its impact coming from the centre, whence every figure derives its power and name, meets the gaze and movement of the devotee as he circumambulates it. Profile after profile meets his vision, each a fresh leaf in the book of revelation of which every temple is a copy. Effect and effectiveness of the Prāsāda are one to the eye, mind and realisation of the devotee.[2] In the rite of circumambulation he himself draws and becomes the outermost perimeter to the building; he 'com-prehends' it while walking round it; sees the images not from one side but covers them by his look, one at a time, during his approach and onward progress; while he identifies the image thereby evoking its name, the total power of the place which the image occupies is sent as it were into his presence from the centre of his devotion.

The sculptures on the outside of the Prāsāda are stationed around its body; and while they give an exposition of its meaning they are also its ornaments. By their sequence they form belts around the body (ākṛti) of the entire temple and its several projections. The latter often form part volumes of their own, massive monumental supports of miniature replicas of the whole temple, each with its own

[2] The usual position of the spectator in front of a relief or, from various angles and distances, if the sculpture is in the round, does not comprehend the effectiveness of the rite of circumambulating an extensive monument.

superstructure (śikhara; śṛṅga; Pl. III).[3] Thus the ultimate meaning of the temple is brought near to the devotee; at every turn he sees the figures on the walls forming the basis of an ascent[4] towards one high and central shape, the vase above the Āmalaka, the sacred vessel (kumbha) which is part of the finial and is placed "at the end of Prakṛti" ('Agnipurāṇa', CI .. 13), beyond the forms of the manifested world, in the deathless (amṛta) region.

In belts around the body of the temple, and in vertical sequences where one image is superimposed on the other, the figures are part of the space-body of which the outside of the monument, the Prāsāda, consists. They do not form groups except such as are unavoidable by their juxtaposition on symmetrical and repeated offsets and recesses. They do not enter into any 'composition' which would extend further than the single buttress or beyond the console on which the image is placed (Pls. III, XLIV, LXXI). If more than one figure are part of the image they are carved in front of a single surface, they are collateral, auxiliary to its meaning and complete its form. This is how the single images whether they consist of one, or of several figures in front of the single facets, or in their niches, have their own wholeness as works of art (Pls. III, VI, XV, XXX, LXXI). Over and above such perfection as these images or groups may have compositionally a further power is vested in them. They are not 'pillar figures' as those of the doorways of Gothic cathedrals; they do not function architecturally; the stress of weight and support is unknown to their constitution. No aspiration moreover draws them upward, for each has its place and this it occupies with effortless grace and exuberance of modelled form. The final sculptural integument of the temple is dynamically one with the monumental progression of its mass. From it the figures step forth with a driving power not altogether their own. While they are images they are at the same time the ultimate conclusion of that part of the wall to which they give its highest accent. Where however they turn towards the wall they illustrate their oneness with its intrinsic movement on which they lean as their support (Pls. XIX, XX).

It is thus from the centre that the dynamic movement of the mass of the temple proceeds in the main and intermediate directions showing forth as sculptured form in its ultimate levels of progression. Its multiple embodiments, the images, are bound together in the regularity of their horizontal sequence. It is reinforced, and assigned its own extensiveness in space, by the fillets and mouldings with their substantial projections and the deep bands of shadow which accompany them, above and below the rows of images. In addition, these horizontal ties are crossed over or making way for the dark shadows or the strong light, held according to season and hour, within the vertical chases and the salient and re-entering angles of the Prāsāda.

A deeply enmeshed net of light and darkness provides the frames to the buttresses with their rows of sculptures. In this reduction to a context of light and

[3] In South Indian temples the relatively flat offsets of the perpendicular walls are crowned each by a miniature chapel (kūṭa, koṣṭha, pañjara, etc.).

[4] The realm of images, excepting Drāviḍa temples, 'begins' on the superstructure from the Śukanāsā downwards; only on a higher level, above the Vedikā of the Śikhara, images once more face the eight directions.

darkness the innumerable and changing gradations of the shadows cast by and playing over the carvings receive monumental firmness (Pl. III). The indefinitely flexed and modulated bodies of the images, their rounded volumes, appear levelled to a considerable extent by the strong light; thus they do not dissolve the compact monument into almost innumerable carvings but keep its surfaces enlivened by rhythmical accents of line and shade, even in the strongest glare which would render a plain surface dead with too much light. Having come forth—ontologically from the centre of the dark sanctuary, the images in the light of the day are an exposition of its meaning, beneficent to eye and mind alike.

The dynamic expansiveness of the mass of the Prāsāda has its correspondence in the plan of the building in the shape of a cross with recessed angles or having an outline which results from a rotation of the square. The static perfection of the small square of the dark Garbhagṛha with its plain walls is translated into the body of the temple, the 'body of God', a likeness of the manifested universe and its primordial substance, Prakṛti. It has its effect by giving the fullest exposition of its meaning and forms to the devotee in the rite of circumambulation in which he himself becomes the outermost perimeter and limit of the monument in the centre.

Such an understanding of monumental form by the ritual encompassing movement is a realisation as much by the eye as within one's whole living person in motion. During this rite the bodily presence of the Bhakta expands and comprises the Prāsāda. While doing Pradakṣiṇa, the devotee is the perimeter of the temple and of its effectiveness; he comprehends its full extent. Prior to it however he had approached the sanctuary by the main entrance passing across the structural halls in front of it. During this approach (abhigamana) in the interior of the building, he was immersed in its space and exposed to the impact of the pillars and walls of the Maṇḍapa.[5] While he traverses the Maṇḍapa he is part of the flux of the whole interior towards the Garbhagṛha, in one direction, in its central part and its parallel 'aisles' which is brought about by the rhythmic sequence of spaces marked by the position of the pillars and their vertical structure. Thus acted upon and prepared, the devotee at last is confronted by the entrance of the Garbhagṛha which bids him halt; its door frame, an iconostasis in relief, is raised before him and separates him from the image, in the Garbhagṛha (Pls. LII, V).

In his approach he had been impressed by many impacts, himself part of the interior of the Maṇḍapa which he traversed in one direction drawn by, and leaving behind him, its pillared rhythms. Now his body is made to halt, and thus at rest, his eyes take in the presence of the image in the frame of the entrance. It is here that Indian sculpture is to be understood as relief in the widest sense.[6]

[5] The exterior of the Maṇḍapa is built and carved analogous to the exterior of the Prāsāda.

[6] The image in the Garbhagṛha is frequently modelled in the round in most of its parts; the back which is not meant to be seen is not worked out in detail. The image with the surrounding images of Āvaraṇa divinities is mostly carved in front of a slab; the latter is in a lower relief and is moreover frequently perforated along the contour of the main image. The form of the main image in the Garbhagṛha is an adaptation of sculpture, originally meant to be circumambulated, for the purpose of merely being looked at from the front.

Excepting the image, the doorways (dvāra), and free standing gates (toraṇā), etc., Indian sculpture is meant to be seen while passing around it. Door frames and Toraṇas are forms of

On the outside of the temple, each of the closely set images on the perpendicular wall facets, has to be dwelt upon by itself. For each is complete in its particular meaning and at its particular place. The main aspects, for example, of the God in the temple such as certain Avatārs, in a Viṣṇu temple; or the divinities most closely related to Śiva, if the temple is consecrated to him; or the images of the three great gods, Brahmā, Viṣṇu and Śiva, are placed in 'massive doors' in three of the cardinal points, whereas the entrance itself, generally facing East, frequently has a small image of the main divinity carved at the centre of the lintel.[7] It abounds also in other carvings[8] all linked up as one great composition. Over and above, it frames the main image in the Garbhagṛha.[9]

Facing the cardinal points are the 'doors' where the image of God shows forth. On the actual entrance especially, the small image on the lintel is similar in position to the image of Christ carved in the tympanum above the entrance and is akin to His words: "I am the Door".

Apart from the main images, in their niches, and indispensable to all temples are the images of the Aṣṭadikpālas, the Guardians of the Eight points of space, each in its correct location. The multitude of divine figures stationed between these two kinds of essential images, each on a facet and having a console of its own, are Nāgas, Śārdūlas, Apsarās, Surasundarīs, Mithunas, etc. (Pls. XLI, XL, XI, XXXIII), and certain specific images of the lesser gods.

Each such type of the 'surrounding divinities' is repeated in many variations of posture and movement on the walls of the temple; like the chorus in an Indian Yātrā performance announcing the particular passage of the play not once only, but by repetition in the four directions of space. Repetition and symmetrical response are the rule in the horizontal and also in the vertical; so that the mind of the devotee becomes moved afresh by the beauties of the Divine and its graces at each angle, assured of its boons and of fearlessness.[10] There is no scope for narration in the juxtaposition of these figures. Each is the form of an enduring state of being in which it is absorbed while its gestures give it an actuality by which the mind of the devotee becomes arrested and is made to dwell on the particular state thus quickened.

structural architecture and provide the ground for the display of reliefs. Their arrangement is closely allied to paintings such as are made even to-day on scrolls (paṭ, in Bengal; to be seen in vertical succession): these would have their carved correspondence on the jambs;—scrolls to be rolled and unrolled horizontally which were known to ancient India ('Mudrārākṣasa', I; 'Harṣacaritra', V; cf. Kramrisch, 'Viṣṇudharmottara', Pt. III. 2nd ed. p. 7; introduction) seem to have been the prototypes of the carvings of the yoke-shaped beams, ending as these do (Sāñcī, Stūpas I; III) with a carved spiral on either side suggestive of all the painted matter 'rolled up' and of which only the central part is exposed on the beam.

[7] Instead of the main image, that of Lakṣmī may occupy this place.

[8] Those of the River-goddesses, etc.; and of the Dvārapālas.

[9] This refers to a Prāsāda without Maṇḍapas.

Where one or several Maṇḍapas are attached to it, the entrance into the Garbhagṛha is at the far end, inside the axial sequence of the Maṇḍapas. The outer entrance to the temple, and which belongs to a Maṇḍapa, is either similar to the main entrance or it is an open 'arch' way (Khajuraho).

[10] The mudrās 'varada' and 'abhaya', convey the two latter meanings and are the indispensable gestures of a divine image.

In the images occupying the reveals or recesses on either side of an offset, as for example on most of the Khajuraho temples (Pls. XX, XIII), the relation is given form of the volume of the figure to its axis on the one hand and to the space which the image is made to fill on the other. But even though the image may not be so favourably placed as to display the complete possibilities of its plastic volume in space and yet being part of the dynamic mass of the temple, such figures as are carved with their backs to the wall, in front view, appear to have arrived on their consoles driven thither by the impact of the buttress behind them (Pl. XLIV). There, even though the image stands straight or is seated (Pl. VI) in rigid symmetry, its volume is yet disposed in dynamic balance around it; the chest of the standing figures curving forward, has its counter weight in the roundness of the hips so that these figures with their backs to the wall, seen as modelled volumes, seem to swing to and fro from their feet upwards in ever varying curves as if rebounding from renewed contacts with the wall and its compacted energy.

The figures seem to resile charged with energy from the surface which they touch,—and not only from that of the wall of the temple but from any surface, be it one of their own body, leg against leg as they cross over, or as the hip is touched by an arm, the back by a scarf, the arm is clasped by a bangle, the bosom by a garland of jewels. Tactile subtleties contribute their share to the effect of these sculptures. In ancient India the sense of touch was given a training and purpose of the highest order.

'Nyāsa' (placing, marking, assignment) is the ritual touching of various parts of the body commencing with the place of the heart and ending with the hands (aṅga-nyāsa). While a mantra, a sacred, rhythmic formula is recited it is thought of as being located in the heart, head, in the crown-lock, "three eyes", chest and in the hand.

While the Mūlamantra, the 'root-mantra', the rhythmic formula of the main divinity, is recited the devotee passes both his hands three or seven times over the whole body from the feet to the head and from the head to the feet (vyāpaka-nyāsa). The whole body and its parts, the hand and the fingers, from the thumb to each of the fingers (kara-nyāsa) and also each of their phalanges are touched and quickened thereby as living seats of God. Various parts of the body are thus assigned to different divinities.[11]

His body is made conscious to the devotee in his daily rites as the seat and place of God. This consciousness he wins by the rite of touching it at sensitive and vital parts.

Nyāsa however is not only performed to the living body of man, but also to that of the image of stone or wood, etc. ('Mahānirvāṇatantra' XIII. 289-91). As the body of the devotee so also is the body of the image touched in six places (ṣaḍaṅga nyāsa). The constituent elements of the world and its principles are assigned to it from the feet to the place of the heart, etc. By thus touching it ritually, it is felt alive with the breath of the cosmos.[12]

[11] 'Agnipurāṇa', XXV.

[12] 'Mahānirvāṇatantra', XIII. 293-297; the 8 groups of the letters of the alphabet are thus assigned; subsequently the constituent principles of the universe are assigned, beginning with Pṛthivī Tattva, the principle 'Earth', to the feet, etc.

Such rites performed daily and regularly cannot but have a lasting effect on those who practise them and those who, moreover, make the images on which they are performed.[13] The sense of touch becomes not only refined by practice but is a means of realisation and of knowledge. Endowed with so qualified a sense of touch, the craftsman produces the kind of sculpture which is so lavishly represented on the temples.

The smooth limbs of the images of the gods are always 16 years old; they are resilient with the sap of life and with breath. The latter makes them not only smooth and supple but also weightless in appearance despite their ample curves (Pl. LXXII).[14] They are particularly fit not only for dancing but also for flying, the many Gaṇas, Vidyādharas, etc., although they never have wings. Ends of garments flutter to enhance their movements and be a foil to their rhythms; whereas folded scarves clasp their fullness and are carved as if they were a special type of jewellery, accentuating through the contrast of their own shape and texture that of the modelled body.

Garments, jewellery and coiffure of the images are a selection and enhancement of those worn in the respective country where the temple was built. The preference of the sculptor however is for the bare body and he makes sparing use only of garments; worn in the shape of a 'dhotī', the cloth clings to the body and is recognisable, as a rule, only by such patterns as are engraved on the modelled shapes of the limbs (Pls. XVIII, XIX, XXIII, XXXIII); and by carving the hem of the cloth, petal-like (Pl. XXX) or as if it were one more ornament of the smooth limbs (Pls. XXI, LXII). Thus all forms of apparel accentuate and accompany the smooth roundness of the figures and their movement; only the headgear and coiffure are additional volumes of sculptural consequence; the high crowns (mukuṭa) of the greater gods, add height to the image (Pls. LXVII, LXX) whereas the chignons which the lesser gods and goddesses wear at the back of their heads add their globular or horn shaped bulges as required in each particular instance, to the balance or the linear composition of the image (Pls. XIX, XV, LX). Coronets, chaplets, diadems, matted hair, etc., add to the breadth or the height as required and to the adornment of the egg or globe shape of the head (Pls. XXXIII, XXXVIII, XL). Straight or aquiline but always powerfully salient noses are thus balanced (Pls. XVII, LXI).[15]

The single figures are always 'in movement' even when they appear to stand still; then even their movement is threefold. As part of the dynamic mass of the wall they share in its impact and appear driven forward; even when they are almost completely carved in the round they are steeped in the drive from the centre

[13] Vedic rites ('Śatapatha Brāhmaṇa', III. 2. 1. 5-6) had preceded the performance of Nyāsa on an image (pratimā).

[14] Adolescent appearance as well as Perfection are denoted by the number 16 (16 digits make the fullness, the totality of the moon) with reference to the images of the gods.

Supple, breath-borne weightlessness belongs also to images like those of the Tīrthaṅkaras whose iconography requires a rigid appearance ; even if, in addition, the quality of the sculpture is mediocre, as for example in the image on Pl. LVII.

[15] Most of the faces of Indian images having been damaged by the Muslim iconoclasts, the noses suffered most and only a few images carved in stone, and most of the metal images have escaped defacement.

of the temple. It carries them, sustains them in the most exacting contortions, bears them aloft when they are represented as flying and adds power, breadth and dignity to their stance when they stand firmly planted on both feet (samapādasthānaka). This erect stance with the weight of the body evenly distributed, right and left, is classified as 'samabhaṅga' or the even bend. It is the first variety in the classification of stances, they are classified in the surface, as the even bend, the slight bend (abhaṅga), the triple bend (tribhaṅga) and the excessive (triple) bend (atibhaṅga).[16]. Even the strictly motionless stance is understood as a particular phase of movement; it balances the body, which remains in tension. This classification leaves out of account the writhing in space of the sculptured form around its axis. The third kind of movement is that of the arms and hands, their gestures. These belong throughout to the class of 'schemata', the gestures expressing permanent states pertaining to the nature of divinity, which assures fearlessness and grants boons. When the hands of these divinities hold or brandish a weapon this action too is a permanent quality of their nature; they cut across ignorance, slay the demon, etc., and these actions are correspondingly expressed as their epithets.[17]

The carved figures are upheld in their being by the total monument, the walls of the temple with its progressive impact. To this movement, greater than their own and of which they are passive part, is added the movement of each figure with reference to its axis, turning and writhing around it if viewed in space, as sculpture (Pls. XIII, XIX), and bent variously towards it when viewed from the front, as image (Pls. XIX, etc., XVI, XIV). To the 'schemata' of the divinities of the higher hierarchies are added the movements of the lesser divinities whose 'mudrās' and 'hastas', the attitudes of their hands and arms, are 'schemata' and 'phorai' as well.[18] These attitudes and gestures moreover, while they represent the particular movement assigned to them, are part of the total rhythm of the body.

The gods represented by Indian sculpture belong to definite types for they body forth definite aspects of divine being; the peaceful (śānta), the terrific (ugra), etc. The iconographical physiognomy of the face is also that of the body; the body of the terrific image for example is inflated with divine fury as are the bulging eyes, etc. Typological iconography is a highly specified science;[19] it comprises the wide

[16] J. N. Banerjea, 'The Development of Hindu Iconography', p. 289, gives a good summary description of these stances.

[17] For example; Durgā Mahiṣāsura-mardinī; Durgā, the slayer of the Demon Mahiṣa; Śiva Tripurāntaka: the ender of Tripura.

[18] This distinction made by Plutarch is introduced here so as to differentiate with the help of an accepted Western terminology a kind of movement which is particular to all Indian images, though not to every Indian sculptural representation of figures. The gestures expressing movement and actions on the other hand are known under the term 'phorai'.

The hand holding a mirror, flower, or a weapon would show a movement of the class of 'schemata'; the hand arranging the hair, holding the hem of a garment which threatens to slip down, etc. to the class of 'phorai' though the latter category with regard to these sculptures tends to get merged in the former.

[19] The respective passages of the 'Viṣṇudharmottara' III. and the 'Īśānaśivagurudevapaddhati', III., at a distance from each other of several centuries are some of the large body of iconographic texts carefully followed by the sculptors; they contain specially vivid descriptions of the divine moods and their counterfeits by art; cf. also the Buddhist 'Sādhanamālā'.

range of emotions classified in 9 categories.[20] Combined and rarefied they are the substratum of the divine countenance while in its structure of ideal proportions ethnical traits are not forgotten which belong to the people in whose midst the images were made.

Innumerable degrees of bliss and august serenity are expressed in the faces of most of the celestials, the gods (Pls. VII-VIII, XXXVII, XXXVIII) and glendoveers (Pls. XXIV-XXVIII), and they are set off against the relatively few types in which 'terror', gleesome 'disgust', etc., are given shape on the basis of an inflated or emaciated appearance (Pls. XXIX, LIX). Where however 'the supernatural' is the main theme and horror and dignity accompany it the face of the animal, the Lion mask, is resorted to (Pl. L).[21] Its wide application and that of the less frequent "death-shapes" are the indispensable counterplayers to the eviternally beatific youth of the other gods.

Their radiance reflects the features of the people who worship them; they are differently proportioned in North India and in the South;[22] their countenance indeed varies in expression from one part of the country to the other and in each age according to the prevailing aptitude of the realisation of supreme bliss and peace. Irrespective however of these and other limiting conditions the many degrees in which beatitude shines forth from the face of the image are carried on unruffled expanses of modelling as delicate, taut and as non-human as are the shapes of flower-petals and ripe fruits. All these faces shine; they have a silent radiance of which the lips tell nothing nor do the eyes ever smile. No glance is cast, no thought communicated from between steady unwinking lids (divyadṛṣṭi)[23] where long eyes in full view sail across cheeks—though the face be shown in profile—; no sockets impede their course. High brows are raised in perennial wonderment. Strung bows, tendrils and antennae combine in their lines which are carved records of the vibrations and tensions of mind. Under their arches the eyes gaze into unknown distance without, and depth, within. They do not perceive, are not organs of sense, but a place of meeting of the outer and inner worlds. Such a place of exchange and contact however is also the whole smooth surface of the images. On it the light and air outside touches upon and is met with by the inner light, pulsation and breath.

This particular quality is not confined to any type or province of Indian temple sculpture. It arises from existence itself realising itself in an enduring recognition,

[20] The 'Samarāṅgaṇasūtradhāra', LXXXII, 2-3 speaks of 11 Rasas adding 'Preyas' and 'Pratyākṣa' (?) to the usual nine, i.e. 'śṛṅgāra' (erotic), 'hāsya' (laugh exciting), 'karuṇa' (pathetic), 'vīra' (heroic), 'raudra' (furious), 'bhayānaka' (fearful), 'bībhatsa' (loathsome), 'adbhuta' (supernatural) and 'śānta' (peaceful); 'Viṣṇudharmottara', III. XLIII. 1 f.

[21] See Ch. on the 'Kīrttimukha', the Face of Glory.

[22] According to the most ancient iconometrical injunctions ('Bṛhatsaṃhitā', LVII, l.c.) and thus shown by images of all ages.

[23] The above remarks on 'divyadṛṣṭi' and the way in which the eyes are shown in sculpture when giving form to divinities refer only to this special and widely represented branch of Indian art. In painting however the scope was great for showing the fleeting glances and facial expressions following all possible physiognomic reactions to psychological experiences and states. This can be seen in Ajaṇṭā, Bādāmī, Bāgh, etc. and read in the 'Viṣṇudharmottara', III. XXXVII; and in detail also in the 'Samarāṅgaṇasūtradhāra', LXXXII, dealing with 'Rasadṛṣṭilakṣaṇam'. In the next chapter of this compendium which deals with the "64 Hastas" the position and movement of the hands and fingers are described and related to those of the face and its parts and of the head.

an ever active memory, completely made conscious to itself. The place of this realisation is the body. The different physiognomical types particular to the different parts of India, are its substratum. The schools of Indian sculpture differ as much as the human types reflected in the images of the gods. The metaphysical realisation to which the images give shape requires the figure of man as reference; on becoming an image, made by art, in stone, etc., it is transformed and transubstantiated. The frame however, of this body made by art is measured according to the perfect proportion of the body of man.[24]

Navatāla or nine face lengths is the generally accepted rule concerning the height of the images of the gods.[25] One Tāla is subdivided into 12 aṅgulas.[26] Below are given, according to the 'Śukranītisāra' IV. 4, the proportions of images according to their relative height of the figures—up to the root of the hair on the forehead. The generally accepted proportion of nine Tālas being that of the gods, 8 Tālas would be that of the goddesses. Tālamāna, iconometry, however is not unanimous on this; according to the 'Vaikhānasāgama' XXV,[27] Daśatāla, "10 Face lengths" images are those of Brahmā, Viṣṇu and Śiva; their images belong to the highest of the 3 sub-varieties of Daśatāla proportion;[28] the Great Goddesses would conform in their proportion with the middle variety of the 10 Faces height. The respective proportion depends on the place which the god holds in the divine hierarchy; the 'Matsyapurāṇa' CCLIX. 1-2, moreover makes the proportion of the images correspond also to those of the types on which they are based. The image of Viṣṇu as Rāma or Varāha has 10 Face lengths, whereas it has 7 Face lengths only when it represents his Dwarf incarnation (Vāmana).

Indian iconometry knows of 9 main varieties of proportions of the images ranging from 1 Tāla to 10 Tālas, corresponding to the following total number of

[24] Cf. also the rule for the perfect proportion of the body of man, as well as of the Mahāpuruṣa (or the image of Buddha): the height from the soles of the feet up to the root of the hair on the forehead is equal to the width between the tips of the middle fingers when the arms are stretched horizontally (a fathom; Nyagrodha-parimaṇḍala).

[25] See also 'Pratimāmānalakṣaṇam' 85-86, transl. with notes by J. N. Banerjea, op. cit. p. 406.

[26] Proportionate measurement expressed in aṅgulas: 'Bṛhatsaṃhitā', ch. LVII; 4-5; 16-17; 'Viṣṇudharmottara' III. ch. XXXV; cf. also 'Mānasollāsa' III. ch. I. 200-205.

In usage, a Tāla—which means 'palm', i.e. the inner length of the hand including the fingers—is stated by the learned to be the (length of) the face; cf. 'Mānasollāsa' III. I. 196-7. The length is usually subdivided into 12 parts or 'aṅgulas'. Aṅgula, as a subdivision of Tāla, bears no direct reference to a 'finger's width' although it seems that originally the proportionate measurement of images had the aṅgula as its module and not the Tāla.

[27] In South Indian images the length of the face is however 14 aṅgulas. The Daśatāla or 10 Tāla proportion is discussed below, in this connection.

[28] Each 'proportion', Daśatāla, etc. is subdivided into 3 varieties, uttama, madhyama and adhama; the highest, the middle and the least. 120 aṅgulas being the mean height, 124 is the highest and 116 the least height of a Daśatāla image ('Vaikhānasāgama). The 'Bṛhatsaṃhitā', LXVIII, dividing the types of men according to their proportions into 5 classes, each 'nyagrodhaparimaṇḍala', assigns a height ranging from 96-108 aṅgulas (96, 99, 102, 105, 108) to the respective types of men. These would approximate to the Aṣṭa- and Nava-tāla types. Further sub-varieties are also known in South Indian Tālamāna; latitude in following the canons is given to the image maker, and this too is classified (see J. N. Banerjea, op. cit., p. 357).

aṅgulas successively : 12, 24, 48, 60, 72, 84, 96, 108 and 120. The series is built up by adding 1 Tāla or 12 aṅgulas throughout. The total height, in each of the 9 types of proportionate measurement, is distributed in 9 divisions, face, neck, etc. (see Chart), in close correspondence to the Navatāla or standard type of 108 aṅgulas. Out of the nine varieties, the 4 types from Saptatāla to Daśatāla have the widest currency.

VERTICAL PROPORTIONS OF 4 MAIN TYPES OF INDIAN IMAGES.

Type of Image	7 Tāla*	8 Tāla	9 Tāla	10 Tāla
Face	12†	12	12	13
Neck	3	4	4	5
Neck to the horizontal line connecting the nipples ("heart")	9	10	12	13
From these to the navel ("belly" ; udara)	9	10	12	13
Navel to genitals ("lower belly" ; vasti)	9	10	12	13
Thigh	18	21	24	26
Knee	3	4	4	5
Leg	18	21	24	26
Foot	3	4	4	5
				1
Total Height	84	96	108	120

* 1 Tāla=12 aṅgulas.
† The figures give the number of aṅgulas.

The rules are : The proportions of the trunk are the same in the 4 types ; the distance from the root of the neck to the genitals is divided into 3 equal parts, in each case ; neck—heart, heart—navel ; navel—genitals ; the thigh and the leg, throughout, are each twice as long. Of equal height, in each canon, are also neck, knee and foot. The actual lengths of these change ; the face however remains the same, *i.e.*, 12 aṅgulas throughout, but for the Daśatāla.

This last and highest standard is built up on the Navatāla, the purest in proportion (1 ; $\frac{1}{3}$; 1 ; 1 ; 1 ; 2 ; $\frac{1}{3}$; 2 ; $\frac{1}{3}$), by adding one aṅgula in each section ; thigh and leg being as usual twice the height of the "heart", etc. One aṅgula, moreover, is added to complete the number 120. By these artifices the highest type of proportionate measurement is constructed befitting the highest hierarchy of divine images. It approximates most closely the "sectio aurea" in the classical statuary of the West ; there the navel divides the total height of the figure—and of the perfect human body in this proportion.[29]

[29] The Nava-tāla and Daśa-tāla proportions represent also two out of the three canons of classical antiquity, the 'navatāla' being that of Vitruvius. The entire height of the figure as 9 face lengths is also laid down as the norm in Byzantine painting, in the 'Painter's Book from Mount Athos'.

The Tāla system, in the Sapta and Aṣṭa-tāla types, is relevant, with regard to the total height only. Their several proportions however are not regulated by it. The Tāla or face length is not the module of these images.[30] Their proportions are based on number, which is correlated to the main divisions of the body. The module is the aṅgula; the measures of the single division are its multiples. At the same time,—excluding the height of the face itself—the organic proportions of the Navatāla type are adhered to (see Chart). Thus the less generally valid, the less perfect proportions are admissible for images lower down in the hierarchy of the images; they are fit for dwarf and child incarnations.

In the general, the Navatāla type, the main proportions are worked out on the principle of organic differentiation similar to that of Byzantine art,[31] the only difference being that ⅓ 'Face length' is given in the Indian image to the knee, whereas in the Byzantine icon no height at all is provided for the knee and ⅓ 'Face length' is added as height of the skull. The Indian Navatāla image thus has relatively long legs and a relatively short trunk—the images of goddesses, having this proportion, especially those whose bodies sway and turn around their vertical axis in space, are seen with foreshortened trunks on pillar shaped legs. (Pls. XIII, XV).

Height, not included in the canon, is added above the line dividing the hair from the forehead. This is considerable. Most of the crowns of the Greater Gods surpass the height of their faces, and the head together with the crown forms one sculptural unit (Pls. VI, XVII, LIV, LXII, LXX); the—invariably crowned—images of the gods thus exceed the proportions of the body in its likeness to that of man.

The Indian system of proportionate measurement of the body of the image is based on number, organically correlated to the body of man and its main divisions, a face length being the module. From this system, laid down as Navatāla, modifications ramify; while they maintain its principle as far as possible, they also have recourse to the lesser unit of measurement, the aṅgula (1 Tāla = 12 aṅgulas), according to which a more mechanical subdivision of the total height is effected.[32]

As far as the proportions of the images are based on number so are their isocephalous rows on the upright walls of the temple (Pl. XLIV) akin in their vertical rhythms to those of the groups of mouldings coherent in their proportions and forming a broad band on the socle (adhiṣṭhāna) of the temple; on its walls,

In these types of proportionate measure of the image, ancient Vedic numbers survive. The length known as a 'puruṣa' or a 'vyāma', a man's length or a fathom, was the unit of measuring the Fire-altar. This length is variously given as 120, 96 and also 84 aṅgulas (cf. Part II, note 12).

[30] In South Indian (metal) images of a relatively late period and also in present practice, the total height is divided into a number of Tālas (10, 9, 8, 7 or 5) cf. 'Some Hindu Śilpaśāstras' by W. S. Hadaway, 'Ostasiatische Zeitschrift', 1914, p. 37. This agrees with the ancient Nava-tāla type.

[31] E. Panofsky, 'Die Entwicklung der Proportionslehre, etc.' ('Monatshefte für Kunstwissenschaft', 1921-22, pp. 188-219). The height of the body being 9 facial lengths, that of the trunk is 3, thighs 2 and legs 2 ; ⅓ is the height of skull, foot and throat.

[32] The more ancient treatises on Tālamāna, the 'Bṛhatsaṃhitā', LVII, etc. measure according to aṅgulas only.

similar though narrower belts of architectural profiles alternate with the belts of images; though the limbs of the latter are more richly interlaced their proportions in the vertical are as pure and also allow for modifications as those of the many variations of the zones of architectural mouldings. Thus the images do not only come forward from the walls, but are part of them also in their proportions. They occupy each its proper position according to the Vāstupuruṣamaṇḍala.[33]

[33] See pp. 53, 97, and the identification of the Pratihāras, the 'gate-keepers' of the gods, with the Planets and the Wardens of the eight directions ('Viṣṇudharmottara', III, Ch. LXXXVII, 36-37).

SYMBOLS OF ENTRY AND EXIT: THE DOOR AND ITS IMAGES

Approaching the image or Liṅga in the Garbhagṛha (Pl. V) it appears framed by the door which leads to this inmost sanctuary. With the wings of the wooden door opened, during Pūjā, the image is seen by the devotee in the middle of the door; the frame of the door is also that of the image; the distance between door and image is translated into colour and atmosphere. Having the image for its centre and subject, this picture is framed by the door-way with its carvings on sill, jambs, and lintel. The several parts of the door-way as given in the 'Bṛhatsaṃhitā' form a geometrical progression; the width of the threshold being equal to that of the door-jambs, the width of the door-way or entrance is double of each; and its height is twice the width. Similarly also are the parts of the door-way proportioned, assigned as they are to various images and carvings. At the bottom are the large figures of the Guardian divinities of the door, etc.; they occupy ¼ of the height of the door.

These pure proportions of the early texts are the basis on which are worked out the many variations of the symmetry of the door and temple (Pl. V). Each Prāsāda is a composition of its own; in it the original proportions and themes are composed each time in a new consistency.

The name for the antepagments of the door-jamb is 'śākhā', meaning 'branch'. A number of branches were fixed in the ground, tied and bundled together originally; 3, 5, 7, or 9 contribute their stems to the varied vertical mouldings of the door-jambs (Bṛ. S.LV. 14). The horizontal themes of sill and lintel, add their balance; the augmentation of the lintel by repeating and varying its horizontal themes twice and thrice, similarly the raising of the threshold by one step or more, increase the effectiveness of the door from a place of entry to one of display.[34] The door "frames" the image and this frame is wrought with many carvings. It appears as if the many divinities carved on the door frame belonged to the image in the Garbhagṛha, were its 'parivāra' or "surrounding" divinities.

The meaning of door and image is closely connected. The divinity to whom the temple is dedicated has his symbol or image in the Garbhagṛha; his image, as a rule, is also carved, on a small scale, on the centre of the lintel. He presides over the entrance and his gate-keepers (dvāra-pāla) are stationed below, to the right and left, at the door-jambs.[35] These guardians of the threshold flank the gods and symbols of the entrance.

[34] The incorporation of the free-standing Toraṇa into this surface of display can be seen from the rock cut example in Nasik, of 100 A.D. approximately, onwards. The division into rectangular panels, each with a relief composition of its own is derived from such Toraṇa compositions as are preserved in Sāñcī. See also Part VIII, note 6.

[35] The Dvārapālas bear the weopons, etc. by which they are recognised as belonging to a particular god; they are Śiva-dvārapālas, or those of Brahmā, Viṣṇu etc. cf. 'Rūpamaṇḍana', II. 13—17; III. 65—70; IV. 102—107.

Carved on the centre of the threshold ('udumbara'; 'bhuvaṅgama') is a long stemmed full blown lotus, symbol of this universe in which divinity is established, symbol also of the state of dispassion of the Bhakta in which divinity is revealed to him. None may tread on it.[36] It is the mark of the threshold, above it, the image in the Garbhagṛha appears raised to the Bhakta who approaches it; and, while he or the priest is about to enter the innermost sanctuary he too is raised to the status of divinity.

In this respect the door is God through whom man enters into the presence of the Supreme Principle which is established in the Garbhagṛha and has its seat in the consecrated image. To be able to enter into the Supreme Presence, man has to undergo a transmutation, for only when he has acquired a celestial body himself is he qualified to pass the company of the gods and confront the Supreme Presence which is beyond form and dwells in the image of the divinity of the temple. The transformation or regeneration which man has to undergo is promoted by the divinities carved on the door-jambs.[37]

Most conspicuous and significant are the large images of the River-goddesses, often accompanied by their retinues, their figures being set against the several Śākhās. Above their groups are carved and repeated in many panels such shapes and configurations, in which life is young and quick; procreative couples on the posts, and baby-shapes of Gaṇas ("quantities" of celestials) amidst creepers rambling around the door-way. Serpents are interlaced on the door-way of Viṣṇu temples, especially.[38]

Thus they enclose the door ascending in an unbroken continuity of swaying creepers, superposed and in panels, each filled with a sinuous pattern of limbs rounded with the sap of youth; all these are sculptural metamorphoses and elaborations of the theme of the River-goddesses for it is from their waters that they arise.

The Rivers have their source and origin in heaven. Thence they descend to earth.[39] On the entrance of the early temples their images are carved to either side of the lintel ('pataṅga'; 'ūrdhvapaṭṭikā'). On its middle the image of the main

[36] Ī.P. III. ch. XIII. 29. The priest enters the Garbhagṛha with the right foot first, without touching the threshold of the door.
'Viṣṇudharmottara', III. ch. XLVIII. 16.

[37] The symbolism of the threshold, but for the central lotus stalk and flower, varies in its devices; hosts of gods dance, rejoice, are present at the moment when the threshold is being passed. Thus the compartments of the door sill are replete with them; or else Kīrttimukhas or Śārdūlas (see below) flank the lotus stalk, etc.

[38] Temple of Rājīva Locana, Rajim (ASI; C.I. Photograph, 1903-4, No. 2191). The names of the antepagments denote the themes which are carved on them, 'patra'; gandharva-śākhā, etc., the one covered with a leaf pattern, the other showing dancing genii (Cousens, 'Archit. Ant.', op. cit. p. 27).

[39] Cf. Part I. p. 3. The descent of Gaṅgā and Yamunā is narrated in a rock carving at Udayagiri, Bhopal, c.I., c.400 A.D. (Coomaraswamy, 'Yakṣas', II. Pl. 20). In temples of the Gupta age (Deogarh; ib. Pl. 21) the images of the two River goddesses are carved to the right and left respectively of the door lintel, also if rarely, in mediæval times, of which the Vyomakeśvara temple (opposite the entrance to the Liṅgaraja Temple, Bhuvaneśvar) is an example. In this small shrine, of c. the 10th century, the position of the River goddesses is the same as on the temples of the Gupta age.

divinity of the temple, and to either side of it those of other great Gods are carved.[40] This then is the celestial region whence the rivers have descended, Gaṅgā, the most sacred of all, celestial Mandākinī, and also Yamunā. From heaven they have come to earth ; in the later temples their images are stationed on either side, at the bottom of the door, the current and ripples of flowing waters are in their swaying stances. To look at them is equal in effect to the ritual bath in their waters, especially in the most sacred water of the Ganges. The energy of the waters is so great that the bath itself confers Dīkṣā, initiation ('Maitr. S.' III. 6.2) : Ablution, transmutation, and initiation are effected at the entrance. This indeed is its initial and essential meaning in sacred architecture for initiation is derived from 'in-ire' meaning 'to enter'. The power of the flowing waters is in their celestial nature and origin. None are as sacred as those of the Gaṅgā who in her celestial form is Śakti.[41]

The presence of the Rivers purifies the devotee from all taints of his human state. It is equivalent to a bath taken in the sacred waters.[42] The entrance to the Garbhagṛha is the sculptural metamorphosis of the natural T īrtha. The door-way is an iconostasis of the descent of the Rivers, of Śakti ; and of the ascent of life competing for its heavenly origin in the creepers rambling upwards on the 'branches' (śākhā) of the frame, in the multiform concatenations within their stalks and, on each single Śākhā, in the sequences of lovers ('mithuna'), prancing chimaerae (śārdūla) and jubilant spirits (gaṇa) (cf. Bṛ. S. LV. 15). All these have their

[40] The celestial region is also indicated on the lintel by a frieze of the Navagrahas, the nine planets, in some temples (especially in Orissa) ; there, the image of Lakṣmī is generally carved in lieu of that of the main divinity of the temple.

[41] In their iconographically complete 'images', the River goddesses, Gaṅgā and Yamunā, are carried by their vehicles (vāhana), the Makara, the first of all the sea-monsters and the tortoise, respectively. In the first is embodied the power of the water itself, which is fearful and benign ; the latter does not refer to the water itself but to the stability at its bottom. The Vāhanas however need not be represented nor any water vessel as attribute of these Nadīdevatās while their figures are carved, as a rule, to the side of the threshold from the seventh century A.D. onwards ; their images sometimes are very large and fill the length of the door jamb (Kharod, Bilaspur, C.P. ; ASIAR. 1909-10, Pl. V.a.) whereas elsewhere they are assimilated to those of Tree goddesses (Vanadevatās). The iconography of the entrance is not everywhere complete ; plain architectural shapes of the Śākhās (Raikona Temple, Nalgonda Distr.) belong as much to relatively late temples as purely floral scrolls and lozenges only constitute the carvings of the door jambs of earlier temples (Sitteśvar Temple, Candrāvatī, Jhalawar). The widest possible latitude was given to the craftsman to draw selectively from the iconographical repertory of the entrance.

River goddesses attending upon or accompanying a Nāga are represented in the Amarāvatī reliefs (Coomaraswamy, Yakṣas, II. p. 70). A Yakṣinī Sudarśanā standing on a Makara Vāhana however is carved also in Barhut (Barua, 'Barhut', III. 74). Nāgas, dwarf shaped Gaṇas, etc. belong to the wider circle of the River goddesses when they figure on either side of the threshold.

The Goddesses, as shown by the 'Īśānaśivagurudevapaddhati', III. XII. 20-21, as well as by a North Indian inscription of the Vaidyanātha Temple, Baijnath (Kangra) are River goddesses (Vogel, 'Gaṅgā et Yamunā dans l'Iconographie Brahmanique', 'Études Asiatiques', 1925, pp. 387-88), whenever they are carved to the right and left of the threshold whether they are equipped with all, or most of their attributes of identification as at Kharod (Bilaspur), Bajaura (Kulu), Dah Parbatiya (Assam) or on a door frame in the Indian Museum, Calcutta, or not.

[42] cf. 'Brahmavaivarta Purāṇa', II. X. 48-52. cf. Part I.

support (dhṛ) on these waters, are borne by it. Thus is illustrated the knowledge that the waters are Dharma ('Śatapatha Brāhmaṇa', XI. 1.6.24), the support of Life and generation; of a new birth and a transformed body.

Upwards and downwards are the images arrayed at the entrance when its broad frame is seen as a surface of display. 'Historically' too, the river goddesses have descended from the high positions on either side of the lintel to their stations on either side of the threshold; from there now the creepers ramble upwards, to the lintel. Beheld however in the dynamic impact of its carved Śākhās, the Rivers and the host of gods seem to have thronged out from the Garbhagṛha : in this dark 'cave' they have their source.

Having come forth from the darkness, young and dazzling in their vigour, the river-goddesses conduct from the level of the threshold not only the glance of regenerate man. They foster and nourish not only him in his new born state but they strengthen also the seed and embryo (garbha) of the temple which had been deposited to the right of the door—below the door-jamb—and prior to its having been set up (Part IV, p. 126). Thus their presence, position and movement draw upward and reinforce the subtle parts of all the elements which constitute the Seed[43] of the 'body' of the Puruṣa, which is the structure of the temple.

The inception of a new life is beset with dangers. The guardians of the threshold thus are the most enduring images of the door[44] where perils must be warded off and contamination with the impurities of the world prevented. They bear the weapon and traits of the particular god whom they serve in each temple and they frequently exhibit his 'fearful' aspect.[45] Thus they are the agents of the image in the Garbhagṛha, and of its smaller version in the centre of the lintel.

The iconography of the entrance has a double function. It belongs to the main deity of the temple who—as Christ—said of Himself "I am the Door" (John X. 9). In this function the door-frame is also that of the image in the Garbhagṛha, its place of manifestation. In this function too, the Ghanadvāras, the 'massive doors' or niches, on the outside of the temple have come to enshrine various aspects of divinity in which it manifests its presence.

The door however in its original function and open, is at the same time the place of the threshold and entry or initiation. The iconography of the River-goddesses is effective in this function where the door is a structural equivalent of a Tīrtha. The one or the other aspect prevails in the carvings of the entrance. Where its initiatory function predominates, the goddess Lakṣmī, bathed by elephants, is carved as the central image of the lintel and not the special divinity to whom the temple is consecrated. Lakṣmī is Vāruṇī, the energy and wealth of

[43] 'Jaiminīya Up. Brāhmaṇa', III. 6.
cf. 'Vedānta Sūtra' III. 1-2. Comm. Śaṅkarācārya.

[44] They occupy their positions in the earliest and in the latest temples.

[45] Mahākāla, for example, to the left of the door of a Śiva temple (Ī.P., l.c. verse 53); images of Time and Death are necessarily amongst the Guardians of the threshold, assisting the dying to the old life which is preliminary to the new regenerate state. "Every passage is a dangerous one, every gateway a death, but if safely passed through the gateway of a new life ' (Coomaraswamy, in a Review of C. Hentze, 'Frühchinesische Bronzen und Kulturdarstellungen', 'The Art Bulletin', 1940 (?) p. 53.

the Waters. Varuṇa, their Lord, the Asura (RV. VIII. 42. 1), rules over the gods, encloses them,[46] he is unseen and deathless (RV. I. 164. 38; X. 85. 17-18). It is to this greater and deathless form of the Supreme Principle that the door leads as the place of 'initiation'.[47]

Facing the entrance, outside the Prāsāda, in the open (Pls. LVIII, XXXVI), or in the Maṇḍapa (Pl. LII), is the image of the Vāhana, the vehicle of the divinity which is enshrined in the temple. Carved in the round, self-contained as form and symbol, the Vāhana 'conveys' the deity. The theriomorphic image, the Vāhana, is, it appears, as ancient as any temple;[48] while its position is outside the entrance, it confronts the temple or the image in the Garbhagṛha with which it is coaxial. No other sculpture or part of the building is so placed. The Vāhana is a counterpart of the image enshrined in the Prāsāda and framed by the door-way. It leads to the entrance.

[46] In its double function as place of 'exit' or manifestation of the deity and as place of entry of the transformed Bhakta, the door, called Mukha (mouth) is akin to the "Kīrttimukha" (see infra).

[47] In principle, the temple has 4 doors (cf. Part V, notes 69, 73), facing the cardinal points ('Īśānaśivagurudevapaddhati', III. ch. XII. 17). They are Śāntidvāra: the Door "Peace", in the East; Vidyādvāra, the Door "Knowledge" in the South, Nivṛttidvāra, the Door "Turning away from the world" in the West and Pratiṣṭhādvāra, the Door "Firm basis" in the North. These four names are those of the four Kalās, the ontological part-aspects of manifestation, according to Śaiva terminology.

Their hierarchical sequence is, beginning from the lowest Kalā: Nivṛtti, Pratiṣṭhā, Vidyā and Śānti. All these doors however lead to the fifth and highest Kalā, and to the Supreme Essence of the Pure Principles.

[48] Cf. The animals carved in the round on the top of Mauryan pillars (3rd century B.C.) and the representations on seals from Mohenjo-Daro (Sir John Marshall, 'Mohenjo-Daro and the Indus Civilisation', Pl. CXVI. 3 and 5), of an animal figure placed on a platform on top of a pole, and carried in procession. The Garuḍa-Stambha in front of a Viṣṇu temple appears as a lineal descendant of these most ancient Vāhanas. Nandin, the Vāhana in the Maṇḍapa, directs the approach (abhigamana) to the Garbhagṛha (Pl. LII); placed outside the temple it regulates the circumambulation (note 1, Pt. VIII).

THE 'WINDOW': GAVĀKṢA

The closed body of the temple is full of openings not factually but symbolically. As a rule there is only one opening, that of the entrance; in effect and in symbol it is repeated at the cardinal points, as a 'massive door' (ghana-dvāra) or a rectangular niche; in addition there are many niches of varying sizes in the wall, socle and the superstructure of the temple. The major niches hold images which are directly connected with the main divinity of the temple, the smaller ones, which occupy less important positions, on the socle, in any direction, housing lesser divinities. Being thus enshrined in a rectangular frame, the image is singled out, its importance being increased in that it appears manifested straight from the centre. Across the massive door its presence shines forth. The Ghanadvāras possess this primary symbolic function by virtue of their original position as doors in the cardinal points. While the rectangular shape of the niche is retained, its place-value remains by association only, if located anywhere on the perimeter of the temple.

The walls of the temple, as has been shown, are transmuted into carvings and images which are an exposition of the meaning of the Prāsāda. They are bodied forth; Aṣṭadikpālas, Pratihāras, Apsarās and other lesser goddesses, Mithuna groups, Śārdūlas and the like are the furthermost exponents of the Prāsāda, unframed, unshrined, and peripheral shapes of the walls. Framed however in their niches, each a small shrine, pillared and having frequently a superstructure and roof of their own the major divinities are sheltered, each niche being a paradoxical massive-door in which is beheld an aspect of the divinity of the temple.[49]

The wall is full of figures and images; it releases them to the sight one step further than it proceeds itself, as its envoy invested with its power; or it envelops them within its body as does the womb of the temple (garbhagṛha) the main image which is enshrined in it.

The rectilinear niches—with or without their multiform crowning 'roof' shapes[50] are far from being the only symbolical or paradoxical openings on the body

[49] The niches are sunk in the wall, in the temples of South India (Tanjore) and in Orissa; the image is housed within the thickness of the pier. In Khajuraho, however, the pillared niche with its canopy is a balcony-like projection from its buttresses. This is the rule also in Rajputana, Gujerat, etc.

[50] They are replicas in relief of various kinds of the superstructure of the temple and conform with its regional and chronogical varieties, or gables or pediments, consisting of Gavākṣa patterns (Pl. XLVI, bottom, the two lateral miniature shrines; see also note 57).

[51] The vertical, pointed or spatulate termination of the gable or keel arch is plain in rock cut temples from about the beginning of the present era. From about 500 A.D. onwards, the ends of each of the two branches forming the arch, curl up in scrolls, to the right and left of the central extension (Ajaṇṭā) which frequently carries a lotus flower (Paraśurāmeśvar Temple, Bhuvaneśvar; Bundana, Rajputana, etc.; 8th-9th century). The Kīrttimukha is the general finial of the Gavākṣa in the 10th century, in North and South India, but is established there also on earlier monuments (note 68).

of the Prāsāda; while they are "massive doors", the others are "massive windows". These are invariably curvilinear; a circular or nearly circular arch encloses the internal space, a pointed arch outlines the Gavākṣa. The archivolt, the face between these arches, is variously carved.

The shape of this window is derived from the curves of light bending wood, such as bamboo or branches. The outer arch results from two branches being fixed at the bottom and their heads tied together at the top; an end piece of the arch marking the place of the conjoint ends of the branches; or, the extension acts as a prop for a carved symbol, such as a lotus flower which it carries on top; or the mask, called Kīrttimukha, covers it completely, widens the area of the extension and gather in its shape the total meaning of the arch (Pls. XLVI-VIII).[51] The inner arch of the Gavākṣa has a continuous, round curve and is derived from one branch being fixed in the ground at both its ends.[52] Where this double arch is part of the roof, the inner barrel shape as well as the gable arch are kept in position by a thong or withe; the tie-rod together with the arches were copied in heavy bent timber and ultimately in stone or brick; the arch, as a rule remains open at the bottom, the 'tie-rod' forming the base of the image within the Gavākṣa (Pls. XLVII-VIII).[53]

In its largest form as exemplified on the Hindu temple, the Gavākṣa is an antefix known as Śukanāsā; it shields the structural opening of the Śikhara or superstructure (Pls. XLVII-VIII); there it has, on the temple, its original and leading place. It may however be repeated on a lesser scale in the three other main directions, in front of the central buttress. In South India it is placed at each cardinal point of the Śikhara or dome shape of the 'High Temple'. In its particular Drāvidian version beset with flames it blazes forth from the many chapels on each Bhūmi; varied in size and the elaboration of its details.

Such Nāsās (Nāsikā; Kudu) are also repeated horizontally on the Kapotālīs or cornices; there they had their place, originally, as attic windows, in which form they have figured since the days of Barhut. Thus the Gavākṣa is originally a dormer or gable window and it retains as its outline the shape of the arch of vegetation, the shape of Prakṛti.[54]

On Nāgara temples, the offsets of the Śikhara are each enmeshed and covered by an unending web of Gavākṣas;[55] where the Śikhara consists of offsets only it appears shrouded in Gavākṣa-lace; so are the Śṛṅgas and Tilakas; on some temples

[52] Cf. Part IV. The arch described in the 'Āpastamba Śrauta Sūtra', and the arch of the chapel, the Buḍirghar, set up in the celebration of Holi (Part V, p. 159).

[53] A completely circular opening however occurs, though rarely, in Gavākṣa patterns, or the inner arch may appear as gathered into a point at the bottom, in the centre (Pl. XLVIII); these however are variations of the Gavākṣa net only and not of its more important larger versions such as the Śukanāsā, and the various kinds of Nāsās or Nāsikās, Śūrasena, Siṃhakarṇa, etc. ('Samarāṅgaṇasūtradhāra', LVII. 37; 924; 967; 'Kāśyapaśilpa', XXII). The curvilinear edge is responsible for the appellation "nāsā"; cf. Śukanāsā, the parrot's beak.

[54] Cf. the so-called "Caitya hall window" of Buddhist Caitya halls, the "Sun window" which is the correct name of the Caitya hall window. It admits the light of the Sun which reaches the Caitya or Stūpa at the far end of the hall.

[55] See Part VI, p. 214; also Kramrisch, 'Kaliṅga Temples', JISOA, vol. II. pp. 43-60.

the buttresses on the perpendicular walls are similarly overspun.[56] The 'niches' also whether on the walls or on the socle of the temple, are similarly crowned.[57]

Gavākṣa is usually rendered as "round window" or gable window.[58] But Gāvaḥ (plural of 'Gauḥ') are the rays of the sun (Sāyaṇa, on RV. VI. 64. 3).[59] The ray as well as the sun is called 'gauḥ'.[60] The first part of the term Gavākṣa means Sun or ray and 'akṣa ', its second part, means axle, pivot, wheel, curve and eye. Ray-wheel or Sun-arch would be appropriate translations expressive of the symbolic function of the Gavākṣa on the Hindu temple.[61] It is not to admit the rays of the Sun into the temple, for the 'windows' are closed and as solid a part of the wall as are the massive and impenetrable doors. They are not meant to conduct the light of the sun to the image within the dark Garbhagṛha; on the contrary, their original function as windows of the houses of man is negatived on the Hindu temple, the house and seat of God. He is the Light as He is the Door. The presence of the Devatā, the Shining one, sends forth his splendour in the darkness of the Garbhagṛha and upwards across the innumerable 'ray-wheels', 'ray-eyes', or 'sun-arches', the Gavākṣas, by which the body of the superstructure of the temple is covered. The retrovert sense of the Gavākṣa has the same paradoxical logic as the impenetrable door. The house of God is other than that of man; its parts though similar in form and name function in the opposite direction.[62] The door is blocked and so is the window; they are parts of the massive body of the temple.

The deity looks out from the innumerable windows of the temple. In these symbolic wheels and arches, shapes are frequently carved which further illustrate their meaning. In the relatively most ancient Gavākṣas of temples, the face of a celestial looks out (Gandharvamukha)[63] or a lion is framed by its arch as on the Śikhara of the Paraśurāmeśvar Temple, Bhuvaneśvar, forming part of an almost pictographic language, for the Lion is the solar animal.[64] Celestials or Lions look out from the temple towards the devotee on whom the light is shed from its dark source within, across its massive walls and closed windows.[65]

[56] Temple in Barvasagar, Jhansi (ASI. 1915-16, Photograph No. 1945).

[57] Pāpanātha Temple, Paṭṭadakal; also Pl. LXXI, III. note 50.

[58] Modern interpretation by Indians calls it "cow's eye" following a popular etymology forgetful of the original connotation, though the word for cow is go (gav) and 'akṣa' denotes the eye. These two meanings are however not the only ones of the two parts of which the word Gavākṣa consists. The 'Vācaspatya' definites Gavākṣa, s.v., as that by which the rays of the Sun—or the waters—penetrate and pervade.

[59] RV. I. 84-15. The ray is also called "gauḥ"; 'Sāma Veda', I. 2. 33.4; 'Nirukta' IV. 25.

[60] RV. VI. 56. 3; 'Nirukta', II. 14.

[61] Ray-wheel, moreover, would correspond to the construction of some of the earlier Gavākṣas with their radiating internal frame in the imitation of the wicker work by which the inner circle was filled.

[62] These dispositions of the visible, of light or darkness, have their equivalent in 'emancipated' or reverse thinking (Coomaraswamy, 'Angel and Titan", JAOS, vol. 55, p. 403); cf. Maṇiprabhā on 'Yoga Sūtra', I. 29. "Thought is said to be reversed (pratyañc) when it turns against the current"

[63] Jouveau Dubreuil, 'Dravidian Architecture', p. 12.

[64] 'Viṣṇudharmottara', III. ch. LXVII. 8.

[65] The small round apertures in the Jāla or web of Gavākṣas, in Latās, etc., are frequently carved in successively narrowing rings, forming all-round steps which lead to the deep central axle-point.

The Gavākṣas in their retrovert function allow the luminous nature of Divinity to penetrate the solid masonry of the Prāsāda; it leaves its superluminous darkness within the deep eyeholes of the Gavākṣa.[66] On Śikhara, Bhūmis and Kapotas, the rows and webs of Gavākṣas hold in their rounded contours a central darkness, dispersed in infinitesimal points in the texture of the Prāsāda.

[66] The Gavākṣas—especially of the Śikharas of Nāgara Temples which they cover with their web—have come to denote an indefinite number of the shrines of the gods which they indicate 'pars pro toto', and which have been coalesced in one total mansion. On the Bhūmis however of the South Indian Jāti Prāsādas the various chapels of the gods preserve their several shapes intact and bear the variously large Gavākṣas, the Nāsās and Kudus, as frequently repeated, though always detached, shapes (Fig. on p. 187).

THE FACE OF GLORY: KĪRTTIMUKHA

Door, niche and window are the architectural symbols of the passage of man to God and of the nearness of divinity; they are places of initiation and manifestation. To them adornments are added which enrich and illustrate their meaning. They are carved in the likeness of animal and man but do not represent them for they do not portray things seen; they give form to the contents of realisation at their proper place, the door, the niche and the window. Pre-eminent amongst them is the Face of Glory, the Kīrttimukha. Its essential place is at the apex of the Gavākṣa. It figures most prominently on the largest Gavākṣa of Nāgara temples, called Śukanāsā, the antefix of the open arch of the Śikhara (Pls. XLVII, XLVIII, L.).[67] On Hastipṛṣtha temples it looks over the apex of the arch of the façade (Kapoteśvara Temple in Chezarla, Guntur). On Drāviḍa temples it dismisses from its mouth the arch crowning each chapel or each of the attic windows of each chapel in the parapet of the Bhūmis, the storeys of the superstructure; the Kīrttimukha is also carved on its cornices and those of the wall of the temple.[68] But the Face of Glory does not only crown the arches of the window openings;[69] on some temples it does not surmount, but fills the opening of the window.[70] Varied in certain details of its appearance it figures for example on the apex and also within the 'opening' or surface of the Gavākṣas or Nāsās of the Great Temple in Tanjore (Fig. h, p. 187).

The Face of Glory has its main position on the apex of the arch or in its centre,

[67] This blind, necessitated by the open trabeate arch of the brick or stone construction is made level with the façade of the Antarāla, the small porch in front of the Prāsāda; it is its superstructure (Pl. XLVIII). Repeated on a lesser scale on the Śikhara in the remaining cardinal points, it adheres there more closely to the central offset (latā; pāga; Pls. XLIII, XLV, XLVI); on Śṛṅgas and Tilakas it forms itself the central offset by vertical repetition and diminution (Pls. XLVI—IX), an intermediate stage between the Gavākṣa of the Śukanāsā and the Jāla or net pattern covering the whole Latā or offset. This blind does not belong to the original Śikhara made of boughs, the 'Tabernacle'.

[68] On the apex of dormer windows, the Kīrttimukha is carved in the rock, on caves XXVIII and elsewhere in Ajaṇṭā, in the seventh century A.D. Cf. Kont-gudi Temple, Aihole.

[69] It occupies the place of the 'keystone' of the arch on the Toraṇa or halo (Prabhā-Toraṇa; Tiruvasi) of stone steles of images, specially in Eastern India (from about 900 A.D.) and of metal images in South India. Cf. its rôle in the architecture of Java, etc.

[70] Durga Temple, Aihole, sixth century.

The position of the Kīrttimukha on top or at the head of a building has its correspondence when worn on the head of images of divinities; one of the earliest known examples of the Kīrttimukha is carved in Amarāvatī, in a relief of the last period, representing the Rāmagrāma Stūpa; it figures as an ornament in the crown of a Nāga, IInd century A.D.; C. Sivaramamurti, 'Amarāvatī Sculptures in the Madras Museum', Bulletin IV, Pl. LXI. 1. A head of a Śiva image from Mathurā (in the Curzon Museum, Muttra) of the 3rd-4th century has a Kīrttimukha in its headdress. Pearl strings and a pearl pouch, in the middle hang from its mouth; two long paws are carved on either side of the 'Lion' face. Śiva having a Kīrttimukha in the Jaṭāmukuṭa, see Daśāvatāra cave, Elura; a Kīrttimukha figures also in the Karaṇḍamukuṭa of a Dvārapāla from South India, Coomaraswamy, 'Yakṣas', I. op. cit. Pl. 18. '. To this day it is part of the coiffure of the dancers in Cambodia.

but features in addition on the front of the threshold of the Garbhagṛha[71] to either side of the lotus stalk in the centre; it is moreover seen as a repetitive motive along the socle or base of the temples, where it is known as 'Grāsa-paṭṭikā' (S.S. LVII, 956) in Gujarat and as Rāhurmukher-mālā in Orissa; it is also carved on either side of the steps at the base of South Indian temples[72] and forms the 'beginning' or the centre of carved panels of the 'Vedi' (Pl. IX).

Above and below, on the apex and on the base, is the awful visage of the Face of Glory, the Kīrttimukha. The countenances of animal and man are fused in this mask inflated with breath, bulging with power and modelled over the dark grin of death's skull (Pl. L).

It usually has the mien of a lion; and is therefore also known as Siṃha-mukha, the Lion's face. It is horned; the frown on its forehead (siṃha-lalāṭa) is gathered in a third and middle horn between the two stag-or ram horn like extensions of the bulge of the eye globes. These protrude from deep sockets, in the fury of breathing which unites the horns of the dragon with the pouches of the lion's cheeks. The out-breathing of the animal, the globes and curves of its Mask, are held in check by the central vertical, the nose, which inhales with vibrant nostrils, and by the horizontal bridge below the eyes and across the nose, where the breath is restrained between inspiration and expiration. The inspiration is through the nose, an in-drawing of scents which the earth below sends up.

The Kīrttimukha is made by art; multiform and protean[73] it is one of the essential symbols in which the Indian craftsman thinks. It conveys supreme Reality which is the origin and the foundation; it is carved at the apex of the arch, on the threshold and on the base.

This symbol is known in Indian sculptures dating from the beginning of the present era[74] when classical antiquity contributed to it the physiognomy of its own lion masks. It has an equivalent in the Chinese T'ao T'ieh, the 'Devourer', known from the second and first millennium B.C. In mediaeval Europe it is seen for example, in Nôtre Dame la Grande in Poitiers, while in English church architecture it is known as the "Green Man".[75]

[71] To either side of the lotus stalk in the centre; cf. 'Padmapurāṇa', Uttarakhaṇḍa, XI, see below.

[72] Especially in Malabar (Temple in Thirukkadittanam, Travancore, c. 11th century 'Travancore Administration Report', 1115 M.E., p. 6). In this and all other examples, the arch like curve of the side of the steps springs from the open jaws of a Makara, below, and ends in the open jaw of a Kīrttimukha, above.

[73] The components are differently fused, quantitatively; sometimes the face of man predominates even over that of the Lion, etc. (Tanjore).

[74] See note 70 and also horned Kīrttimukha from Sirkap, Taxila; ASIAR, 1919-20, Pl. X, Figs. 25, 31 (cf. "classical" lion's heads from Taxila; ASIAR, 1915-16, Pl. V, g, etc. A Kuṣāṇa version from Nasik is illustrated in ASIAR, 1936-33, Pl. VII.

Kīrttimukhas in the Gupta age are frequent, for example, carved on the railing of Bodhgayā.

Two paws are added to the face (see note 70), for example, also at Rajaona (5th-6th century; "Candimau", ASIAR, 1911-12, Pl. LXXIII); the paws, as a rule, are absent in Indian representations but they form part of the Tibetan version.

[75] H. Marchal, 'The Head of the Monster in Khmer and Far Eastern Decoration', JISOA, vol. VI. p. 97 f. Lady Raglan, 'The Green Man in Church Architecture', 'Folklore', vol. L,

It has its most explicit form on Indian temples from the tenth century onwards, were it is placed on the apex of the Gavākṣa of the Śukanāsā, etc. and comprises it. The Face of Glory generally is an incomplete face and has no lower jaw. Instead, below its tusks, from within its mouth, issues the arch of the Gavākṣa together with the many forms on, within and around it (Pls. XLVI-VIII. L.). The archivolt is filled with a scroll full of Gaṇas and music in its convolutions (Pl. XLVII). On Orissan temples (Mukteśvar, in Bhuvaneśvar, etc.), a bell on a chain dangles from the centre of the archivolt; spirits of the air are seen flying towards it. The outer edge of the arch is variously beset with curly carvings; foam, flames and wings are born there.[76] These belong to and extend from Makaras which lie at the base and form the ends of the arch (Pls. XLVII and XLVI).[77] In this combination, the Face of Glory is known as Kāla-makara.[78] Makaras moreover frequently issue from beneath the pouched cheeks of the Kīrttimukha (Pl. L).

The inner circle of the arch of the Śukanāsā, etc., as a rule, is not closed below, but on the level of its horizontal tie-rod rests an image, a particular aspect of the divinity of the temple (Pls. XLVI-VII), or the inner circle is filled by a lotus flower or the face of a Deva or Asura (Bṛhadīśvara Temple, Tanjore). The lotus in the Gavākṣa in some of the earlier temples (Mukteśvar, Bhuvaneśvar) corresponds to a lotus at the apex. The lotus at the apex is also carved in Eastern India on the Prabhā-Toraṇas of steles; there it precedes, and is analogous in meaning to the Kīrttimukha; lotus (stalk) and Kīrttimukha are also the symbols of the threshold.

The Face of Glory has, in the main, the physiognomy of an animal. In and around this 'animal caeleste', lion and ram, dragon and serpent, fish, bird and man, combine. Breath inflates and death hollows its face.

Whose is the glory, whose the Face? Its forms and names give the answer. The Face of Glory is known as Grāsamukha in Western India, as Rāhur-mukha in Eastern India.[79] It is also known as Kāla. 'Gras' means 'to devour' (cf. the Chinese T'ao T'ieh) and also 'to eclipse'. Rāhu causes the eclipse of the Sun and Moon. His name also designates the eclipse itself. Rāhu is the Caput Draconis,

p. 45 f ; cf. also a corresponding face, in E. J. Millar, 'English Illuminated Manuscripts from the 10th to the 13th century', Pl. XI, from a 10th century Psalter.

The Gorgoneion, "an awful monster's grizzly head" sent up by Persephone from Hades ('Odyssey', IX. 633 f.) is a cognate Head, with glaring eyes, protruding tusks, etc. The monster's Head itself is the monster.

[76] 'Foam' in the present example, flames in Orissa and South India ; wings, not only on the temples of Bali, etc., but also of parrot-shaped 'Su-parṇas' on either side of the Śukanāsā of the Kāśinātha temple, Paṭṭadakal.

[77] In Pl. XLVI, the Makara is replaced by a 'Face of Glory'. Kīrttimukha and Makara are closely related ; see infra. On a Kāla-makara Toraṇa at Terahi, Gwalior (ASIAR, 1914-15, Pt. I. Pl. XVa), female figures issue from the jaws of Kāla.

[78] Stutterheim, 'The Meaning of the Kāla-makara Ornament', 'Indian Art and Letters', N.S., vol. III ; 'Les Déformations de la Tête de Kāla', "Revue des Arts Asiatiques', vol. XII.

Kāla is the first presiding divinity of Rāhu, and Sarpa the second (cf. 'Indian Antiquary', XXXIII, p. 61 f).

[79] In Cambodia, it is known as head of Rāhu ; it is also known as Vanaspati, 'Lord of the Wood' (cf. the 'Green Man'), in Java, and in Assam (ASIAR, 1946-37, p. 58 ; referring to the Deo Parbat Temple, Sibsagar). The Lord of the Wood ((vana) however is the Lord of Light (vana) or intellectual Splendour.

the ascending node of the moon or the point where the moon intersects the ecliptic in passing northwards. Rāhu is also one of the nine planets (Nava-graha) but is not visible, being a planet of an aeon which is no more.

Grāsa and Rāhu are synonymous; they denote the Devourer. The Devourer more specially however is Time, Kāla. These are the three most frequent names of the Face of Glory. Rāhu has the widest currency and content. He has also his own myth:

In the fight of the gods and demons, the gods were in danger of losing. They were not immortal; Amṛta, the nectar of immortality, would make them immortal but would have to be churned from the ocean. For this purpose, the gods required the help of the anti-gods, the Asuras, the demons. The gods negotiate with the demons and they agree that the Amṛta obtained by churning would be divided equally between the gods and demons. The powerful Asuras however carry off the Amṛta and quarrel among themselves as to who should get more and who less. They entrust the Amṛta to the great God Viṣṇu. He however passes them by and gives the drink of immortality to the gods. Rāhu, the Asura, sees this treachery, assumes the shape of a god and gets the drink. But while Rāhu just sips of the Amṛta the Sun and the Moon perceive his trick. They point him out to Viṣṇu who cuts off Rāhu's head. The head however had become immortal by having tasted Amṛta. Hence Rāhu, the immortal Head, the Face of Glory, tries to swallow sun and moon whenever he gets near them. When they are partly or wholly hidden in Rāhu's mouth, they are eclipsed.

The myth of the treachery of the gods and of Asura-power is summed up by Varāhamihira in the 'Bṛhatsaṃhitā', V. 1-3, in the chapter which treats of Rāhu. Some teachers (ācārya) hold that the head of the Demon, though severed (from the body) by Viṣṇu, yet alive by virtue of Amṛta, became a planet (grahạ). He is invisible except at the time of an eclipse (parva-kāla), his shape is like the circle of the sun and the moon. Some say he has the shape of a serpent, others assert he has no shape and yet others believe that he consists of Tamas, Darkness.[80]

The commentary of this passage explains that Rāhu, the Asura, is the son of Siṃhikā, the Lioness. She is Nirṛti, Destruction, the daughter of Diti, "Dividing" ('Brahmavaivarta Purāṇa' I. IX. 41), the mother of the Maruts and the arch-mother of the Demons. Siṃhikā, untimely, asked Kāśyapa, the Seer (ṛṣi), for a son. Furious, he gave her a son, as cruel as Yama (Death) and Kāla (Time), Antaka (the Ender); the learned called him Rāhu, says Parāśara. It is Rāhu who gives both good and bad luck to man (Comm. Bṛ. Saṃh. V. 2).

Rāhu who is Tamas, Darkness and Death, is the son of the Lioness. The Lion is the Solar animal. His figure is the device on the banner of Sūrya. Rāhu is also called Svarbhānu 'Splendour of Radiance'. Svarbhānu, the Asura, overspreads and

[80] Abbreviated.—This traditional knowledge however is discussed from a 'modern' angle in the Rāhucara chapter of the 'Bṛhat Saṃhitā'. Rāhu is also known as Bhūchāyā, the shadow of the earth (cf. however the Balinese name of the Face of Glory, which is Boma, the 'son of the Earth goddess', Bhūmi). The interpretation as Bhū-chāyā, however, does not concern the Face of Glory; whereas Boma, son of the Earth goddess, in his terrestrial origin, illustrates by analogy the origination of the Face of Glory in the ground (bhūmi) of divine being.

conceals the sun with darkness (RV. V. 40. 5-6; Ś.B. V. 3. 2. 2), being greater than the sun, the manifest divinity.

Tamas: Darkness, and Svarbhānu: 'Splendour of Radiance', or Vanaspati, Lord of the Light; Kāla: Time and Death, and Asura are the names of the Face of Glory in the polarity of its portent. Asura is derived from 'asu', "vital breath" and 'ra', "who gives" (RV. V. 41. 3). It is the Supreme Spirit who, breathing, gives the Breath of Life.[81]

The Face of Glory on the Hindu Temple has its essential position on the apex of the Śukanāsā, at a definite proportionate height of the superstructure; above it practically no images are carved on the trunk of the Śikhara of a Nāgara temple; from it downwards extends the realm of figured shapes (Pl. XLIII-IV, XLVIII).

The Kīrttimukha is a mask made up of the face of the Lion (Siṃhamukha), of Death's head (Kāla) and the Dragon's head (Rāhu, Tamas). The Lion, the Solar Animal, the Splendour (Yaśas; tejas), on the flag of the sun, the symbol of justice and power, is the Destroyer of fiends. The mantra, the magic formula, on giving a lion to Mahādevī, the Great Goddess, is: "Do thou destroy my enemies" ('Mahānirvāṇatantra', XIII. 257). It is similar to the mantra of Rāhu: "Enemy of Soma, the Moon, destroy my enemies" (ib. XIII. 111).[82] The lion as destroyer, is an embodiment of but one side of power; the solar animal is Power altogether. In Vedānta, it is said that the Supreme Lord (Parameśvara) is a Lion. The Supreme Spirit (Paramātman) is the Lion (Siṃha), in the Narasiṃha-avatār of Viṣṇu, and Nara is the creature (jīva).[83] The 'Kālikāpurāṇa (XXX. 130 f.) speaks of Nārāyaṇa or the Supreme Spirit as Brahman. Nārāyaṇa is the Siṃha or Lion part of the Narasiṃha Avatār.

In the 'Mahābhārata' (I. 19. 7-11), Viṣṇu as Nārāyaṇa cuts off Rāhu's head. Only the Supreme Spirit can by its death-bringing gesture give and restore life eviternal to itself, to its immortal Head, severed from the fallible body of the world of dichotomy in which strife and deceit of Suras and Asuras take place.

In the mask of the Kīrttimukha, the life-giving power breathes forth in lion features the splendour of radiance which belongs to the solar animal; the Lion face, Siṃha-mukha, is that of Svarbhānu; its eyes blaze 'like lightning' ('Padmapurāṇa', Uttarakhaṇḍa, XI). The sun, the Eye of the All (RV. VII. 63. 1), is behind the

[81] RV. X. 10. 2 and X. 11. 6. Sāyaṇācārya explains Asura as 'prāṇavān', breathing, prajñāvān, 'pro-gnostic'. Asura is 'Prāṇa dātṛ'.

[82] The Vedic Mantra of Rāhu is given in RV. IV. 31. 1.

[83] 'Citsukhī' or 'Bhāṣyabhāvaprakāśikā' on 'Brahmasūtra Śaṅkarabhāṣya'; Dedication verse.

The Lion is seen to emerge from the high crown of Virāṭa-Puruṣa above this image of Viṣṇu, in a relief in Bādāmī (R. D. Banerji, Memoir 25, ASI, Pl. XIV b).

On the ridge of the Śukanāsā, on temples of central India and the Deccan an image of the 'Lion and the man' is placed immediately behind the Kīrttimukha and exceeds its height. In the temples of Orissa, etc., the figure of a lion literally springs from the Śikhara. See the following chapter.

mask,[84] behind even Death's skull; the mask is dilated by breath, the outbreathing of the Supreme which is and makes the world.[85]

The Lion-face[86] carries the attributes of the Dragon or Serpent above and below its bulging countenance. Above are the Dragon's flaming horns. The horns are rays (RV. VII, 55. 7. comm.).[87] The triple horns unite the 'natures' of the 'Lion' and the 'Dragon' in the triple unity of Time.[88]

The dragon, the Serpent component of the Kīrttimukha has no chin. The majority of Kīrttimukhas on Indian temples are without lower jaws.[89] Thus Vṛtra is described (RV. V. 45. 6) the All-coverer, who has neither hand nor foot (RV. I. 32. 7). The missing lower jaw is a more forcible representation than the open mouth, of out-breathing, sending forth, emitting the breath of life. Could the mouth be closed the progression of life would be at an end. Thus, a consecrated person should smile with his mouth shut, so that he may retain his intellectual fire (tejas; 'Taittirīya Āraṇyaka', V. I. 4). Vṛtra, however, who has in himself splendour ('Pañcaviṃśa Brāhmaṇa', XX. 15. 6), who enveloped the world ('Tait. Saṃh.' II. 4. 12. 2) when as yet there was no distinction of being and non-being, life and death, day and night (RV. VIII. 100. 7) and who is wealthy, "comprehends within him all gods, all knowledge and all oblations" (Vāj. S. X. 5. 2), breathes out his splendour, wealth and sovereignty (cf. RV. I. 80. 6) into manifestation.[90] This was when his jaw had been smitten by Indra's bolt; manifestation came forth from the smitten Dragon, the Enveloper, at the moment of his death. This Death does not die (Ś.B. X. 5. 2. 3); it is a condition and ever renewed accompaniment of manifestation : it is immortal like Rāhu's head itself which is Death's open secret.

The Lion's head, and the Dragon's head are modelled on the frame of Death's head. The deep holes of the fleshless sockets of the eyes are filled entirely by their blazing orbs. It is a re-conditioned face, not that of any mortal

[84] In some representations from Eastern Java (Stutterheim, l.c. Fig. 11) and the Sunda islands the Face consists of a single circle, the eye. Its bulging shape fills an outline of Gavākṣa shape, thus truly a Gavākṣa or Sun-arch though no longer recognisable as window; cf. also the Kīrttimukha in the Gavākṣa, as in the Durga temple, Aihole.

[85] Cognate with this Lion-sun component in the ronstitution of the mask of the Asura are the 'birds' carved on the Prabhā-toraṇas of images (Suparṇas or Haṃsas; Kramrisch, 'Pāla and Sena Sculpture', Rūpaṃ, 1929, Figs. 14, 15), and also to either side of the Śukanāsā, for instance, of the Kāśināth temple, Paṭṭadakal, but they are not frequent amongst the Āvaraṇa or surrounding symbols of the Face of Glory and feathery forms alone curl from and around the edge of the Gavākṣa (Pl. XLVII). Su-parṇa (RV. I. 35. 87), 'well feathered' is the name of the small sun-birds. Well feathered and winged is the Gavākṣa below the Face of Glory. The feathers sometimes are flames: Agni was first generated from the Breath of heaven (RV. X. 45. 1).

[86] The Lion is the Vahana of Rāhu according to the 'Matsyapurāṇa' (XCIX. 7).

[87] Agni is 'tridhātu śṛṅga', his horns are three (RV. V. 43. 13); Brahmā has 4 horns (RV. IV. 58. 2).

[88] The succession of past-present-future (cf. the Trident of Śiva) is converted into simultaneity in the Face of Glory, the mask of the God-head.

[89] Where the classical influence prevails or persists, as in the more or less 'human' faced mask, the lower jaw is present.—The T'ao Tie'h also is without a lower jaw (Pelliot, 'Jades Archaiques de Chine', 1929, Pl. XVII).

[90] Coomaraswamy, 'Angel and Titan', JAOS. vol. 55, p. 400. "No essential value would be really changed in the 'Puruṣa Sūkta' by a substitution of Vṛtra for Puruṣa".

creature (jīva); it is the mask of Paramātman, the Supreme Spirit, under the Lion's guise. In death's skull, the lower jaw fallen away after the decomposition of the flesh, is not seen. In the Face of Glory it is covered by tusks, transformed into streamers, hidden by scrolls, indicated but disguised, gone over from the mask of death into the arch of manifestation (of the Gavākṣa) and the curling foam of Breath. Inasmuch as the Kīrttimukha is modelled as the Death-head, it is the mask of Kāla, Time, the Devourer.

As Kāla, the Kīrttimukha, Rāhu's head, devours sun and moon. Even though hidden by Rāhu, the Eclipse, sun and moon are not swallowed by the open mouthed devourer, Time. He sets the measure of their courses by eclipsing them and setting them free again to meet his dark power.

The Face of Glory, the Kīrttimukha has thus three aspects. (1) It is the Death-head of Time (Kāla), the Devourer (grāsa), of Rāhu, the Eclipse. (2) Death's head is vested with the insignia of Ahi-Vṛtra, the Dragon, the ophidian carrier and source of the solar power, the monster which envelops the universe and emits it. In this aspect the chinless, horned, fiery mask covers the reality 'Puruṣa', while (3) from its Lion's look and breath, the Supreme Spirit, Brahman goes out into the world.[91]

Death and the Living Breath, Dragon and Lion, out-pouring and indrawing coincide in the Monster's head, the Face of Glory. This Supreme identity of contraries constitutes the mask of the Godhead, the Kīrttimukha.

The Kīrttimukha, the head of Rāhu who is Svarbhānu, radiant Splendour and Tamas, Darkness, is a seat of the superluminous darkness which has its architectural receptacle in the Garbhagṛha. Prior to its manifestation the Light is in the Darkness, for "verily this was at first Darkness (Tamas) alone. It abode in the Supreme" (Maitri Up.' V. 2). Thus the 'Mahānirvāṇatantra' (IV. 25), hymns the Great Goddess: "Before the beginning of things Thou didst exist in the form of Tamas, which is beyond speech and mind; and of Thee, by the creative desire of the Supreme Brahman was the entire universe born." The world is the outbreathing of the Supreme. Breath in the shape of foam and curls is exhaled from the open mouth of the Kīrttimukha. It passes along the arch of the Gavākṣa, the arch of the Sun and of manifestation. The curls of breath turn hither and thither, up and down, in multiple shapes, foam of the celestial waters, feathers of sun-birds, movement in which is dissolved the body of the Makara which is foremost amongst the monsters of the sea (Pls. XLVI, XLVII). The movement is densest in the archivolt where it acquires greater definition as vegetation-creeper, curving upwards, convoluted and full of spirits (gaṇa) and their music or, a bell is carved in the centre of the archivolt, (Mukteśvar Temple, Bhuvaneśvar, etc.), straight from the Lion's mouth for "all musical sounds are in that of the bell" ('Matsyapurāṇa', LXXI. 10) and sound is the quality of the element ether (ākāśa), the first and all pervasive, in the hierarchy of manifestation. The movement of Breath is shown by the rhythmic path of the creeper. It is the symbol of Nature 'naturans' and 'naturata', or Prakṛti. The Brahman whence she is engendered comprises her in her

[91] The "three bodies" (tanavas tisraḥ) of the Grāsa or Kīrttimukha are also those of Śiva who is Kāla, Puruṣa and Brahman ('Mahābhārata', XIII. 47. 17).

transcendental aspect as Parā-Prakṛti, in the form of Tamas. Prakṛti manifest however is the ambient curve of the Gavākṣa, the Arch of Nature, in which the rays of splendour have their circumference. Thus a Lion may fill the Gavākṣa, or any aspect of divinity or the mask of the Godhead itself.

The carvings of the Gavākṣa and its arch proceed from the Kīrttimukha and finally return towards it; as much as the creeper rambles downwards, so much also its coils compete upward until they are gathered at the apex, in the centre, where in some of the masks vibrant nostrils sniff up curls and coils, conglomerated in heavy ornament.[92]

Thus inspired and replete, the Siṁhamukha dismisses from its upper jaw, on either side some of its contents, Makaras, for example (Pl. L.) The Makara, moreover, is closely associated with the Kīrttimukha,[93] in the Kālamakara Toraṇa, where the Kīrttimukha crowns and the Makaras flank the arch of Gavākṣa (Pl. XLVII) or gate, etc. In this relation the Siṁhamukha, the head of the Lion, the Solar animal, is the station of the sun, and the Makara (Capricorn), the gate of the gods, their way of ascent.[94]

Around the Kīrttimukha stories were woven, some having Rāhu's myth for their background while in others the shape of the mask of the Godhead is seen worn

[92] Vegetation creeper, foam of the celestial waters, sunbirds and rays, the symbols proceeding from the Kīrttimukha and belonging to the Gavākṣa give form to contents such as are hymned in the 'Taittirīya Āraṇyaka', I. 1.2-3 : "O Waters, whose steeds are the winds, whose lords are the rays of the sun, whose body is formed of shining rays. . . . May the heavenly waters and herbs be auspicious to us and may they bring happiness to us".

Vegetation creeper, 'foam' and Kīrttimukha in three quarter profile and in profile, see Pl. IX.

[93] Cf. Pl. XLVI, where Kīrttimukhas are substituted for the head of the Makara on either side, at the base of the arch of the Gavākṣa. The Makara may have a Dragon's head or that of a Lion or bird (Mathurā Toraṇa, 'Ep. Ind.' II, Pl. III).

[94] The Makara, the Dragon element in the constitution of the Kīrttimukha, is collateral with it in many variations ; it issues from the Face of Glory (Pl. L) or, more generally, from the ends of the arch at the base where the Kīrttimukha is the apex or finial (Pls. XLVII-VIII). The Makara, Vāhana of Varuṇa, figures also by itself amongst the sculptures of the temple, at the base, as one of the 'animals' (p. 147) or it is part of the corbel of the capital, the Śīrṣa (Pl. LXXVIII). In the latter instance the jaws of the Makara are of essential significance, for in the mouth of the monster (Bartṛhari, 'Nītiśataka', 4) is "a thing of splendour". Festoons of pearls are frequently seen to issue from the mouth of the Makara, and also from that of the Śārdūla and the Kīrttimukha. Re. Makara, see Coomaraswamy 'Yakṣas', Part II, (Smithsonian Inst. Pub. 3059, pp. 44-56); and 'An Indian Crocodile' ('Bulletin of the Boston Museum of Fine Arts', 1936). The 'jaws' as a place of entry and exit have the ambivalence of the Door and are carved in this double function, with figures proceeding from or swallowed by the mouth of the Makara, for example: on a Kuṣāṇa Torana, ASIAR, 1906-07, Pl. LVI, jumping out of the jaw of the Makara, Devatās, flying forth from it ; cf. also ASIAR, 1903-04, Pl. LXV, Fig. 11. The arch is shown to issue from the Makara's mouth, together with the Devatās, ASIAR, 1922-23, Pl. XL f, but the movement of the arch can also be read in the opposite direction as being swallowed. Figures rushing to be swallowed or fighting unvanquished in the mouth of the Makara, are seen on Pl. LXXVIII and ASIAR, 1909-10, p. 75, Fig. 6 ('Kinnara' armed with sword and shield about to be swallowed by Makara) ; or the Makara is shown in its dual operation, as on a carved frieze of the Gupta period, from Sārnāth (ASIAR, 1914-15, Pl. LXIV. d.) where a Yakṣa is seen emerging jumping from the open jaw, while another Yakṣa is about to be devoured by the Makara.

or made by manifested divinity. One legend, similarly recounted in the 'Padmapurāṇa' (Uttarakhaṇḍa, X. 10 f. XI. 36-44) and the 'Skandapurāṇa' (Viṣṇukhaṇḍa, Kārttikamāsa Māhātmya, XVII) narrates how Rāhu as messenger of Jālandhara, the Asura, demanded Pārvatī from Śiva whom he was about to wed. Śiva thereupon produced a terrible being from his third eye. Lion-faced, with lolling tongue, the eyes like lightning, hair on end, looking like another Narasiṃha it rushes at Rāhu; but Śiva stops it and bids it to devour itself. This is does leaving only its head, the Kīrttimukha.

Śiva thus, from his wisdom-eye sees and produces a reflex of Rāhu which commits the act of self-sacrifice. It is part of Śiva's Consciousness.[95] Śiva as Mahākāla shares in the name and features of the Kīrttimukha (Kāla).[96] It is furthermore similar to the head of Narasiṃha, the man-lion Avatār of Viṣṇu whose meaning is given in the 'Citsukhī'.

A Liṅgāyat legend,[97] narrowed in significance, tells of Śiva-Śaṅkara-Śarabha. He seized Narasiṃha who had become excessively proud after having killed Hiraṇyakaśipu—the brother of Siṃhikā who is Rāhu's mother. Out of Narasiṃha's severed head, Śiva made the Kīrttimukha.

The mask of the Godhead is also the face of the great gods. In this world of dichotomy, of good and evil, where the Asuras, fallen, are the Titans or demons, the gods regain the integrity of the Godhead at the moment of strife and death when the Face of Glory of the Asura is beheld in the God's own countenance.

"The wife of Kāśyapa gave birth to two sons, Rāhu and Vāstu. The head of Rāhu was cut off by Viṣṇu; Vāstu was put down by the gods" ('Śāradātilaka', III. 2. Comm.). Rāhu and Vāstu are brothers. Vāstu is laid to rest at the base of the Temple and is its 'plan'; Rāhu's head is fixed above, on the pinnacle of the Śukanāsā of the Śikhara; below it is the realm of images and appearance. Rāhu's head is also on the apex of gates; it is repeated moreover on Gavākṣa emblems throughout the superstructure, on all the Bhūmis of South Indian temples, and on the cornices of the walls. There it is carved in the fullness of its meaning, as the Head; and Prakṛti, the arch below.

On the threshold of the Garbhagṛha only the Head is carved marking the passage into transcendental nature; the Head, moreover is repeated in bands as

[95] The legend of the Purāṇas ends saying that the Kīrttimukkha should be represented at the entrance of Śiva temples and should be worshipped first on entering. Hence it is always found on the front of the threshold of the shrine; worshippers sprinkle it and are careful not to step on it. In this version, only the Kīrttimukha of the threshold is taken into account.

[96] The images of Śiva in his terrific (ugra) aspects, as Aghora, Bhairava and Mahākāla have bulging eyes, inflated cheeks, tusks, etc. The basic structure of these faces is that of man whereas it is that of the lion in the image of Śiva as Śarabheśa.

The Kīrttimukha, moreover (see note 70) has its place in the centre of Śiva's Jaṭāmukuṭa. This has its noblest shape in Elephanta where it crowns the face of Tatpuruṣa in the image of Mahādeva.

[97] 'Seven Liṅgāyat Legends' (from the 'Anubhāvaśikhāmaṇi'), 'Indian Antiquary', IV p. 216. They are said to be based on a work of the thirteenth century.

Grāsapaṭṭi and Rāhurmukher-mālā,[98] as an enrichment of some of the mouldings of the base of the temples. There, the 'animal caeleste', the solar animal as Śarabha,[99] figures for all animal-nature sacrificially transmuted.

The sacrifice of the lower self, the self-sacrifice, has its legend in Vāstu as well as in Rāhu. Vāstu is Existence and its extent. He regulates the proportions of the temple according to cosmic order and cyclical numbers. He is the metaphysical plan of the temple. Rāhu, as his brother,[100] is imaged on the walls and essentially on the superstructure of the temple. Between Rāhu and Vāstu is the realm of appearance or concrete form (mūrti); both give it sustenance: Vāstu gives its frame work and Rāhu fills it with the inexhaustible wealth of the forms of nature (Prakṛti). Above Rāhu they are not seen for as much as he emits he also devours them. He is Time the Devourer, particularly the Eclipse and also the Planet of an aeon which has passed. This great Asura rules over the destinies of men, brings good or evil.

Vāstu as 'extent' of all things built by men is space ordered by art; Rāhu as his brother is the Time-agent and quickens its form. Thus the two sons of Kāśyapa, the Seer, are the "demons", in the sense of the Greek 'daimon' of the builders of the Temple. Rāhu's likeness is higher in position while it yet has its place in Vāstu's extent. In it is envisaged the Asura, who is Svarbhānu and Tamas as well, in the Supreme identity of contraries which is in the Godhead only, the Whole.

[98] Cf. also the enrichment consisting of Gavākṣas which is called Gavākṣamālā ('Raghuvaṃśa', VII. 2).

[99] AV. IX. 5.9; V.S. XIII. 51.

[100] The myths of Rāhu and of the Kīrttimukha tell of the Asura at the various stages of his 'fall'; they give diminished accounts of his wholeness.

ŚĀRDŪLA, LION AND LIONESS

"Thou art a Lioness, winning the sun-gods (Ādityas), winning sacerdotal power (Brahman), winning regal power (Kṣatra). . . . Thou art a lioness, bring thou hither the gods for the sacrificer" ('Vājasaneyī Saṃhitā', V. 12).[101] These words are recited by the sacrificing priest over the four corners of the High Altar, the Uttara Vedi ('Śatapatha Brāhmaṇa', III. 5. 2. 10-13). He takes the earth for making the High Altar from a square pit and shifts it with the words: "Thou art a Lioness overcoming the enemies, be thou meet for the gods. Through thee may we worst our enemies" (V.S. V. 10; Ś.B. III. 5. 1. 33).

"The offering reaches her before it reaches Agni, for this High Altar is in reality Vāk, the uttered Word." (Ś.B. III. 5. 1. 23). The offering inwardly made, the desire and resolve to sacrifice, find utterance first in speech, in the rhythmic formula, by which the altar is consecrated in its four corners in the intermediate directions; invested with power, its substance, earth, carries the offering to the sacrificial Fire, Agni, as does the rhythmical utterance. Vāk, the uttered Word, is Power manifest; the rhythmical utterance is a lion; earth, the substance, thus imbued, is a lioness, one in each of her four corners where power is assembled to ward off the evil ones and to worst the enemies.[102]

Vāk, utterance, articulate voice, is the substance of the Word. The Word prior to its utterance as articulate sound, prior to its manifestation, is Universal Consciousness; by stages it becomes manifest, as articulate voice in man and as the Word which is the substance or body of the universe.

Vāk, the uttered Word, has come down and reached manifestation from its unmanifest stage (avyakta) where it is the undivided Universal Consciousness, not as yet discerned as the mind (manas) or the intellect (buddhi) of the Universe.

Vāk, the uttered Word, is a lioness. Come into manifestation from undifferentiated Wholeness, her nature is ambiguous, winning and also destructive. She seizes everything. The 'Śatapatha Brāhmaṇa' (III. 5. 1. 21-23) tells of Vāk in the battle between the gods and demons how not having been accepted as a sacrificial fee she went away from the Ādityas. It is then that she becomes a lioness and seizes everything. The gods call her and also the demons. The gods succeed by promising that the offering shall reach her before it reaches Agni, the Fire.

The gods—the universe in its ordered aspect—win over the Lioness: uttered Word, the Lioness, attached to the gods, is rhythmical utterance, or metre; it is unassailable as, for example, the metre Virāj, in whose form "tigers went forth" (Ś.B. VIII. 2. 4. 4) or the metre Aticchandas, in whose form "lions went forth" (Ś.B. VIII. 2. 4. 5).

[101] 'Taittirīya Saṃhitā', 1.2.12; Ś.B. III. 5.2.11; 13.
[102] See Part III. p. 95.

Tejaśśabda, the Fiery Splendour of the Word, has become audible in the metres. Śārdūla-lalita and Śārdūla-vikrīḍita, the sport and play of the Śārdūla, are further names of metres.

Śārdūla is also the name of an animal shape 'made by art'. (cf. kṛtrima-grāsa; 'Samarāṅgaṇasūtradhāra', LVII. 777). It is also known as Virāla in Orissa[103] or Vyāla (S.S. LVII. 643), particularly in South India ('Mayamata', XVIII. 77). Śārdūla means a tiger, leopard, panther; a demon, a kind of bird, or the animal Śarabha which is stronger than a lion, has 8 legs and of which there is no likeness on earth.

In Indian sculpture, tiger and lion are interchangeable shapes and denote the foremost amongst all animals.[104] The Śārdūla is also called Siṃha-virāla, if its head is that of a lion; Nara-virāla if the head is that of man[105] and Gaja-virāla if it has the head of an elephant. It is represented rampant, but also in other postures. Endowed with the shape of the Lion, is the Siṃha, the group of the animal and the man which is carved in the round, at the base of the temple[106] (Pl. II) and also on the ridge of the Śukanāsā;[107] tiger, lion, boar, ram, bird and elephant combine where it rears, fearsome and playful, in relief on the walls of the temple,[108] in the recesses between piers (Pl. III).

[103] N. K. Bose, op. cit. p. 105.

[104] The physiognomy of the Lion is coined with an admixture of surviving classical and Achæmenian features, in early Indian sculpture and later (cf. also G. Combaz, L'Inde et L' Orient Classique, vol. II. pp. 16-17.—Lions are also preserved from Gandhāra with a strong admixture of Scythian traits; in mediæval Indian sculpture the Scythian component is the most conspicuous.

Worked in gold, figures of lions are inlaid in a bracelet with precious and semi-precious stones, in circles, crescents and triangles (in the Peshawar Museum, ASIAR, 1919-20, Pl. XXIV. C); they encompass the axis of movement at the places of shoulder and hip joints with flames of their jewel colours. In the mediæval stone sculptures, a fleece of curls (Pl. II; however damaged) or a scroll (Pl. LXXVII) mark the joints of these animals full of Power (śakti) and rhythmic movement.

The Śārdūla, complete with rider, and the fighting knight are carved in ivory, in Begram.

[105] Kramrisch, 'Indian Sculpture', Fig. 92.

[106] Cf. also Gadarmal temple: Badoh, Gwalior, ASIAR, 1919-20, Pl. XLIII. b., figure of a large lion on the plinth of the temple.

[107] See note 122. On Orissan temples a Siṃha 'flies' or leaps from the apex of the large Gavākṣa. Also in Bengal; Temple in Ghutgaria. ASIAR. 1925-26. Pl. IX.c; and, at the corresponding height from a corbel of the Śikhara, on temples of the Kumaon hills, etc. The Lion seated, is frequently placed below the Āmalaka, in Orissa. See also note 83, and infra.

[108] The Lion and the Śārdūla appear at different periods, in the various schools, in different parts of the sacred architecture: the lion figures as lowermost section of the pillar of Pallava temples, as bracket in the Cālukyan buildings, lion or Śārdūla are brackets of capitals in the Maṇḍapas of Candela temples in Central India, etc; on the wall, in procession in friezes on the base of Hoysala temples, etc. etc.

Śārdūla and Makara are hypostases of parts of the Kīrttimukha, *i.e.*, the Lion and the Dragon, but they each have a body being fully 'animal'. Kīrttimukha and Makara, Śārdūla and Makara, are frequently carved near each other and are also combined (Pl. L); on the side slab of the door steps of the Nārāyaṇa Temple, Aihole (Cousens, 'The Chālukyan Architecture', op. cit. p. 50, Fig. 16), etc. These carvings are related in their themes to those on the threshold of the Garbhagṛha; the 'Lion face', a long scroll issuing from its mouth is for example on the side of the door steps of the Śambhuliṅga temple in Kundgol (Cousens, l.c., Pl. XCII).

This protean animal made by art, has always the body of a lion, and in its more important versions, also its face. It is a symbolic shape and corresponds, within manifestation, to the Face of Glory, the Mask of the Asura.[109].

The original position of the Lion shape is in the corners of the Uttara Vedi, the High Altar. Similarly too, the Lions have their places in the corners of the Throne of the Supreme Spirit (Paramātman) or of Sūrya,[110] the Sun-god, and of the Buddha. The Siṃhāsana, the lion throne, is the figured equivalent of the Uttara Vedi. Thus, on the temple, the lions are not only at the bottom, on the Vedi, but also on top, on the Vedi of the Śikhara, where they support the stainless Āmalaka; they are also carved below the section of the Śikhara called Vedi, where the Lion (called Udā-siṃha, the 'flying' lion, in Orissa) springs on a corbel from its body.

Vāk, uttered Word, the Lioness, is as dangerous as she is beneficent, such is her nature as an element of the sacrifice and also as the Word which is the substance of the universe. The Lioness is Power, is Śakti;[111] Vāk, one with her in power and effect, is Māyā or Prakṛti, Nature. She is the power and effect of Parameśvara, the Supreme Lord, the Lion. This makes the Kīrttimukha, the Face of Glory, and the Śārdūla, who is Vāk and Prakṛti, so closely connected in the carvings of the temple (Pl. LXXVII). The Śārdūla shares the features of lion and dragon, and has the body of the lion;[112] the Śārdūla is more body than head; with powerful curved chest and sinuous thighs it rears; this mounting wave is its natural shape and gait "for just as man walks two footed and erect, so did the animals walk two footed and erect (Ś.B. III. 7. 3. 1) when they, as images discharged by creative thought (Paśyantī Vāk), embodied the Word in its fiery Splendour (tejaśśabda).

The Śārdūlas, carved on the temples are images of the words which had lain dormant in the unmanifest; they lift their heads and toss their manes, in close

Śārdūlas, half animal body, half scroll, the latter issuing from its mouth; and a Kīrttimukha, the centre of a scroll torus similarly originated, are part of the mouldings of a pillar (Pl. LXXIII from Kekind, Rajputana). Both these symbols are amongst the most frequently employed motives of architectural carvings.

A plethora of Śārdūlas and Siṃhas for example is on the rock-cut Pañca-Pāṇḍava Maṇḍapam in Mamallapuram (seventh century A.D.) where the seated Lion shape is also the lower part of the shaft of the pillar; rearing, it is shown on the brackets of their capitals; above the cornice a frieze of Śārdūlas is at the base of the upper storey. Similar friezes are peculiar to South Indian temples from then to the 13th century (Viṣṇu temple, Narttamalai, Pudukottai) and later. The animal proceeds in its various possibilities, tiger-lion following upon a horned dragon-lion with bird-beaked elephant trunk, etc. in permutations familiar to sculptures of 'super-natural' animals from the days of the Indus civilisation.

[109] The designation 'leogryph' is not suitable as the bird component is comparatively rare and restricted to the head only.

[110] 'Īśānaśivagurudevapaddhati', III. XIII. 6. The names of the Lions are "Stainless, Essence, Worshipful" and "Supreme Bliss". cf. JISOA, vol. X, Kramrisch, 'Temple, Door, Throne, etc.' p. 216.

[111] And thus the Vāhana of Durgā, the Great Goddess.

[112] While in many of the images the Animal can neither be classified as male nor as female, Siṃhāsanas generally are supported by male 'lions' (Pl. LVI).

sequence forming themselves the creeper-pattern, the wave of Prakṛti (Pl. X);[113] they rear and turn, lashed by their riders, whom they carry on their backs, and who are part of the wave, being themselves the Śārdūla's counter players. They are armed, ready to attack but stayed by the Beast and protected. Perfervidly ingenuous, the Beast and the figure of man form a recurrent pattern, rising and falling in rhythmic incandescence. Never is the rider thrown off; when he means to attack he is carried along and when he submits he is protected by the Power of Nature, and of Rhythm.

Vāk, who is Māyā, is the Chimaera,—never slain by Bellerophon. The Greek myth tells of him that he, though mortal, after having slain the Chimaera, tried to fly to heaven. This temerity was punished by Zeus who caused his fall. The animal, full of genius, the Chimaera, such as she is widely represented in Indian temples, is never killed. Her end comes differently. She vanishes, being Māyā, illusion, at the moment of Knowledge when she is resorbed in the Universal Consciousness. The story of King Dilīpa ('Raghuvaṃśa', II. 57-62) tells of this moment.

During twenty-one days King Dilīpa accompanied the cow given to him by Ṛṣi Vasiṣṭha.[114] On the twenty-second day the cow is attacked by a lion. The king draws an arrow but his arm is magically numbed. The lion says he is a servant of Śiva,[115] eating his appointed food. Dilīpa offers his own body to save the cow and asks the Lion to spare the 'body of his fame' (yaśassarīraṃ), his body of Splendour (yaśas), rather than his mortal body. The Lion consents; when the king presents himself to be devoured, the illusion (māyā) vanishes.

Confronted with the realisation by the king of his body of Splendour, the terrific Lion is nowhere to be seen for his body itself is made of the Splendour (tejas) and is but one Glory of King Dilīpa. The Fame and Glory of the Kings has at all times its emblem in the Lion or Tiger.[116]

In the group of the 'Lion and the Man' (Pl. II), the beast with open mouth and raised paw is about to devour, but its over-powering presence protects man, defiant, supplicating, small and part of the group in the closeness of the contact of its two figures and the continuity and response of their themes. Elsewhere the rearing Śārdūla safely carries its rider, while another warrior, with the sword of knowledge drawn, crouches below and seizes the tail of the beast,[117] or he proffers the shield

[113] This is a frequently recurring device, collateral with the door to the Garbhagṛha; (Temple in Tumain, Gwalior, ASIAR, 1918-19. Pl. XIIa).

[114] Twenty-one or three times seven is the extent of these worlds; 22 indicates the 'Beyond'-manifestation (cf. the 21 enclosing stones of the Gārhapatya hearth, Ś.B. VII. 1.1.13; VII. 1.1.32-35; the 21 knobs of the golden plate, the sun, which are the sun's rays, shining downwards (cf. Ś.B. VII. 4.1.10).

[115] Lion or tiger not only support and surround the throne of Divinity as His place of manifestation; Śiva (Parameśvara) himself is the Lion, Śiva takes the shape of the tiger (vyāghra), lion (siṃha), deer (mṛga), boar, etc. and of birds ('Mahābhārata', XIII. 45.127-8); see also note 108.

[116] 'Aitareya Brāhmaṇa', VII. 4.1.10. "The Tiger is the Lordly Power (rājanya) of the wild animals. The Rājanya is the Lordly Power".

[117] Lakṣmaṇa Temple, Khajuraho, bracket of Maṇḍapa pillar; the bracket next to it is illustrated on Pl. XVIII.

of dispassion (vairāgya), the protective weapon by which 'Nature' is held in check. If the whole group is placed on the head of an elephant, that "storehouse of darkness", the Lion, frolicsome after having overcome the darkness, scatters the brilliant pearls[118] that trickled down from the forehead of the elephant.[199] The Lion scatters the pearls, but being no ordinary lion but a Śārdūla, metre and rhythm itself, the pearls are collected in strings and festoons, in many rhythms (Pl. LXXVII). Taken from the 'storehouse of darkness', they now belong to the Lion; he gathers their strings in his mouth and as much as he is himself part of the Face of Glory, he holds them and sends them forth as his own; or he wears them as a necklace (Pl. II) and has his limbs edged with similar pearly chains of curling fur.

The group of the Lion and man is carved in the round and placed in front of the body of the temple. It shows man as he approaches the Centre, under the threat of the Lion; man draws the sword of Knowledge and protects himself from Māyā with the shield of dispassion. On the walls of the temple and the pillars of its halls, man rides the monster, Śārdūla, whose prancing gallop has the rhythm of Nature and inspiration.[120] Hers is the fiery splendour of creative thought;[121] her shape is rhythm itself. This noble beast embodies at the same time the lordly power of the wild animals; and represents the Lordly power (rājanya) in general; man, who rides it, copes with it, is particularly the Kṣatriya, the warrior, the royal knight;[122] it is his body of Fame (yaśaśśarīraṃ), his royal Splendour.[123]

In South Indian temples the rearing Śārdūla (Vyāla), is the general theme of Maṇḍapa pillars such as those of the Kalyāṇa Maṇḍapa, Mārgasaheśvar Temple, Viriñcapuram, ASIAR, 1919-20, Pl. VIIa. The Śārdūla above the elephant is equal to the Śārdūla above the Makara; the Śārdūla moreover frequently has the trunk of an elephant.

[118] "Like a lion who having overcome that storehouse of darkness, the elephant, jumps about scattering brilliant pearls"; Sirpur stone inscription, 8th-9th century; 'Ep. Ind.', XI. p. 190. "Lion intent upon vanquishing the heavenly elephants"; "large pearls hanging from the mouths of the lions acquired by breaking open the temples of the elephants" ('Ādipurāṇa', 231-32; I. A. vol. XIV, p. 105); cf. strings of beads issuing from the mouth of the Śārdūla, on the back slab of Buddhist images, for example, from Nālandā, ASIAR, 1928-29, Pl. LVII.

[119] This is a more facile way of acquisition than having to extract the pearl from the jaws of that other embodiment of darkness, the Dragon.

"Pearls that trickled down from the foreheads of the elephants of his (the king's) enemies that were slain by him as by a lion"; Gurjara Grant, about Śaka 417. 'Indian Antiquary', XIII. p. 84.

[120] The Śārdūla, different from the Kīrttimukha, is not shown as out-breathing. She is either inhaling or retaining the breath, commuting it into power (see infra).

The head of the Śārdūla proper is also without the component "Death head" which belongs to the Kīrttimukha proper; being Vāk, she is Life.

[121] The Śārdūla is at the same time the form of Paśyantī Vāk and Tejaśśabda as well as of Virāṭa Śabda, the Word which is the 'rhythmical body' of the universe.

[122] The group of the Śārdūla (and the knight) has been taken to refer in Orissan temples to the Kesarī dynasty (M. M. Ganguly, op. cit. p. 203); there the Lion is shown rearing with its triumphant rider; in front, below the lion is the small figure of an elephant—and in the 'Hoysala' temples of the Deccan to a ruler of that dynasty (Cousens, 'The Chālukyan Architecture', op. cit. p. 105). It is represented on carved panels (Mukteśvar temple, Bhuvaneśvar, Orissa, 10th century; Tripurāntaka temple, Balagamve, Dharwar, p. 107) and as statuary carved in the round the group of the Lion and man are placed on the ridge of the widely projected Śukanāsā (Dakṣiṇa Kedareśvara temple, Balagamve, c. 1075 A.D.; also temple at

The most exalted temple-type, the Meru, must be built by a Kṣatriya only as its patron, the architect being a Brāhmaṇa or a Vaiśya.[124] The royal patron is most closely identified with his temple by the symbol of the Śārdūla. On the walls of the temples of the Candella dynasty, in Central India, images of the Śārdūla alternate with images of the Apsarās and other goddesses (Pl. III).

The Śārdūla, an animal of perfervid ingenuity, composed of rhythm, is an embodiment per artem of the Lion, the Lordly Power of the wild beasts, who is Prakṛti, Śakti, Māyā. This image, composed of Rhythm, is Vāk. Vāk is Life ('Aitareya Brāhmaṇa,' X. 6. 38). The pilgrim who circumambulates the temple and whose eyes dwell on its images "wanders in the trek of the Apsarās and the Gandharvas and the wild beasts" (RV. X. 136. 6). He is cognizant of all that is knowable in this universe, says the commentator, he is qualified to confront and to ride the Śārdūla.

Rattehalli, Dharwar ; Pl. CXII) exactly as, for example, on the Viśvanātha temple, Khajuraho, and at the place where in Orissan temple (Liṅgarāja) the Lion above the elephant springs forth.

This scene has been interpreted as representing a patronymic legend related in an inscription from Gadag ('Ind. Ant.' II. p. 301) explaining the origin of the Hoy-sala dynasty which implies the slaying of the tiger and its subsequent adoption as emblem of the Hoy-sala ("slay or Sala") dynasty. The tiger in the image of the Śārdūla, however, is never represented as slain. This local adaptation of an universal Indian symbol is of secondary interest only.

[123] Cf. lion crests and lion flags ; the latter are described in the 'Ādipurāṇa', l.c. ; "On the lion flags, lions about to spring, appeared intent upon vanquishing the heavenly elephants. The large pearls hanging from the faces of the lions looked like fame acquired by breaking open the temples of great elephants". The lion is "dharma". It figures on the flags of sun and moon, 'Viṣṇudharmottara', III. LXVII. 8 ; LXVIII. 3.

[124] See part V. note 42, p. 143.

Royal patronage, Lion and Śārdūla, the many images of Śakti, and the Mithuna groups, seem to belong to the world of the Kṣatriya. The architect, it is enjoined, should be a Tāntrik ; p. 10.

Surasundarī, which means Celestial Beauty,[125] is but one of the names and types in which the image of Śakti is carved on the walls of the temple. Śakti is Energy, the primordial Power and substance of the world. Māyā,—the visible world, measurable in its forms,—belongs to Brahman as Śakti ('Vedānta Sūtra' I. IV, 1-7). She is herself the "ability to act";[126] her image is placed next to that of any of the gods. By her activity she attracts and helps the devotee; she is his guide and appeals to all. While every man is not equipped for riding the Śārdūla, he may be led by Śakti and grasp the meaning of her hands (hasta),[127] postures and actions. While the Śārdūla is the 'angel' of active man, the various images of Śakti assist his contemplative and passive nature. The images of Śārdūla (Vyāla), and Śakti are collateral; they alternate on the walls of the temples of Khajuraho and on the capitals of the pillars (Pls. III, XVIII). The rearing body of the animal and the shape of the woman are seen to sway in similar curves; they are one in nature and form though different in functions and appearance, for Śakti is Vāk, the "active power of Brahman proceeding from him" (ṚV. X. 125) and the Śārdūla is Vāk.

The plan, with the fretted outline of the buttressed fort, of the temple (Figs. on pp. 251, etc.) is akin to a yantra or linear diagram used by the worshipper for a localisation of each of the aspects and powers of God in their hierarchy with regard to the Centre, the immovable Principle. In the Śrī-yantra, the various positions are held by goddesses or powers who are known as Yoginīs,[128] conjoint energies by whom is effected the work of the Transcendental Power, Mahā-Śakti. They are placed in the yantra in a hierarchy of position, proceeding inward and corresponding to an increasing secrecy and sacredness until the centre is reached where the Supreme Yoginī is, the Mahā-Śakti. Close to the perimeter, yet secret in their power, are a group of Yoginīs; where they reside is the Place of Fulfilment of All Hopes (sarvāśāparipūraka-cakra). They are the Attractions (akarṣiṇī) of and by the intellect (buddhi), of and by the sense of "I" ness (ahaṅkāra), of and by the faculties of knowledge and action who, decked in love provoking fashion, draw towards themselves the intellect, the notion of "I" ness, all the faculties of knowledge and action, the senses and the body, thought and memory and while they overwhelm them and

[125] 'Samarāṅgaṇasūtradhāra', LVII. 645.

[126] 'Śak' means "to be able to do something" ; 'ti' denotes capability.

[127] 'Hasta' is an attitude of arm and hand, or of the hand only ; it is a near synonym of 'mudrā'. The action, shown by the respective gesture, conveys one or many definite meanings.

[128] 'Tantrarāja-Tantra,' ch. IV, 72-73 ; in the Śrīyantra, 16 Śaktis (gupta yoginīs), the Attractions, are stationed on the 16 lotus-petals near the circumference of the circle. Outside the circle, and within the square enclosure of the yantra are the Dikpālas, the Guardians of the regions and other groups of divinities. The Āvaraṇa-devatās, the surrounding divinities, in both these zones, have their images and correspondences on the walls of the temple.—Yoginīs are attendants of various classes of the Great Goddess who is herself called Yoginī ('Jñānārṇava Tantra', XVI. 140 f. 'Tantrarāja Tantra', V. 28. Comm. Manoramā.)

fulfil their desire they leave them, increased in power, in the region where hopes and desires attain their multifarious objects. With the help of these Śaktis a transformation is then effected of the mind (manovikāra), the faculties and the rest; they approach the Centre in which there is no separateness.

It is in this sense that a further group of beauteous Śaktis is described as Maids (paricārikā) and others are called Messengers (dūtī) of the Transcendental Power, the Mahā-Śakti. In their lotus-hands they carry, each of them, a 'mudrā', a raiment, a mirror and various kinds of vessels[129] (Pls. XI, XII, XIV, XLI, LI).

The Śaktis or Yoginīs are working energies subservient to the Great Śakti. On the walls of the temples they are figured in all directions as Celestial Beauties. They perform this work by the side of the gods whose activity their presence releases. Indian astrology knows the Yoginī as a cosmic power. It moves from day to day, from place to place, in all directions.

By the side of the eight Regents of the directions of space, by the side of each of the several groups of gods, the Celestial Beauties are placed embodied in their archetypal forms. They display them in rhythms and gestures and by their attributes which they have in common with the Yoginīs.

In the macrocosm they operate as branches and part aspects of the Transcendental Power, conjointly with the Supreme Principle as Yoga-māyā, the manifestation of the universe. In the microcosm, with reference to man, Yoga-māyā is the power of reintegration; the Yoginīs are maids and messengers, the 'angels' of the Transcendental Power. The Attractions in the outer circle of the yantra, the Celestial Beauties on the walls of the temple, serve man, the devotee; they satisfy his response to them so that, increased in power, released from their attractions and transformed, he proceeds in his devotion towards God in the innermost sanctuary of his heart and in the temple. They help man towards reintegration, akin to those celestial damsels (apsarās) who appear at the time when he, a knower of Brahman departs from this world: "Him approach 500 celestial damsels, 100 carrying scented powders, saffron, turmeric and the like, in their hands, 100 carrying fruits, 100 carrying various ornaments and 100 carrying garlands. They adorn him with ornaments befitting Brahmā himself. Thus adorned with Brahmā ornaments and knowing Brahman he goes to Brahman."[130]

The Celestial Beauties belong to the Āvaraṇa-devatās, "surrounding divinities". Their number is large. Their figures are repeated on the temples, all round the walls, to either side of each god, and as on the Kandarīya and Devī Jagadambā Temples, in all the three belts of sculpture. (Pls. I and III). Such supererogation in carving their figures, alike in type yet indefinitely modified in each instance by a particular rhythmical consistency, shows repetition itself as a power in whose comprehensive rhythm are interwoven the images in rows and storeys. It is made concrete by art in the figures of the gods and the celestial women who, though they resemble the human shape, are unlike it. For the divine (daiva) and the human form "are born from one parentage. The divine form is

[129] In the yantra of Bhuvaneśvarī, the Maids (paricārikā) have their place outside the lotus-petals; 'Śāradātilaka', ch. IX, 38—40; the Messengers (dūtī) surround the Primordial Śakti imaged as Tripuṭā (ch. X. 92).

[130] 'Kauṣītakī Brāhmaṇa Upaniṣad', I. 4.

endowed with more intellect (buddhi). The human form is not so endowed with intellect.''[131]

The form of the Celestial Beauties is of embodied intellect; by art this intellectual (paramārthika) body is made concrete.[132] It is different from the physical body of flesh and bones and which is of the earth. The qualities of the celestial body are those of the atmosphere, pervaded as it is by the light of the sun and where blows the wind and the gale of the Spirit. It is the region of movement; the celestial bodies are built up by movement only. In the ''air-world'' (bhuvas; antarikṣa) the gods dwell; man moves in it and breathes. In its movement, his living body is of the air-world and one in nature with that of the gods. Indian sculpture, whose subject is the gods, knows only of this celestial body. It consists of movement and is resilient with the breath that courses in its smooth channels.

Other names and forms, other image of Śakti are: Apsarā,[133] Nāṭakā,[134] Yakṣiṇī[135] and Dig Devī.[136] Being active power and causal stress, her image is an embodiment of movement; as Apsarā she is the movement in the atmosphere, as Yakṣiṇī she is the movement in vegetation, as Nāṭakā she is the movement in the body of man and is shown as a dancer. Her iconography describes her various 'places'; they are not sharply defined. Her associates, such as bough and tree (Śālabhañjikā; Pl. LX)[137] and flowering vines (Pl. XVIII) declare her images as Yakṣiṇī.

Vibrant power is the celestial beauty of her images; they all resemble the Great Goddess whose 'eyebrows are the entrance arches of the Palace of the Lord of Love'[138] and whose eyes are like fishes, playing in the lake of the beauty of her

[131] 'Matsya Purāṇa', ch. CXLV. 14-16.

[132] 'Garuḍa Purāṇa', ch. XV. 45-68.

[133] Apsarās are the celestial dancers in Indra's heaven (Pls. LXVIII, XL). Their name signifies ''moving in the water'', in the celestial vapour; they are the movement in the atmosphere while the Yakṣiṇīs are the movement in the trees.

The Apsarās are the consorts of the Gandharvas and are also known as Surāṅganās or celestial damsels (cf. Surasundarī). The 'Tantrarāja Tantra', IV. 58-70, tells how to control Apsarā and Yakṣiṇī.

[134] Nāṭakā, as a rule, is the designation of the dancing female figures on the walls of the temples; cf. ''Mayamata'', XVIII. 6, where Vyāla (=Śārdūla) and Nāṭakā appear by the side of each other.

[135] Yakṣiṇīs ('Tantrarāja-tantra', XVII. 50-53) are young and beautiful woman-spirits in fine raiments who give the Sādhaka all worldly goods he may desire. In this limited function, however, they carry the heritage of their past when Yakṣa was equivalent with Divinity (Devatā; see also the images represented and inscribed in Barhut, Barua, op. cit.).

[136] Dig Devīs or Dig Nāyikās are the Women of the Quarters; they are frequently referred to in inscriptions (Candela Inscr. 'Ep. Ind.' I. p. 212; inscription from Ittagi, dated A.D. 1112. 'Ep. Ind.' XIII. p. 36 f.) of which some, for example, 'Ep. Ind.' XIII. p. 205, describe how the ''precious pearls of the king's stainless virtues adorn the girdles of the Ladies of the Quarters of Space'' or how the Dignāyikās ''wove the fame (of the king) into pearl strings which they ever wore'' ('Ind. Ant.' VI. p. 65, grant of Govinda II Rathor, 750-810 A.D.).

[137] The group of the 'Woman and Tree' is known as Śālabhañjikā; or Śālabhañjī (S. S. LXVI. 30-32). Cf. Coomaraswamy, 'Yakṣas', I. p. 32 f.

The Śālabhañjikā is frequently carved on the brackets of capitals or forms the bracket of the Ucchālaka (Pls. XVIII, LX).

The Nāṭakā, Pl. LXIV, also forms a bracket, but of the ceiling of the Maṇḍapa.

[138] 'Brahmāṇḍa Purāṇa, Lalita Sahasranāma', 6.

face. This beauty in her belongs to God and is His reflex; He is seen himself to assume the state of Śakti so that he may be confronted by His own felicity with all its contents.[139] Śakti reflects by her Form (rūpaṃ) the Light (prakāśa) which is God.[140] She mirrors the Light of Consciousness-Bliss (cidānanda). Because she acts as its mirror, she is also shown holding a mirror in her hand (Pl. XIV).[141] If the boughs of her tree are like her arms and the curves of the creeper like her own movement,[142] if the tree-woman is one idea and composition, the mirror-woman is another type or sculptured group of Śakti; the former being a reiteration of the underlying theme by two kinds of shape, that of vegetation and that of woman, their interplay, affinity, and identity as movement, the latter enacting the drama of the reflection seen in the mirror and of the living being. "The reflection of the face seen in the mirror is nothing in itself as separated from the face; so is the living creature (jīva) in itself nothing, a reflection of Consciousness in the mind—that self-abiding Consciousness in its true state am I" [143] says Supreme Consciousness of itself. Śakti exemplifies it, on her own level, with luxurious grace and sadness, or any of the emotions which belong to the human face.

While Śakti looks at herself in the mirror or experiences herself in her movement to which she yields, while she produces it, she becomes conscious of herself in any of her shapes and wondering she knows and greets herself.

Wondering she enters the palace of her person and touches her body in a new awareness (Pls. XIII, XV, XVI) while she discovers her egoity, her own and particular "I"ness in the many tasks which she performs as part and maid of the Great Goddess.

In her wondrous beauty, where the 'person' meets her Power, Śakti bends over Ahaṅkāra, the "I" concept, which is but herself tainted by her entry into this world of duality (Pls. XVIII, XIX). The goddess is near to losing her divinity while her beauty becomes animated by emotions (Pls. LX, LXIV, XIII).[144] So far and no further do these angels descend for the sake of the souls in bondage (paśu) whom they introduce to the higher hierarchy.

[139] This relation is that of the 'enjoyer' and the 'enjoyed' (bhoktā; bhogya). Abhināvagupta who lived at the time when the most ingenuous and diversified images of Śakti were carved (c. 1000 A.D.) says: "The God of unsurpassed felicity is called the enjoyer. Desire and such other contents of His self are what he enjoys. It is for this reason only that he assumes the state of Śakti" ('Tantrāloka', śl. 190; comm.).

[140] The beauty of Śakti lies in the coincidence of her form and meaning, it is a projection of her image as it is in God, into visibility by means of art. Her perfection is not only in her dance of productive intentness (Pls. XXI, XXII), but also in her destructive will as the dancer of death. Cāmuṇḍā, the seventh Mātṛkā, is carved as a dancer, on mediæval temples (Bhūleśvar Temple, 'Bulletin of the Deccan College Research Inst.', vol. IV. Fig. 7); and in earlier reliefs.

[141] The mirror is "pure knowledge" (V.D. III. ch. XLVIII. 16). The mirror is one of the attributes of Pārvatī, and also the Lotus flower.—Goddess and mirror within a lotus flower in full bloom are carved in Barhut (Barua, op. cit. Pl. XXXI).

[142] Latā is both creeper and woman; a slender girl, any woman.

[143] 'Hastāmalaka', 3 (Sāyaṇācārya, 'Śaṅkara Digvijaya').

[144] Hindu, Buddhist (Pl. XXXVIII) and Jain (Pl. XX) images are referred to here without discrimination as the principle "Śakti" is realised by the orthodox and also the unorthodox devotees and craftsmen alike.

The problem of egoity (ahaṅkāra) is particularly given shape in mediæval Indian sculpture. It may be due to some extent to the infiltration of new, Northern elements (Gujars, Ahirs,

India thinks in images; the image (mūrti) itself is beheld as a divinity. "Mūrti (image), the wife of Dharma (the Order of things in the cosmos and Righteousness in man), is Form, luminous and charming. Without her, the Supreme Spirit (Paramātman), whose abode is the whole universe, would be without support."[145] Her charm and attractions are those of the Anima Mundi, cosmic vitality, active in the middle region (antarikṣa), in space. There the temple has its extension.

etc.) into the people of India, and intensified by the strain and apprehension caused by the Muslim invasion.

Its expression differs in kind and degree in the various sculptures (Pls. XIV, XII, XVI, XVII) not only in their countenance but throughout the whole figure or also the whole group and its parts. The perfection of movement has not everywhere the same serenity (Pl. XX against Pls. XVIII, XIX). Vehement in its resilience it finds its balance in the upper part of the body (Pl. XX) ; in another image the body stiffens in dancing frenzy in a vertical of high tension (Pl. XXI). Emotional overemphasis leads to a tortured expression of some of the figures, to a cramped linear movement (of the fluttering scarves, for example, Pls. XXI, LXIII), to harshness in the contrast of modelled form and the flat ground of the relief (Pl. XI), to a violent antithesis of light and the deepest shadows (Pl. XXI) and to an elimination of modelling (Pl. LIV) in sculptures of a subsequent phase. Starkly assertive, the "I" conceit subjects the 'curves of life', the sinuosities of the vibrant form of Śakti, to impervious accents (Pl. LIV). They lend zest and incisiveness to some of the carvings (Pl. XLII) while in less gifted hands (Pls. XL, LXIII) they deaden Indian sculpture.

[145] 'Brahmavaivarta Purāṇa', II. 1. 145.

THE IMAGES OF IMMANENT BREATH

The celestial dancers, the Apsarās, have their bodies built not of the gross substance of earth, such as flesh and bones, but of the attributes of air consisting of movement, "bending, stretching, jumping and running".[146] Thus she dances at the festival of the gods in Indra's heaven (Pl. LXVIII; 'Mahābhārata'. III. 43. 28-32). Gandharvas make the music and join in the dance in Indra's city Amarāvatī. That he enters Amarāvatī is said of a dying person;[147] he is released of the earthly sheath of his body as is the initiate, who enters the inner temple.

In full worship there is always dancing and singing before the Devatā for his entertainment. This is Rājasīka Pūjā, expansive worship of God. In Sāttvika Pūjā, in which is worshipped the Essence (Sat), the Supreme Spirit, the dance is that of the mind and the senses. It is the dance of Śakti in her various forms. These are carved on the walls of the temple (Pls. XXI, XXII, LXIV) and show their "body of movement" which belongs to the air and is supported by immanent breath. For the air, when inhaled, is changed; it is believed to increase in volume by the heat of the body; not all of it is exhaled, the major part of its increase remaining. Thus the vital forces are increased and also the lightness of the body; the more the air (prāṇa) is kept in, the lighter becomes the body.[148] This is the object of the control of breath (prāṇāyāma) which is a prerequisite in the training of a Yogī. The lightness of the body (laghutva; 'Śvet. Up.' II. 13) is felt in its effect as a soaring, a staying in the air. The power of levitation, inwardly experienced through breath, releases the images of the dancing, flying hosts of gods, of Apsarās and Gandharvas, of the Vidyādharas, the wizards and of numberless Gaṇas and other celestials (Pls. XXIII, LIII, LXIX, LXXIV, LXV, XXIV, LV).

Prāṇāyāma is part of the knowledge of the sculptor by actual practice or by his awareness of it. Another means of concrete realisation, similarly at his command is by touch, as practised in Nyāsa, the ritual act of assigning or locating divinity at its proper place in his own living body and in the form of the image. Such a constantly repeated concrete experience by touch of shape three dimensional, rounded and also breathing, is part of the equipment of the craftsman, as a Sādhaka and Yogī. He applies it creatively on the image which he carves. Prāṇāyāma and

[146] 'Garuḍa Purāṇa' XV. 25. The body consists of the five elements: earth, water, fire, air and ether. Skin, bones, nerves, hair and flesh are the five attributes of earth; bending, running, jumping, etc., are the five attributes of the air.

[147] This meaning is implied in Mbh. VII. 7. 20.

[148] The air inhaled (pūraka) increases in volume by the heat of the body 5 times while it is restrained or the breath is held (kumbhaka) and when exhaled (recaka) two-fifths only pass out and the remaining three-fifths are retained.

Nyāsa develop in him a subtle sense of the living form, not only sustained, but also shaped, as it were, by breath. In his carvings he makes palpable the 'body of breath' by a modelling in which the shape of man, free from the gross weight of the earth, the bones and muscles which belong to it, is given transubstantiated form as the breathing body of the gods.

With breath restrained the vaulted chest (Pl. LXXIX) lifts the sentient face into regions where pain is no more but a memory (Pl. XXV), and offerings are made of sound from many instruments (Pls. XXVII, XXVIII, LV), or full of detachment, the flight is across clouds of ignorance. They are cut by the sword of knowledge in the hand of the Vidyādhara. Gaṇas are often seen flying in crowds and Vidyādharas are accompanied by Apsarās or they fly singly. Trenchant, their backs arched like scimitars, with sword drawn and mace swung across their heaving shapes, the Devas soar fighting (Pl. XXIII); in another relief they are composed into a pattern of the cosmic wheel (Pl. LXIX) which keeps rolling through the cycles of time, they urge it on wielding their swords and driven themselves in its rotation; knowledge is ground by the wheel of time and its swish is the rhythm of a ceiling panel.

Breath, the vital manifestation of the Spirit, is the support and prime mover of all action; it is shown having formed a body of its own which is particularly that of the Gaṇas (Pls. LXV, XXIV, etc.). They are mere quantities (gaṇa = quantity), look like windbags (Pl. LXV), hosts of them. Their bodies inflated by air race in gusts across the atmosphere, support the Vimānas, the chariots of the gods (Pl. XXIV), and produce the music out of the sound which is immanent in the ether and in the air. Full of it, they play it on different instruments and make it as articulate as their air-borne, air-filled bodies are made by the sculptor. They —and not caryatids—carry the superstructure and walls of the temple (Pls. LIII, LXVI, XXXIX).

The inward realisation of lightness, weightlessness, non-existence of the physical body in a state of concentration on the Supreme Spirit and on His manifestation, the Word, and the hearing of its music are shown in the images of the Gaṇas who, while resembling the shape of man, are unlike it. Their bodies made of breath move in the air.

"Breath goes out with the sound HA and enters again with the sound SA; the living being is indeed always repeating the mantra Haṃ-Sa. Haṃ-Sa" ('Garuda-Purāṇa', XV. 78). Breathing is the rhythmic formula which is constantly said of itself. The Haṃsa mantra is the "seed of the Universe", the breath of life (prāṇa-bīja). Its visual symbol is the Haṃsa, the royal mallard, celestial swan (Pls. XLII. LXXV) who is the vāhana of Brahman. "The Haṃsa dwelling in the Light . . .[149] signifies the unity of Paramātman, the Lord beyond and without qualities, and all that has proceeded from him. It is thus also His symbol as Antarātman, the immanent Spirit ('Śāradātilaka', XXI. 64 f) which is consciousness as the manifestation of Supreme Consciousness (Cit).

In the shape of the celestial swan it is carved anywhere on the base of the Prāsāda or on the ceiling of the Maṇḍapa, flocks of birds in shapes ever renewed in

[149] Haṃsavatī Ṛk. RV. IV. 40.5; 'Vāj. S.' XII. 14; Ś.B. VI. 7.3.11; 'Kathopaniṣad', V. 2.

the course of thousands of years,[150] in procession, or in couples confronting each other. Where, as in Pl. LXXV, a lotus in flower is shown between two swans, the words addressed to the Goddess have found a visible equivalent: "I worship that pair of swans who are Haṃ and Sa, dwelling in the mind of the Great, who subsist entirely on the honey of the blooming lotus of Knowledge" ('Saundarya Laharī', 38).

As form (rūpaṃ) and figure (ākṛti) of a verbal symbol, the Haṃsa bird carved on the temples means that union towards which fly the hosts of celestials, the Gaṇas, Vidyādharas and Gandharvas and whose dancers are the Apsarās. They are given form, are bodied forth by art as images of the power and the movement of the Breath and the Spirit.

[150] From Mauryan capitals (3rd Century B.C.; Rampurva) to contemporary South Indian temple reliefs and metal lamps. The Sasanian shape of the bird proved to be the most enduring (Pl. XLII). The Haṃsa, except in the classical, "illusionistic" representation of the Kaniṣka casket is but rarely shown flying (Pl. LXVII); even though they surround flying Vidyādharas, the birds are not represented in flight.

MITHUNA

The State of Being a Couple

"Just as a man closely embraced by a beloved woman knows nothing more of a without or a within, so also does the Person (the spiritual person of man) embraced by the 'prognostic' (prajñātmanā) Spirit know nothing more of a without or a within. This is his true form in which his desire is satisfied, the Spirit and the whole of his desire. He has no desire any more, nor any pain." ('Bṛhadāraṇyaka Upaniṣad', IV. 3.21).[151]

This state which is "like a man and a woman in close embrace" is a symbol of Mokṣa, final release or re-union of the two Principles, the Essence (Puruṣa) and Nature (Prakṛti). This symbol is carved, on the door jambs of the Garbhagṛha and on the walls of the temple, repeatedly, in the many forms in which limbs are conjoined in close embrace (Pls. XXX-XXXIV).[152] The name of this conjoint symbol of Puruṣa and Prakṛti, as Mokṣa, is Mithuna, 'the state of being a couple'.[153]

Mithuna as symbol of Mokṣa, ultimate release, means a union, like that of the Fire and its burning power, which is inseparable from, and in, the Fire from the beginning. Mithuna as practised and beheld by the Sādhaka is a re-union, for in the beginning the Puruṣa, the Essence, was "like a man and a woman in close embrace. It desired a second. Himself the Puruṣa divided into two. So were born man and wife. He united himself to her" ('Bṛhadāraṇyaka Upaniṣad', I. 4. 1-4).[154]

Prakṛti as Supreme Śakti is within God, hidden in His own qualities ('Śvetāśvatara Upaniṣad', IV. 10). Within Him, by means of his mind (manas), he entered into union (Mithuna) with the unspoken Word (Vāk) (Ś.B. VI. 1. 2. 6). The divine 'bi-unity' comes about by "Śiva's need of Śakti for accomplishing the enjoyment of unredeemed man (paśu, lit. the animal) and his final release" (Śrīkumāra in 'Tātparyapradīpikā', the commentary on 'Tattvaprakāśa' I. 3).

Man's separation from God and the world of dichotomy in which he lives result from the bi-sexual polarity in divinity, and from the subsequent exter-

[151] Translated by Coomaraswamy in 'La Doctrine de la "Biunité" Divine', É.T., 1937, pp. 289-301.

[152] The 'Tantrarāja Tantra', XXI. 88-96 treats of the offerings made to the 50 Mithunas.

[153] Mithuna as an enrichment on the door-jambs (śākhā) of the Garbhagṛha is enjoined to be carved in the 'Bṛhat Saṃhitā' LV, 'Hayaśīrṣapañcarātra', 'Agnipurāṇa' CIV. 30; 'Samarāṅgaṇasūtradhāra', XL. 30-34; etc.

The earliest Mithuna yet known is carved on one of the earliest historical monuments yet known, *i.e.*, of about the 2nd century B.C. in Sāñcī, Stūpa II. Marshall-Foucher, 'The Monuments of Sanchi', Pl. LXXVII. 20a. Mithuna is one of the permanently recurrent themes of Indian sculpture. A 'classical' Mithuna, on a gold ornament, is reproduced in the 'Journal of the Asiatic Society of Bengal', 1912, p. 283.

The Buddhistic connotation of Mithuna is the union of Buddha and Prajñā.

[154] See note 151.

nalisation of the Conscious Śiva as the object of his own Self-enjoyment. In order to regain the primordial wholeness (Brahmajñāna) the yogin practises bodily, mental and intellectual exercises and the devotee (sādhaka) observes the rites as his means of accomplishing (sādhana) final release. In such exercise (yoga) there is a coupling (maithuna) of the active and the changeless Principles.

The symbolic union (yoga) in the flesh with the assistance of a Śakti may be practised only by Sannyāsins who are far advanced on the road to metaphysical realisation, while the highest class of Avadhūta[155] does not require this sacrament and may not unite with a woman. The Sādhana in which the Sādhaka is assisted by his Śakti is called Latā-sādhana.[156] In its performance the Śakti is as much woman (latā) as she is a vine or creeper (latā). "As the creeper embraces the tree on all sides, so do thou embrace me" ('Atharva Veda', VI. 8.4.). "For when one is with a mate, he is whole and complete" ('Śatapatha Brāhmaṇa', X. 5. 2. 8.).[157] Thus Gaurī is described as Ardhāṅgī, the half of Śiva's body, "embracing Śiva as the Mādhava creeper clasps the young Āmra tree with her bosom like a cluster of blossoms". ('Yogavāsiṣṭha, Nirvāṇaprakaraṇa', XVIII. 3).

Gods and ascetics therefore should be represented in their love sport (krīḍā, līlā) on the walls of temples[158] but ascetics practising the game of love should not figure on the habitations of men[159] for their game is none of the three purposes of life.[160] It is a symbol of final release, its fourth and ultimate purpose.

[155] Avadhūta is a man who is above caste and the ordered life (āśrama ; *i.e.*, its four successive stages as celibate student, householder, recluse and Sannyāsin) and ever contemplates the Supreme Spirit only. The lowest type of these Sannyāsins live in the family. In the third class, conforming with the rules of Yoga and Bhoga, the Sannyāsin may satisfy the desire of a woman who approaches him. In the next two classes he is competent to practise Yoga with the assistance of a Śakti. In the highest, the sixth class, he may not unite with a woman.

[156] The rules relating to Latā-sādhana are given in the following Tantras: Śiva Saṃhitā, p. 45 ; Prāṇatoṣinī, p. 618 ; Gandharva Tantra, p. 60 ; Kaulāvalī, p. 29, etc.

[157] In Orissa, (cf. 'Utkalakhaṇḍa', XI. 'Ind. Ant.' XLVII. p. 217) it is said that Mithuna figures on a building prevent the building being struck by lightning.

In the lightning is seen the union and identity of the immanent spirit of man and the transcendent Spirit. "The Person seen in the lightning—I am He ; I indeed am He ('Chānd. Up.'. IV.13.1. 'Kena Up.' 29-30). No lightning will strike the building where this union is imaged.

[158] T. Bhattacharya, 'Some Notes on Mithuna in Indian Art.' Rūpam, 1926, p. 22f, quotes 'Suprabedhāgama', XXX. saying that "Śivakrīḍā, Harikrīḍā and Tapakrīḍā should particularly [be made]"—a reference which could not be verified from the Tanjore Ms. of the 'Suprabedhāgama'.

Mithuna carvings showing shaven headed and other ascetics occur on the temples of Orissa ; also in Khajuraho, etc.

[159] 'Mayamata', XVIII. 111.

[160] Kāma, Lust, with the discipline of its satisfaction, is the third of the 4 purposes of life which are lawfulness (dharma), the acquisition of wealth (artha), the satisfaction of lust (kāma) and the attainment of final release (mokṣa).

ĀMAḶAKA

The Āmalaka is the crown of a Nāgara temple. Above the truncated body of its Śikhara it clasps the shaft (veṇu; Pl. I)[161] and is surmounted by the finial (stūpikā) with the vase (kalaśa) as its most conspicuous part. The Āmalaka has a cogged rim. Its solid shape is that of a ring stone; it may be compared to an indented wheel, the spokes being shown as ribs of its ring shape (Pl. I). The Āmalaka is not only the crown of the main Śikhara (mūla-śikhara, mūla-mañjarī) of the temple, but also of every Mañjarī or Śṛṅga that leans against, or is arrayed on, its body (Pls. I, II, IV, XLIII, XLV and XLVII). Its shape furthermore is the basis of the finial above the superstructure of the Maṇḍapa (Pl. I); it may moreover, be doubly present (Pls. III, IV) having its larger and main shape surmounted by yet another smaller shape.[162] Where, as in Orissa, etc. the Latā type of the Śikhara is dominant each of its Bhūmis itself terminates in an Āmalaka; carved in the corners it is assimilated in its shape to the square section of the Śikhara and forms an Āmalaka quoin.[163] There is no Āmalaka on the superstructure of a South Indian Drāviḍa temple. Its position, function and meaning are transferred there to the cupola of the High Temple, the Vimāna or Harmya.[164]

The Nāgara temple is the most widely represented shape of the Hindu temple, in time and place. The Āmalaka is the crown above the Śikhara; it is at the same time a ring around the emerged part of the internal and invisible pillar of the temple, a capital of the 'Veṇu' of which the truncated body of the Śikhara is a sheath (veṇu-kośa).[165] It is the highest part of the Śikhara; separated from its truncated body, it is the base on which rises the finial. Its function and meaning are two-fold; it is the crown of the superstructure, the sheath, and a cogged ring around the internal pillar of the temple. As crown it is the loadstone which locks together the pile of the Śikhara; as ring-

[161] The earliest yet known crowning Āmalaka of a structural temple has been unearthed in fragments at Nāgarī, Chitor, Rajputana. Mem., ASI, No. 4, p. 126. It belongs to the fifth century A.D. Cf. Cunningham, ASR. IX. p. 43, describing small shrines complete with Śikhara and Āmalaka, at Tigowa, C.P.

[162] They are called Āmalasara and Āmalasarī respectively (J. Burgess—H. Cousens, 'Architectural Antiquities of Northern Gujerat', op. cit. p. 27). They may be seen on temples of Central India, the United Provinces, the Central Provinces; for example on the Mahādev Temple at Nohta, where an Āmalasara of enormous diameter is topped by a smaller Amalasarī; ASIAR, 1912-13, Pt. I. pl. Va, and in Gujarat, etc.

Cf. also, ASIAR, 1927-28, Pl. LIIA, a Triśūla supported by three Āmalakas (stūpa II, Nāgārjunakoṇḍa).

[163] The blocking courses formed by the Āmalaka quoins (of the koṇa-pāga, karṇa) have the shape of a ribbed square cushion (Pl. LXXI; Osian, Rajputana) or of a rectangular clasp (Orissa). Cf. 'Viṣṇudharmottara', III. ch. LXXXVI. 7-8.

[164] This has also been recognised by K. R. Pisharoti, in an article on 'Āmalaka', 'The Calcutta Oriental Journal', Vol. I. p. 191; note 19.

[165] In the South Indian temples, it has been shown, the walls of the High Temple form the emerging part of the central pillar which is also called 'grīvā', the neck.

stone or capital it rises above it and is the final clasp of the neck of the pillar itself invisible and having for its sheath the truncated body of the Śikhara.[166]

The superstructure reduces the extent of the temple from the surface covered by its plan and perpendicular walls, to the point of the finial which is beyond the superstructure. This ascension is made haltingly, pausing at every Bhūmi or level (Pl. LXXI) and coming to an end of its own at the pinnacle of every Śṛṅga (Pl. IV), which is but a station on the steep upward slope and curve towards the summit. "The stations on the way to Brahman are conductors of the soul, not marks of the road nor places of enjoyment" ('Vedānta Sūtra', Comm. IV. III. 2-7). Śṛṅga clings to Śṛṅga; (Pls. IV, XLIII); and all the Uro-mañjarīs lean against and are urgent in their competition towards the top where they come closest to the root-Śikhara and the central Pillar. As much as the piers and offsets proceed from the perpendicular walls, away from the centre of the temple, so much do the Śṛṅgas and Latās compete towards—or leave off—and, reduced in number or extent, reach the inner sheath (veṇu kośa-antara),[167] the topmost course of the Vedi (skandha) and the Pillar with its Āmalaka. It is a long ascent (dūrohaṇam) made by the eye on the basis of shape and form. This ascent is an architectural analogy to the recitation of the Dūrohaṇa mantra, "By repeating the Dūrohaṇa Mantra the sacrificer ascends to heaven" ('Aitareya Brāhmaṇa', XVIII. 6. 20). The sacrificer must already when alive ascend to heaven and gain a footing in the sun which shines on high; then he descends again to the earth. Thus the sacrificer who has arrived in the celestial world takes foot solidly in this world.

All this is performed by the repeated recitation of the Dūrohaṇa Mantra, its verses and pauses;[168] all this is performed too by the ever renewed effort at climbing the Śikhara with the help of its smaller replicas. By this repeated and renewed effort, the apex is reached and the mass of the structure is reduced. The many Bhuūmis, Mañjarīs, Śṛṅgas and Latās fulfil their purpose in different ways on the various temples: with a seeming independence and a high flung tension (Pl. I); in a choral sameness of step, reglemented and united (Pl. XLIII), or with a rhythmical interchange of ascent and pause,—of vertical curve, and platform; together with Āmalaka—sustained by one chain of thought carried in its long course (Pls. LXXI and IV).

The upward journey approaches its end the nearer it leads to the Central Pillar of the temple which emerges from the High Vedi, a straight passage in its vertical direction though not factually, right from the Garbhagṛha and its centre. Above the crown and ring of the Āmalaka there is no competition, only a meeting and concurrence from all directions in the point of the finial; it rises bud-shaped or in the likeness of a fruit (mātuluṅga) from the vessel, the Amṛta-kalaśa (amara-kāraka) which makes immortal because "Viśvakarmā made the Kalaśa from the different parts (kalā) of each of the gods" ('Mahānirvāṇa-tantra', V. 181). So the substance of the Kalaśa, which is gold, as a rule,[169] contains the properties of

[166] This part is also played by the pyramidal Bhūmis of the South Indian superstructure.

[167] 'Samarāṅgaṇasūtradhāra', LVI. 288; or Skandha-Kośāntara; 276.

[168] S. Lévi, 'La Doctrine du Sacrifice', pp. 88-89.

[169] The jar (Kumbha; Kalaśa) of the Stūpikā is of gold; it may be substituted by copper, silver, stone, brick or stucco (saudha); 'Mayamata', XVIII. 195.

each of the gods up in the deathless (amara) region, straight above the Nidhi-Kalaśa in the foundation of the temple in which were placed the treasures (nidhi) of the earth.[170] The 'treasures' would be transmuted into Deathlessness in the High Vase in which their several colours, scents and shapes would have entered through their presiding divinities. As above the temple, so also is a vase below the temple. In the Vase (kalaśa, kuṃbha) of the finial (stūpikā) are collected (from the root 'stup' to collect) all the properties of all the objects and their potencies and merged in Amṛta, the Deathless. Into this vase, the Golden Prāsāda-puruṣa is laid.

The finial (stūpikā) with its point (bindu) above the Kalaśa, above the Āmalaka rises from the centre of the Central Shaft (veṇu). Its pillar shape is clasped by the ring of the Āmalaka. But it is not the only pillar so clasped. Here it is the Central Pillar of the Hindu Temple; elsewhere, the pillar in itself denotes the presence of the Buddha and is carved in relief, in Amarāvatī for example. In regular intervals, like the Bhūmis of a Śikhara, Āmalakas clasp its shape. The Āmalaka here functions as a ring. Through a number of rings passes a central pillar or shaft. This is the original function of the Āmalaka as ring-stone or naturally holed stone, Svayamātṛṇṇā, the self perforated "brick" (iṣṭakā) in the Vedic Agni. Three such self-holed stones were placed, the first on the golden man in the centre of the bottom layer, the second in the centre of the third layer and the third upon the centre of the completed fifth layer. They represent the three worlds; the holes afford to sacrificial man, himself identified with the golden Puruṣa a passage to the highest region.[171]

The third naturally perforated stone is placed upon the last, the fifth layer of the Altar; the Āmalaka too, is placed above the platform of the Vedi of the Śikhara. By its position it signifies the celestial world, below which the temple has its extension in space (antarikṣa), the mid-region—between heaven and earth.

The central pillar of the temple thus is alike to the Passage in the Fire-Altar; through it sacrificial man, the devotee, attains to the Highest Point where he is altogether liberated from the conditions of space and time. This straight, short way however is only for those who ascend from the Centre, from within the darkness in the mountain to the light above. Figuratively, the Pillar strikes the ground in the centre of the Garbhagṛha, a shaft of light. Nothing retards their ascension, it is instantaneous. The pilgrims from afar, however require the conductors on the way upwards. They are stationed on the outward shape of the temple, in its architecture. The temple as a monument thus serves a similar purpose as the icon (mūrti). The highest kind of devotion need not dwell on either and ascends

[170] The Nidhi-kalaśa need not necessarily be present in the foundation.

[171] The Āmalaka and more precisely, the cupola (Śikhara) of the High Temple (Vimāna) above the Bhūmis of a South Indian temple, would correspond in their topmost part to the "roof plate of the domed house" and represent an architectural equivalent of the Sundoor through which one "escapes altogether" as pointed out by Coomaraswamy, 'Some Sources of Buddhist Iconography', 'B. C. Law Volume', p. 473, note 12; and also in 'Pāli Kaṇṇikā', JAOS, 50; 1930; 'Symbolism of the Dome', op. cit., I.H.Q. 1938, and 'Eckstein', 'Speculum' 1939; also 'The two Reliefs from Bharhut', JISOA 1938, l.c. 'Svayamātṛṇṇā, Janua Coeli', 'Zalmoxis', 1939, could however not be consulted.

straight from the Centre within the cavity, within the heart, to the Highest Point.[172]

The central pillar 'pillars apart' heaven and earth (AV. X. 8. 2). It is a pillar of light, extending downwards from the sun in the zenith and rests on the earth ('Aitareya Brāhmaṇa', V. 28. 1). Its sheath (veṇu-kośa), the superstructure of the temple, shines with innumerable Gavākṣas (ray-wheels) in all the directions, a light-house on which 'revolves' the Āmalaka with its cogged rim. Its indentations sum up the buttresses and projecting angles of the total building; together with it they seem to revolve around its vertical axis, which divides while it unites, heaven and earth (cf. RV. X. 89. 4).

The Āmalaka effects and symbolizes the passage to heaven; it is the architectural symbol of the celestial world; viewed as sculpture, it is a three dimensional shape of the filaments of the lotus or of a halo with its rays.[173] The disc of the sun looks like the pericarp of the sky-lotus of which the petals are the directions of the compass and the filaments the solar rays.[174] The rays of the sun, in another inscription[175] are seen as "the round wooden rings of the sacrificial posts (yūpa)".

The naturally perforated or ring-stone[176] is the prototype also of the many carved stone discs which have been found in various sites.[177] They have a large, round hole in the centre, as a rule; a ring-stone however having no hole has been found in Mathurā. Its solid centre is filled with the carving of a lotus-Āmalaka shape.[178]

The Āmalaka ring-stone on the shaft of the Pillar of the Śikhara symbolises the celestial region where the rays of the sun spread like the filaments of the lotus of the zenith ('Bṛhadāraṇyaka Upaniṣad', VI. 3. 6). This region is above the body of the temple, above the truncated superstructure, around the Central Pillar; there the Central Pillar gives up its shaft and emerges from the Āmalaka as it

[172] The complete and unconditioned liberation (mukti) is distinguished from temporary and conditional states known as: 'sālokya, sārūpya, sāmīpya' and 'sāyujya'. The last is a becoming one with God; the first, a dwelling in the same world with God; it is attained by image worship.

[173] Cf. the Śakti-cakra like the rays of the sun "on the white lotus of eight petals" ('Kālottara Āgama', quoted in 'Īśānaśivagurudevapaddhati', Pt. III. ch. V. 11 f.).

[174] 'Ep. Ind.' XVIII. p. 49f; Cola Inscription, Cape Comorin, 'Travancore Archaeol. Series', III. p. 85 f.

[175] Rewa inscription of Malayasiṃha; Memoir, ASI. No. 23; R. D. Banerji, 'The Haihayas of Tripuri and their Monuments', p. 135.

[176] Is a symbol of re-generation. Those who pass through it are, as it were, born again. Crooke, op. cit. p. 322. Cf. the Muktidvāra in Satrunjaya, etc. The ring stones having "undulating surfaces" (Marshall, 'Mohenjo-Daro and the Indus Civilisation', pp. 61-62, Pl. XIV. 6) may, more closely even than the others, be connected with the corrugated shape of the Āmalaka.

Maurice, 'Indian Antiquities', 1793, also tells of the belief in a new birth of the soul by passing through holed stones. Self-bored stones are used as 'lucky stones'.

[177] Taxila (three from the Bhir Mound, one from Hathial); others have been found in Sankisa, Kosam (near Allahabad), Rajghat (Benares), Patna, etc.

[178] ASIAR, 1930-34, Pl. CXXX. 1. On its outer rim is carved the figure of an animal with the body of a lion, the wings of a bird and the head of man.

Havell, 'Handbook of Indian Art', pp. 8, 57, 112 and also in his 'Ideals of Indian Art' p. 171, connected the Āmalaka with the Lotus, if differently from the present context.

were in its inmost core only, as finial (stūpikā).[179] Inasmuch as the Āmalaka has retained its meaning as ring-stone it is a symbol of passage, of exit from this world and entry into heaven. In its appearance however on the monument it is the crown of the temple. In it are gathered the slopes of the Śikhara; their multifarious profiles are commuted into the unity of its solid and comprehensive shape.

In South Indian temples where the shape of the Āmalaka is unknown, the cupola of the High Temple (vimāna; harmya) takes its place.[180] In this connection, the High 'little temple' (harmikā; hammikā or 'little palace') on top of the Buddhist Stūpa has its particular significance. In name and position this Harmya is identical to the domed High Temple on top of the Bhūmis of the South Indian Prāsāda. Its shape too, where it is shown to be a chapel with a vaulted roof[181] is cognate with that of the South Indian High Temple and its cupola. On other stūpas however no such chapel is shown within its square railing and surmounted by successive tiers of slabs, increasing in area. Instead, the square railing has the shape of a closed casket with a railing pattern for its sides; on which rest the tiers of slabs, successively increasing in area.[182]

The self-same combination however of the closed casket whose sides consist of a square railing, surmounted by an inverted pyramid of slabs, is placed on top of the capital of pillars, either structural or carved in the rock and contemporary with the stūpas and their 'caskets'.[183] The contents of such a casket are known for they are also taken out of the casket and carved above the pillar capitals. In one instance[184] an Āmalaka is carved above the railing of the 'casket'. In this way

[179] The Āmalaka has been shown to have an equivalent in the flat stones which are used to cover the opening of the top of the 'spire of Toda-huts' "where certain relics are intended to be hidden from the public gaze", Simpson, 'Origin and Mutation in Indian and Eastern Architecture', published in 'Transactions of the Royal Society of British Architects', 1891, p. 253.

In Barhut relief representations (R. Chanda, 'Beginning of the Śikhara of the Nāgara Temple', 'Rūpaṃ', 1924, Figs. 1-3) a ring shape from which emerges the finial "shuts up the hole at the top of the dome".

Such shapes have played a part similar to that of the Āmalaka; there however the 'ring-shape' etc., rests on the dome, etc. itself and is not separated from it by a central shaft, as it is on the temple; such a separation would be meaningless in case of a structure; the super-structure of a temple however is a monument, it functions symbolically and not structurally. The vision of the celestial region and of the Cosmic Pillar became symbolic form by the transposition and transformation of structural shapes. To the same extent are the body and limbs of the images reminiscent of the shape of men although they are unlike it.

[180] The term Mūrdheṣṭakā ('Mayamata', XVIII. 117; 'Kāśyapaśilpa', XLII. 1-2), the head, or top 'brick' is the place where the finial is fixed; also the 'pidhānaphalakā' of a wooden structure ('Tantra-Samuccaya' Pt. I. ch. II. 49-50;) cf. Coomaraswamy, 'Pāli Kaṇṇikā—Circular Roof Plate'; JAOS, 50, pp. 238-243.

Although the Āmalaka has no place in the South Indian Vimāna as a whole, its shape, though modified, is yet recognisable as part of the capital of Pallava and Cola pillars.

[181] Barua, 'Barhut', Pt. III. Pls. LII, LIII.

[182] For example in Ajaṇṭā, Cave IX; Karli, etc. Cf. the increase in area in the opposite direction of the Bhūmis in the super-structure of the temple.

[183] At Bedsa, P. Brown, op. cit.; See also note 191.

[184] On a structural pillar at Besnagar, see P. Brown, op. cit. Pl. IX, Fig. 4.

it is made visible. Generally however the Āmalaka is shown within the casket whose sides are opened up for this purpose; only their posts are left at the four corners.[185] On some of these pillars, the Āmalaka in its receptacle is placed above the lotus (Bedsa, Karli) or pot (Ambivale, Nasik) shaped capital. The lotus as well as the pot are inverted, they are seen from above downwards, their petals and contents are showered from a celestial world to the earth below. Correspondingly, in a wooden temple it is the rule according to the 'Tantrasamuccaya' I. II. 48, to measure the rafters of the Śikhara from its top downwards; it is understood spreading from above to the walls of the temple below. In this inverse measuring the Highest Point of the temple is taken as its 'origin' and starting point, which it is ontologically; the temple as symbol of manifestation begins from the Bindu, the point limit between the unmanifest and the manifest. This point is situated above the Āmalaka.

Indian pillars of later ages, from the Gupta period onward, retain the Āmalaka without or within its casket as constituent part of their capitals. These have many variations and elaborations but, as a rule consist of the capital proper, called Bharaṇa, 'bearing' (S.S. LVII. 69; LXIII. 56)—on many types of pillars it has the shape of an Āmalaka (Pl. LXXVI)—and a kind of bracket capital, called Śīrṣa or head. The intervening part, if present, is called Hīragrahaṇa.[186] Below the Bharaṇa a 'collerino' may be present, called Vīrakaṇṭha.[187] Vīra denotes the sacrificial fire and Vīrakaṇṭha is the space of an inch from the edge of the hole in which the sacrificial fire is deposited. This connotation has its origin in the same

Cf. the corresponding representation of a 'surrounding railing' carved below the tree which is meant to be shown surrounded by it; Barhut, op. cit. in the scene of the Jetavana Jātaka (Pl. XLV).

[185] In Bedsa, Karli, Nasik, etc. The thin corner posts are replaced by the figures of Gaṇas who act as Karyatids; their bodies are placed slantingly like brackets; the straight corner posts disappear. This change can be seen on the capitals of pillars of one and the same cave, the Vihāra 3, in Nasik. The same type of Āmalaka with the figures of Gaṇas, etc. as 'struts' *i.e.*, 'corners' of the casket occurs in Ajaṇṭā, Caves I and II, whereas in cave XXVI, Yakṣiṇīs with their trees act as struts.

[186] South Indian texts know the capital as Bodhikā or Poṭikā ('Kāśyapaśilpa', IX. 1 f).

The wrongly called 'cushion' capital of the pillars in the caves of Bādāmī (6th century), the Dhumar Lena in Ellora and the Śiva temple in Elephanta (7th century) consists of an Āmalaka without any 'casket'. More than one Āmalaka forms the capital of the Iron pillar in Delhi (415 A.D.). Cf. the proportion of the Āmalasāraka of the pillar, 'Viṣṇudharmottara', II. Ch. XXIX. 58.

The names Hīragrahaṇa, also Hīra or Hīraka occur (S. S. LIV. 24, LVII. 253; 497); in Gujarat, Hīragṛhas are the corbels intended to hold the lower tenons of bracket figures (Burgess-Cousens, op. cit. p. 24).

Hīragrahaṇa, 'containing or enclosing the diamond', may originally have referred to the corbels (such as in Bedsa, Karli, Nasik, etc.) forming an inverted pyramid of slabs above the Āmalaka in the casket, while Hīraka may denote the Āmalaka, the stone whose meaning is as precious as a diamond.

[187] S. S., LXIII. 57. "Vīragaṇḍa', an instance of popular etymology.

South Indian Vāstuśāstras use a somewhat different terminology for the parts of the pillar. The word Vīrakaṇṭha however is retained (and translated by P. K. Acharya as "warrior's neck") in 'Mānasāra' XV; the name of the capital, Bodhikā (Poṭikā), derived from 'awakening' and 'enlightenment', refers to the liberation which is attained by passing across the Āmalaka as ring-stone and Mukti-dvāra.

place where, on the Uttara Vedi, the last Svayamātṛṇṇā had come to lie. Both the terms belong to 'surrounding shapes', of the immanent Breath (ātman) in the Altar, or of the sacrificial Fire.

As many as are the uses of the Āmalaka, the cogged ring-stone[188]—and especially of the highest of these Svayamātṛṇṇās, denoting the celestial world—so manifold also are the meanings of its name. Etymologically it is derived from the root 'mal', "to hold" or "to gather"; this meaning describes it in its function as a ring. Its name moreover is differently written and frequently begins with a short 'a'; Amala means without impurity, stainless; thus the name Amala-śilā 'pure stone' was given to it, especially by the Buddhists.[189] Another of its names of this kind is Amala-sāra, Pure Essence.[190] Both these names are descriptive of the High Region, the celestial world; of which the Āmalaka—as ring-stone and Mukti-dvāra, door of liberation—is the symbol denoting entry and final integration.

When however, as generally in Vāstu-śāstra, Āmalaka begins with a long 'a' it is the name of the fruit of the Emblic Myrobalan, whose shape it remotely recalls. Closer, however, than this resemblance is its affinity with the circle of lotus filaments which are likened to rays.

The Āmalaka moreover in early Vāstuśāstra is also called 'Aṇḍa', the 'egg' (see Part VII, p. 273). The interchange of these two images has its background in the 'Chāndogya Upaniṣad', III. 19.1: "The sun is Brahman. Such is the teaching; and its exposition is this: In the beginning, this was indeed non-existent; it became existent; it came into being; it became an egg; it lay for the period of one year; it broke open; then came the two halves of the egg shell, one silver, one gold" and Śaṅkarācārya's commentary: "What is emphasized is not the negation of existence (but the absence of differentiation of Name and Form). As a matter of fact, the term 'sat', 'Existent', is found to be used in the sense of 'differentiated name and form' and this differentiation of name and form of the universe is mostly dependent upon the sun". The Brahmāṇḍa the 'world egg' is the true 'Dhātu-garbha' and is enshrined as such in the Harmikā or casket above the Stūpa.[191]

[188] As end of the cross-bar on the throne of Buddhist divinities, ASIAR, 1928-29, Pl. LVII. Or, similar to its use on the pillar, on the Āyakakhambas of a Stūpa (Gumadidurru, ASIAR, 1925-26, Pl. XXXVb; and in symbol-ornaments stuck into the coiffure of Terracotta figurines, on plaques ('Annual Bibliography of Indian Archaeology' XII. Pl. V.) Not only in the capital, but also as part of the base of a pillar comparable to the lowest Svayamātṛṇṇā is the Āmalaka shown in relief representations from Nāgārjunakoṇḍa (ASIAR, 1927-28, Pl. LI.).

[189] Beal, Buddhist Records II. pp. 136-7. Foucher, 'L' Art Gréco-Bouddhique', op. cit., I. p. 96. note.

[190] 'Samarāṅgaṇasūtradhara', LVI. 49; 154, etc., Āmalasāraka. Āmalasāraka however would be synonymous with Āmalaka.

[191] In this connection it may be possible to see some light thrown also on the corbels or bracket capitals of pillars, etc. where an inverted pyramid composed of tiers (Hīragrahaṇa) rises above the Āmalaka. Their symbolism might be referable to that of the spheres above the sun, from Svarloka upwards.

The successive increase in area of the single 'slabs' serves a purpose akin to that of a bracket capital on the pillars, whereas no such purpose is served by the same shape on top of the Stūpa. The slabs of this inverted pyramid share with the pyramid of slabs of the temple the function of a solid cover.

Above the Āmalaka is the Stūpikā, the finial, frequently made of gold, or gilded. Its most conspicuous part is the round body of the jar, the Kalaśa. "The golden Kalaśa, a 'high seat', on the summit of the god's dwelling, looks as if it were the sun's orb that had arisen on the lordly mountain of sunrise.[192] The Kalaśa is likened to the sun and the temple is "the Mountain where the Sun rests at midday.[193] Meru, the support of the Sun,[194] and "the one Sun that never leaves the Meru" ('Aitareya Brāhmaṇa', XIV. 6.44, Comm.)[195] are symbols of the ultimate state of illumination of the Sādhaka for whom the sun neither rises nor sets. "For one who thus knows the secret doctrine of Brahman, it does not set nor does it rise; for him it is day, once for all" ('Chāndogya Upaniṣad', III. 11.3).

To the Sun these worlds are linked by means of the quarters ('Śatapatha Brāhmaṇa', VI. 7.1.17). Beheld from above, the temple spreads from its finial to the four quarters, while seen from below it is a step-way (sopāna mārga) to ultimate release (mukti).[196]

The Āmalaka, below the golden orb of the Kalaśa-sun, the ring of spotless rays, is the celestial world in which dwells the sun as the pericarp which is above and in the centre of its halo of filaments and its wider sheath of petals (padma-kośa). The Āmalaka and also the dome of the Harmya represent the lowest celestial level of an extra-cosmic Empyrean.[197]

In the Kalaśa—sun, all the gods are merged in the Deathless; the Āmalaka consequently is sacred not to one god only but to the Three great gods, Brahmā, Viṣṇu and Śiva. This is the meaning of the Āmalaka as the fruit of the tree (the Emblic Myrobalan). Its legends are recounted in the Purāṇas.

The Tulasī is sacred to Viṣṇu and the Bilva is Śiva's tree. Once when all the gods and sages (ṛṣi) had assembled at the Tīrtha of Prabhāsa, Devī, Śiva's Śakti, wanted to worship Viṣṇu and Lakṣmī, who is Viṣṇu's Śakti, wanted to worship Śiva. Deeply touched, their eyes welled over with tears of joy. Where the tears fell to the ground, Āmalaka trees grew up "since they were born from

[192] 'Ep. Ind.' XIII, pp. 46, 56 ; Kanarese inscr. narrating the building of the Mahādeva Temple at Ittagi, A.D. 1112. In many other inscriptions too, the golden Kalaśa is likened to the sun (Khajuraho inscr. of the year 1001-1002, ib., I. p. 144 ; in a 12th century inscr. from Pithapuram, ib. IV, p. 44. f. etc.).

The Kalaśa is made of gold, silver or copper ; Ī.P. IV. ch. XXXIV. 20 f. The word 'finial' in the present context is taken to denote the entire object above the Āmalaka or the cupola (śikhara) of the South Indian temple.

[193] Deopārā inscr. of Vijayasena, 'Ep. Ind.' I. p. 314.

[194] Hansot Plate, 756 A.D. (Broach) ; 'Ep. Ind.' XII. p. 203.

[195] The sun called Digbhrāja, the illuminator of the regions.

[196] Buddhist stone inscription, 8-9th century ; 'Ind. Ant.', XVII. p. 308.

Each Śṛṅga or miniature Śikhara has its Āmalaka in the hierarchy of celestial regions (Pls. IV. XLV) whether these shapes are distinct units as on the temples of central India, or form one sequence of architectural form as in Rajputana (Pl. LXXI), Aihole (Fig. p. 183) or in Orissa, where the Āmalaka-quoins appear as mouldings of the 'Koṇaka pāga'. In these positions they do not symbolize the sun in the 4 quarters ; the corners of the temple, as a rule, are in the intermediate directions.

[197] See Coomaraswamy, 'The two Reliefs from Bharhut in the Freer Gallery', l.c., p. 150.

tears and all the gods and sages saw Brahmā, Viṣṇu and Śiva in the Āmalaka tree" ('Bṛhaddharma Purāṇa', XII. 1-35).

Brahmā, Viṣṇu and Śiva dwell in the Āmalaka tree. The 'Skanda Purāṇa', ('Vaiṣṇava Khaṇḍa', XII. 9-23) describes the Āmalaka (Āmardaki) tree. It is the first tree grown in the universe. Viṣṇu is seated at its bottom; Brahmā above and Śiva higher still. The sun is in its branches, the gods are in their ramifications and in its leaves, flowers and fruits. Thus the Āmalaka is the support of all gods.

The Āmalaka, tree of manifested deity, redeeming, supernal tree, has contributed to the temple the image of its fruit. It is raised high on the Pillar, above the trunk of the Prāsāda. Its radiance is gathered in its ring of rays, it is given additional support by images carved below it and placed above the last Bhūmi of the superstructure. Siṃhas, the four Vimāna-pālas or Guardians of the temple,[198] or aspects of the divinity of the temple may, but need not, be placed in this high region.[199] Towards the light which spreads from the Āmalaka to all the regions, the Uromañjarīs, Śṛṅgas and Latās, every shape of the superstructure of the temple is seen to ascend: progressing in series, forming vertical bands and ridges and dark narrow paths, flung toward the summit across all strata, all Bhūmis, and linking up the piers and offsets of the walls with the superstructure (Pls. XLIII, XLV, I, IV). In one competition, from the Vedi, the ground on earth, to the High Vedi of the Śikhara proceeds the ascension of the many units of form. The images cease at the height of the Face of Glory and are shown once more, below the Āmalaka.[200] The long ascension (dūrohanaṃ) has altogether been given form. On some Śikharas, moreover (Pl. XLV), a small figure of man is placed. It is outside the body of the Prāsāda, climbing the mountain of the Śikhara towards the Āmalaka and the Flag placed in the High region. It is the figure of the warrior, the Kṣatriya, the King,[201] who gains here a footing, high on the superstructure, ascending to heaven.

[198] The names of the four Vimānapālas are given as: Nyakṣa, Vivasvān, Mitra, and Kṣattā; 'Vaikhānasāgama', VII, VIII, XLI: see also, Gopinatha Rao, op. cit. Vol. 1, Pt. II. Appendix, p. 5. They are forms of the 'Sun'; see Pl. LXI, Head of a Vimānapāla or Devarṣi.

[199] On temples where the Latās of the Śikhara exceed in height the Mūlamañjarī especially in the Deccan, the Kīrttimukha is carved at the very end (temple of Jhodga; Amṛteśvar Temple in Ratanvalli, etc.)

In Orissa, 'Deul Caraṇīs', a particular form of the Lioness, are carved below the Āmalaka. They are related to the Caraṇas, movers at will, floating through the air; they belong to the group of Siddhas, Brahmarṣis, Devarṣis, etc. ('Harivaṃśa', CXXVI. 2); The 'Kāśyapaśilpa', XXVII. 66-69, speaks of the figures of bulls in the corners of the 'gala' (neck) such as are to be seen on Pallava and Cola Temples (Kailāsanātha Temple, Conjeevaram, etc.) or of images of the 4 Bhūtas, named Āmoda, Pramoda, Pramukha and Durmukha. Their head-god is Yama (cf. Part III, p. 59, the Pecaka Vāstumaṇḍala).

[200] On South Indian temples however, the super-structure too is full of images.

[201] The figure of the Royal Knight with the sword at the right side, is carved in the very act of ascending, under the Āmalaka (Taleśvar temple in Tilasma, Mewar, Rajputana 'ASI. Progress Report, Western Circle', 1905, p. 56). Today even this figure is locally known as the "royal personage who built the temple and who by means of that meritorious act ascends to heaven."

THE TEMPLE AS PURUṢA

The meaning of the forms and figures on the walls of the Prāsāda and its superstructure is held and integrated in the crown of the temple whether it is dome shaped as in South India or has the appearance of an Āmalaka, as on the great majority of temples. Beneath the apex of the dome and under the Āmalaka, the house of God rests on this earth whose extent, architecturally, is covered by the Vāstupuruṣamaṇḍala. In it the temple has its plan, prognosis, and projection on the surface around the Brahmasthāna; its centre coincides with that of the Garbhagṛha. It is there that the Pillar of the temple, passing downwards from the High Temple or the Āmalaka, strikes the ground. The Brahmasthāna, ensconced in the body of the temple, in the Garbhagṛha, is transfixed, as it were, by the vertical shaft of the finial above the dome or the Āmalaka; disembodied, beyond the body of the Prāsāda, it stays in the Empyrean and points into the unconfined. From its point downward the temple spreads the rich folds of its cloak, the sheath of its Pillar, its super-structure and walls. It extends in all the directions, has no façade but is oriented. From its hem or perimeter upwards and inwards it connects all the directions of space and all the constellations in time, in a sumptuous fabric. It coheres in strict measure and is woven with images, each in its place; they are multiform in all the pursuits in which man is confirmed in deathlessness (Pls. XXX, LXVIII, LXXX). The long ascent (dūrohaṇam) from tier to tier and peak to peak, is lit by the 'radiance' of Āmalakas and Gavākṣas; the light of the sun rests upon their curves and mingles with the superluminous darkness which is held in them. Each peak has its sun, each station its light; it is eclipsed by one that shines from a higher plane which, with a greater power, draws towards itself the forms of monumental display. Far above and yet supported by the ground of nature, the high platform of the superstructure levels in its squareness the competition of the multitudinous forms and images. Thence the Pillar of the Temple emerges naked : it is seen from this high level only whereas its immanence in the body of the Prāsāda supports each of its varied profiles and strata, which form the slopes of Mount Meru, the body of this Universe.

All the things indeed of "this wonderful world (saṃsāra)",—its course and the passage that leads beyond it—"are described under the guise of the temple (Prāsāda) : the diverse shapes of all creatures, high and low, encaged in their bodies through their various actions, from the celestial beings (downwards).[202] Thus the kings are admonished in the above inscription, not to turn their minds to sin, but to see the Order of this world in the likeness of the temple and be guided by it, supported by it in the long ascent to the ground above, the High Altar, above which are the rays and the deathlessness of the Sun, the Brahman ('Chāndogya Upaniṣad, III. 19.4; Taittirīya Āraṇyaka', II. 2.2). Below it, all are in the power of death, who has given this residence on earth to sacrificial man so that he may ascend to its summit, and finally transcend it. All is order in the residence

[202] Sirpur stone inscription, verse 21 ; 8-9th century ; 'Ep. Ind.', XI. p. 190.

of God on earth, in the symmetry of the structure, and its plan. Square in shape, it is the Vāstupuruṣa, the place of all the gods. The Vāstupuruṣa, Existence, the Asura, the unruly, expansive, is kept in check, cosmic order covers it and makes it the time-table of its movement every day, every year, in all the cycles of the aeon. All the gods, those of the stars and the suns, face the Brahmasthāna, are turned towards the centre, they have their images placed on the body of the temple, adorning the folds of its robe, the buttresses of its walls and face the devotee. Viewed from above as much as from the Centre—which view no physical eye can take—they have their stations simultaneously, in rhythmic intervals on the body of the temple wrapt in its still mantle of carved stone. Viewed however from outside, and compelling circumambulation, they are the links of its closed body, unfolding its vestment in the many recesses, offsets and piers (Pl. XLIV), the pages in the book of all Time, a consolidated region where the South and the North have the same architectural profiles and only their images are as different as is their orientation.

On the fixed ground, the pillar is struck; it inheres the mass of the temple; like a lighthouse it has, as it were, turned around its axis and has thrown forth its radiance in the shape of images, visible and clear to all. The solid pile of the monument, with its buttresses and recesses and their sculptural exposition, is embodied movement, it revolves with the spirits of the air (Pls. XXV—XXVIII) in unbroken rhythmic form. In it Śakti is active, the power that drives forth the form, and is its substance. The Spirit gives His impress to it, and Yama, the Dharmarāja, gives it definition and finality in the succession of creative movement, at its own time and place.

The temple stands firm; it is a monument of the movement of the cosmos and leads beyond it. It is to be seen and comprehended (darśana) by circumambulation (pradakṣiṇa), to be approached and entered (abhigamana) so as to be born from its dark womb and to ascend its height in an instant of coincidence, to the golden point of reintegration from the middle of the cavity, in the heart. This monument is the seat and house of God. Its substance and shape (ākrti) is Prakṛti ('Agnipurāṇa', LXI. 25 f), the primordial nature of the world; its images which mirror the course of the world (saṃsāra) give liberation ('Kulārṇava Tantra', II. 24). Its total form is the seat (Prāsāda) of the Supreme Spirit.[203]

'At the end of Prakṛti' ('Agnipurāṇa', CI. 13), in the Kalaśa, the golden

[203] The vision of the Temple, the Seat of Liberation, is amplified in the image of Vaikuṇṭha, the World wherein dwells the Supreme Viṣṇu.

Vaikuṇṭha is described as full of many cities. In the centre is the city of Ayodhyā, surrounded by ramparts and gates in the four directions each having a high Gopura. In its centre is the "inner city" (antaḥpura) of Viṣṇu, itself surrounded by ramparts. In the centre of the "inner city", is the hall, "the King's abode" (rājasthāna) and in the centre of the hall is the "Beauteous Throne", the essence of all the Vedas. In its centre is the Yogapīṭha, the Base of Reintegration, and in its centre is the eight petalled Lotus, at the centre of its petals is the Supreme Puruṣa and Īśvarī ('Padmapurāṇa Uttarakhaṇḍa' ch. CCLVI, 7-26; cf. also CCLVII. 120-133).

The temples of South India, the Drāviḍa country, with their Prākāras, or ramparts surrounding the innermost shrine, are the architectural form of Vaikuṇṭha, the 'Un-hindered', pervaded throughout by the Supreme Puruṣa.

Prāsāda-Puruṣa is installed[204] in the Empyrean below the Paramount Point of the finial. The temple as house and seat of God in which dwells His Essence is also His body; the temple contains the whole manifestation ('Mayamata', XVIII. 193) in which He is beheld as Puruṣa, Supernal Man. "The Prāsāda should be worshipped as Puruṣa" ('Śilparatna', XVI. 114). It is both, His house and representation.[205] The several parts of the temple communicate His living presence and are likened to the body of man in the same way as the square of the plan and its partitions are the 'body' of the Vāstupuruṣa. The door is the mouth,[206] the Āmalaka or the High Dome is the head; its Brahmarandhra or foramen[207] is pierced so as to receive the tenon (kīla) of the finial (stūpikā). The image in the Garbhagṛha is the Life (jīva) of the temple concealed in the darkness of the cave, enclosed by the mountain of its walls. The outside of the bulwark, teeming with ordered shapes and figures, is its explicit form. The temple is conceived from inside and visualized from outside; the communication between inside and outside is brought about by the radiating power from within which assigns its place to each and every facet of the walls; the inner dark is extracted through closed doors and windows (Ghanadvāra and Gavākṣa) as a chiaroscuro which adheres to the Prāsāda extended in mid-space and facing all the directions. Tier upon tier in a solidified ascent, its bulk is reduced in the tapering superstructure and carried towards the Paramount Point.

When the building is completed a large flag, as long as the temple is high, is fixed, at the top; the finial is installed and the Kalaśa.

Finally, the rites of consecration are performed: the indwelling essence is established in the temple (hṛtpratiṣṭhā).[208]

As in the beginning, so also on the completion of the building, the rite of auspicious germination (aṅkurārpaṇa; Ī.P. IV. ch. XXXIV. 27; 'Kāmikāgama', LXI. 3; Mayamata, XVIII. 166) is enacted and oblations are given at night. Then at dawn, of another day, the Sthapati, the master architect, and the Sthāpaka, the priest architect, ascend the Vimāna and with a golden needle, perform the rite of opening the eyes (netra mokṣa) of the Prāsāda in front of the cupola (Śikhara) of its High Temple (Harmya).

The Sthāpaka then instals the Prāsāda, in its concrete shape (prāsādamūrti) on its altar or pedestal (dhiṣṇyamūrti) and places in it the Seed (bīja) of the Temple.

Prior to the inception of the building, the Seed of the temple,—its causal stage whence the unmanifest becomes manifest—was deposited in the ground (bhūmi),

204 This rite is performed—not only—in South India to this day; cf. also 'Paurāṇikavāstuśāntiprayoga', Fol. 24 B; 'Bṛhacchilpaśāstra', III. 102.

205 Cf. Ś.B. XIII. 8. 1. 1. where the Vedic funeral mount is spoken of as "house and representation", "gṛhaṃ vā prajñānaṃ vā'.

206 The Śukanāsā is the nose, the Bhadras are the arms, the Aṇḍa=Āmalaka, the head; the Kalaśa, the hair; the Kaṇṭha, the throat; the Vedi, the shoulders (skandha); the door, the mouth, and the image (pratimā) is the Jīva, its life. ('Agnipurāṇa', LXI. 23-25). See Part IV, note 84.

207 Coomaraswamy, 'Symbolism of the Dome', l. c., p. 53. M. Eliade, 'Yoga', p. 306.

208 A summary is given here of their description in the 'Īśānaśivagurudevapaddhati', Pt. IV. ch. XXXIV. 65-93.

in the womb of the Earth,[209] surrounded by all her substances and sheltered by her so that the temple may arise. Now the building is completed, the Seed has germinated, assimilated all the substances and grown into the body of the temple.

In the completed building too, the Seed, having germinated in its substance, is realised in its causal, creative significance in which it dwelt while the temple was being built in the lotus of the heart,[210] of the Guru, the Sthāpaka. Now, on the completion of the building it is brought from the heart of the Guru and placed in the temple. This seed is Consciousness itself (Cit).[211]

The form of the Prāsāda (prāsāda-mūrti) is the monumental embodiment of the Puruṣa, the Essence, [212] it is the form of Consciousness itself.[213]

Then the Yajamāna, the sacrificer-patron, presents the Sthāpaka and Sthapati with gold, clothes, ornaments, etc., according to his ability. The Sthapati makes over a gift of gold to the Takṣan, and receives from him the entire merit (dharma sarvasva) of the work. The entire merit in building the temple, the Sthapati gives to the Yajamāna. Now the shrine is installed. The Sthāpaka and Sthapati who had begun the temple also complete it. Should they be dead, their sons and disciples carry out the work according to the precepts of the Guru. He conducts the work, from the beginning, and should he no longer dwell in the body, his painted effigy is present at the installation of the temple.[214]

The continuity and perfection of the work are assured according to the particular tradition in which it was started. The science of architecture having its origin in Brahmā and being transmitted by an unbroken series of sages preserves its integrity in the planning and building of every temple. Thus it is said that "Brahmā himself is the Sthapati.[215]

When the building is completed and consecrated, its effigy in the shape of a golden man, the Prāsāda-puruṣa, is installed in the Golden jar, above the Garbhagṛha, above the Śukanāsā. The effigy is invested with all the Forms and Principles of manifestation. While the Vāstupuruṣa "Existence" lies at the base of the temple and is its support the Golden Puruṣa of the Prāsāda, its indwelling Essence, sum total of all the Forms and Principles (tattva) of manifestation and their reintegration lies in the superluminous darkness of the Golden jar on top of the temple below the point limit of the manifest. In supernal radiance, the golden Puruṣa of the Vedic Altar ('Taittirīya Saṃhitā', V. 2. 7. 1) appears raised from the golden disc—of the sun—within the bottom layer of the Agni to the finial above the superstructure of the Hindu temple. The ascension of the Golden Puruṣa cancels the descent of the Vāstupuruṣa.

[209] Part IV, p. 126 ; notes 85 and 95.
[210] Cf. Ī.P. III. ch. XXVII. 72-106 ; XIII. 71 f.
[211] Ib. IV. XXXIV. 55-56.
[212] 'Agnipurāṇa', LXI. 11 ; 'Viṣṇusaṃhitā', XIII. 61-69 ; 'Śilparatna', XVI. 114.
[213] As such "buddhyā niścitya mandiram" ('Śilparatna', XIX. 115), "having fixed in mind the temple (with all its parts) from base (janman) to finial, the Sthapati together with the Takṣan should place the lowermost moulding (pādukā)".
[214] 'Īśānaśivagurudevapaddhati', IV. ch. XXXIV. 4 ; 'Mayamata', XVIII. 159-161.
[215] Ī.P. IV. ch. XXXIV. 3. The Yajamāna is Viṣṇu,—the sacrifice (Ś.B. I. 2. 5. 3 ; 9) ; the Ācārya (Sthāpaka) is Rudra.

Within these two movements the Hindu temple has its being; its central pillar is erected from the heart of the Vāstupuruṣa in the Brahmasthāna, from the centre and heart of Existence on earth, and supports the Prāsāda Puruṣa in the Golden jar in the splendour of the Empyrean. Its mantle carries, imaged in its varied texture, in all directions all the forms and principles of manifestation towards the Highest Point above the body of the Temple.

EXPLANATION
OF
PLATES

The Plates (I—LXXX) illustrate the Hindu temple and its sculptures in some of its types mainly in central India and Rajputana.

EXPLANATION OF PLATES

FRONTISPIECE : AMARAKAṆṬAKA

Amarakaṇṭaka in Baghelkhand (22° 41' N; 81° 46' E) is the abode of the chief of Sages ('Epigraphia Indica', vol. XIX. p. 295). From there the rivers Narmadā, Son and Mahānadī are said to flow to the West, East and North. From the days of the 'Matsya Purāṇa' to the present, this sacred site enveloped in its dust and the smoke of its fires, the pilgrims congregated there.

The throng of the people and their leisure fills the space between the shrines in worship—or in ruins. There, under the trees, and near the water, their clothes have been washed and spread to dry; the various daily actions performed outside the temples are as much part of the life at the Tīrtha as are the rites of 'drying up' (śoṣaṇa) the impurities of the subtle body and purifying the bodily elements (bhūtaśuddhi) of the Sādhaka who has entered the temple.

PLATE I. KANDARĪYA TEMPLE

From S.E.; Devī Jagadambā Temple to the north of it, in the back-ground; buff coloured sandstone; Khajuraho (24° 51′ N; 79° 56′ E), Chatarpur State, Bundelkhand, central India. Tenth century.

The Kandarīya Temple is a temple of Śiva, the Devī Jagadambā Temple was dedicated to Viṣṇu.* Khajuraho, the ancient Kharjūravāhaka ('Ep. Ind.' I. p. 139; inscription of the year 1001-2 A.D.), the "date-tree bearing", was the capital of the Candella Rajputs. Only 20 out of its 85 temples have survived; they were built in the tenth and eleventh centuries. Some of the craftsmen inscribed their names (on stones of the Viśvanātha Temple, c. 1000 A.D.). These names however cannot be connected with any of the major figures of which on the Kandarīya temple alone there are nearly nine hundred (ASR. II. p. 419).

The Kandarīya temple measures 102′ 3″ in length, 66′ 10″ in width and is 101′ 9″ high (B. L. Dhama, l.c., p. 9).

The temple stands on a high platform; four small shrines in the corners (cf. plan of the Lakṣmaṇa temple, built in 954 A.D.; p. 255) which made it a Pañcāyatana temple, no longer exist. In plan, the main building, but for small

* The Kandarīya temple was consecrated to Śiva ; Kandarīya means 'of the cave'. Some of the temples of Khajuraho are known under several names. The Devī Jagadambā temple, also called Kālī temple, was dedicated to Viṣṇu. The Lakṣmaṇa temple, also called Rāmacandra or Caturbhuja was also consecrated to Viṣṇu. The Citragupta temple, also called Bharatji temple, was dedicated to Sūrya. The Viśvanātha temple was dedicated to Śiva Viśvanātha, the Lord of the Universe. The Duladeo or 'Holy Bridegroom' temple was sacred to Śiva. The Pārśvanātha temple was dedicated to Jina Vṛṣabhanātha (Ādinātha), the first Tīrthaṅkara.

discrepancies, is similar to the Lakṣmaṇa Temple. It is a Sāndhāra Prāsāda whose Pradakṣiṇa or ambulatory is extended in the Mahāmaṇḍapa; two pillars demarcate the Antarāla (cf. the Citragupta Temple, Pl. V, which also has two corresponding pillars flanking the entrance to the Garbhagṛha); the central square (vedi) of the Mahāmaṇḍapa is co-extensive with the square of the Kandabhitti (SS. LVII. 491), the walls of the Prāsāda,—the distance between the central square of the Maṇḍapa moreover being equal in the Lakṣmaṇa temple, to the side of the Prāsāda. Prāsāda and Mahāmaṇḍapa are contracted as one walled-in building to which are attached the Maṇḍapa and Ardha (half) Maṇḍapa as half-open, pillared hall and porch. Prāsāda and Mahāmaṇḍapa open up with Bhadras and Catuṣkikās in the middle of each side resulting in the appearance of two 'transepts' or a double cross shaped plan.

In the vertical section (Fig. i, on p. 212) the Kandarīya Temple is seen to be a mountain of masonry from the base to finial; it is hollow on the groundfloor with its pillared halls and porches leading to the Garbhagṛha in which is the Liṅga. The floor itself is not on one level but is somewhat raised to form the Vedi or dais in the centre of the Mahāmaṇḍapa; it is raised to an even higher level in the Antarāla where steps lead to the Garbhagṛha. By the high level of its floor the Garbhagṛha partakes in the vertical ascent of the Prāsāda.

Pillars and pilasters support corbelled domes; even within the Garbhagṛha the corbelled ceiling rests on pilasters; the pillars of the Mahāmaṇḍapa are extended beyond their capitals—the extension is called Ucchālaka—and are crowned by heavy bracket capitals, whereas half pillars are set on the seat (āsana), whose back projects slanting outward above the perpendicular part of the wall below it (which is also called Vedī; 'Samarāṅgaṇasūtradhāra', LVII. 29; 126; Pls. I. LI. LXXVI). At the end of this hypostyle, the Garbhagṛha with its walls, the main sanctuary within the temple, is set right below the neck (grīvā) of the Śikhara and the Liṅga has its place below the Kalaśa, the vase of the finial (Fig. i, p. 212). Between them the Śikhara rises, inaccessible to the devotee and to be seen from the outside only.

The several halls, the great Maṇḍapa, etc., and the half-Maṇḍapa (Mahāmaṇḍapa; Ardha-maṇḍapa) each have their separate superstructure with its Āmalaka finial; miniature Maṇḍapas cluster on the superstructure of each Maṇḍapa and are subordinated to it in the same way as are the Uromañjarīs to the Mūlamañjarī of the Vimāna. Similarly also the small trabeate domes of the Mahāmaṇḍapa cluster around the large dome in the centre below the peak of its roof. The pendant, projecting downward from the apex of the dome, is below the Kalaśa on the summit. The superstructures are graded in height towards the Prāsāda, that of the Mahāmaṇḍapa ending below the top of the Śukanāsā. On its ridge, a Siṃha overlooks the cascades of Bhūmis and the stations of the many Kalaśas showing their contents as an emerging bud-like shape (Fig. i, p. 212), the Bījasvara (SS. LVII. 425), the 'seed-sound' or primeval sound. The pile of masonry above the ground floor, but for one small Gavākṣa, has no external opening (Pl. IV); internally, ties made of stone slabs are laid horizontally at the height of the shoulder course (skandha) of the Uromañjarīs from the 'sheath' of the walls towards the internal piers. The compartments so formed are left hollow (Fig. i.) according to considerations of weight and stability. The central 'shaft' of the Prāsāda is ideally present and reaches from the floor of the Garbhagṛha, beyond its ceiling, also beyond the Skandha and across the Āmalaka; it is capped by a flat, inverted bowl shape above the Āmalaka and below the Kalaśa, which is known under the names Padmaśīrṣa (lotus-head); Karpara or Karparī (pan, skull); Candrikā (cardamon? a moonshaped circle) and Daṇḍikā (necklace) (S.S. LVII. 85; 170; 324, etc.). The first two names illustrate the 'piercing of the skull' of the Prāsāda by the bolt of the finial.

The mountain range of the Kandarīya, and of the other temples similarly built, has its peaks arrayed above the longitudinal axis of the building; the deep indentations between them allow space,—it had found its entry into the ground-floor in the wide open balconies—a further participation in the total effect of the monument. It makes the mass appear weightless within a silhouette which shows ascent and descent and renewed ascent from a higher level, leading each time to a summit of its own. The outline of the whole temple has a movement different from that of the several structures which it comprises; rising and falling and rising always higher like the breathing of a runner as the goal lies near. The Śukanāsā is the last halting point (Pls. I, XLVIII, XLIX); its articulation is similar to that of the superstructures of the Maṇḍapa and different from the Śikhara of the Prāsāda of which architecturally it forms part. So close do the Maṇḍapas come to the Prāsāda but here they stop; and none may exceed the height of the Śukanāsā. From there the Mūlamañjarī, in an elastic curve carries its Uromañjarīs and Śṛṅgas towards its high finial.

In deep indentations space lies between the 'towers' of the temple (Pl. I); in dark openings below projecting rooflets (chādya) it stretches along its length, within its body, a band of measured compartments which contradicts the volume of piers and Śṛṅgas and bisects the building; below is the pile of masonry raised on its terrace (Jagatīpīṭha; S.S. LVI. 124, gives its height as half of the width of the Prāsāda).

The progressively arduous and repeated ascent and descent towards the pinnacle of the Śikhara limned against the sky in the lateral view, is not visible in the front view where the several Maṇḍapa roofs seem to coincide in one comprehensive outline and the effect is similar to the steep and direct ascent of the back view. These main views however are but a few out of the indefinite number of positions which are taken during circumambulation. The building is to be viewed from all its corners; each buttress, each facet, presents its three sides, the volume which they enclose and in addition, the volumes which project from them as sculptures and mouldings. The intersections of the horizontal and vertical volumes of the lower part in their continuity are summed up and gathered in the 'staccato' forms of pediments and the storeyed shapes of the superstructures of the Maṇḍapas and these have their response and integration in the large 'legato' of the curve of the Śikhara.

This monumental, sculptured architecture is not to be understood functionally, nor in human terms, by empathy or a feeling into its form. An intricate instrument of precision and enduring stability of concatenated themes and rhythms, it leads to final unity.

PLATE II. THE LION AND MAN

In the porch of the Mahādeo Temple, a small shrine between the Kandarīya and the Devī Jagadambā Temple. The three buildings are raised on the same terrace. The superstructure of the temple of Devī Jagadambā is seen in the background. The image is carved in the round (ghanarūpa); its height is 4′ 8″, the length 5′ and its width is 1′ 6″. Khajuraho, tenth century.

The Lion is a Devourer (grāsa); it is shown here with the whole face (akṣatamukha; S.S. LVII. 643), including the lower jaw, which however is broken off. Similar images may be discerned in a corner of the terrace and on the ridge of the Śukanāsā (Pl. I). The Chinthe, at the entrance to every Pagoda, is the Burmese equivalent of the Lion. It wards off all that is evil.

The group of the Lion and man, a three-dimensional composition in curves, is to be seen laterally; a triangular shape domed by the sweep of the Lion's head and shoulders, springs from a base charged with resilient power; there one globular shape is balanced on a higher level, the other touches the base; these two weights, the haunches of the animal, and the man are also turning points of movement. The group is rich in such pivotal points, in knees, hips, shoulders, elbows and necks. Between those centres of rotation a see-saw balance of poise and active energy is produced by volumes sharply outlined within parallel curves. The economy of the flowing lines of scarf and ornaments on the figure of man, the different patterns of hair, mane and whiskers, closely follow and intensify the modelled shape of which they form part. The beading on the animal's legs and round its neck is cognate in its effect with the cogged rim of the Āmalaka of the temple in the background; it is subordinated to the several large single globes in the group, those of the head, eyes and nose of the lion, and face, head, chignon of the man—the club which he brandishes and also his small shield (they are seen only on the left side of the group). By the response of their physiognomies and heroic bodies, the animal and the man are confronted in similar arcs of breathing chests; while the frame of man yields it by an extreme effort in which is power, defiance and submissiveness, agony, in its literal sense,—it holds the outlines of his back in its grip,—the curve of the animal's front has quiet power and the deep saddle of its back curve, dignity. The Lion but raises its paw while man throws forth his whole weight in the fight by which he wins the monster's protection. Thus the two creatures form part of one group; it has its springiness in their lower limbs which form the balance of its wide base; the actual contest is wrought at the peak of the inner triangle of the group by the meeting of paw and arm; these limbs and the legs have the effect of elastic links in a triangular chain fixed in space.

The height of the outer and inner triangle coincide in one vertical through the joint of the lion's jaws, his paw and the man's knee; the quantitative preponderance of the left part of the group and its repose has its counter-weight in the energy embodied in the figure of man.

In this group are summed up qualities by which mediaeval Indian sculpture is conspicuous. It is neither baroque nor is it romantic; it has nothing to do with idealism but builds with symbol-elements of form the concrete reality (mūrti) of the work of art. The several phases and provinces of Indian art apply themselves, each in its particular livingness, to themes clearly seen and established.

Residues of nomadic formulations, carried through central Asia, are stored in the repertory of mediaeval Indian motives. The tufts of curls on shoulders, haunches (the latter are defaced in Pl. II) and in the face, belong to it.

The pose of the Siṁha with its paw raised can be seen on a signet of the third century B.C. from Amarāvatī (ASIAR, 1905-6, Pl. XLIX. Fig. 12).

PLATE III. DEVĪ JAGADAMBĀ TEMPLE
South wall of the Vimāna*; Khajuraho.

The Nirandhāra Prāsāda was originally dedicated to Viṣṇu. It was a Pañcāyatana temple. The socle more closely resembles that of Pl. I than the one shown in profile on p. 259. The same mouldings, but different in their sequence and proportion, are seen here projecting from the Mānasūtra; the socle grips the ground and makes the walls of the temple appear rooted in it and the several edges of the perpendicular wall appear to rise with a concave flexion. Its impetus is steadied by the entablature mouldings ('mekhalā' and 'antarapatra', combined with 'chādya') in a thrice repeated band whence the Śikhara curves upward and is gathered in the Āmalaka (not shown in Pl. III).

The projection of the plinth (pīṭha) from the Mānasūtra, is an aliquot part of the height of the plinth, (½, ⅓, or ¼) in principle; and projection and height of each moulding should also be proportionately related.

The mouldings of the socle, the Pīṭha, in the temples of Khajuraho, are relatively more restrained than those of the lowermost part of the wall, the Vedikā, where the widely projecting Torus shape of the Kumuda effects a transition from architectural to sculptural form. It accompanies every buttress (ratha) and extends into every recess (salilāntara) with multiple repetitions of its profile, broken thus into a series of square pillow shapes with lateral extensions, like petals. This moulding with its neck, placed as it is above the combined Kumbha and Paṭṭikā below, has, on each buttress, the appearance of a small Stūpa-like monument; its front face moreover is carved in the likeness of a small shrine (kūṭa); its sheltering depth, on the major buttresses, is occupied by an image (Viṣṇu on Garuḍa, on the central Bhadra) while a lotus rosette takes its place on the Rathas. These miniature shrines in relief have an elaborately carved pediment (siṃhakarṇa) composed of Gavākṣas. The pediment exceeds the height of the Kumbha and, oversecting the recess, links the lower mouldings of which it is itself the highest surface, with the forms above the necking; it helps to knit the horizontal mouldings into a pattern of vertical offsets.

Each of the belts of the wall consists of its Jaṅghā or wall surface proper and an architrave of which Mekhalā (or Mālā, Varaṇḍikā or Kapota) is the moulding and Antarapatra the necking; in lieu of the moulding, a rooflet (chādyaka) shades the niches of the Bhadra; its appears supported on pillars (stambha), a veritable shrine for the major images.

Above the Mekhalā is an Ardhaprastara or half-entablature made of the consoles on which the images have their stand. These entablatures form the horizontal clasps of the Bhadras, Rathas and Pratirathas, which are the several buttresses and their offsets in front and also on either side. The vertical panels and facets in every plane, the innermost being that of the broad recess (antara) are beset with images, each on its ancone, and shaded by a cornice or rooflet and

* Photograph by Johnston and Hoffmann, Calcutta. Cf. K. de B. Codrington, 'Ancient India', Pl. LXXII B.

thus within the wall space. With every movement of the eye of the beholder a new perspective shows the images from a different angle; to avoid being bewildered, he has to concentrate on each of them, facing it, and then give his attention to the next, in the same way; their sum making up the iconostasis of the temple walls in all the directions. The single images, each on its panel, do not coalesce in groups; each panel, be it even without lateral pillars, is an abbreviated shrine of a particular divinity. The images approximate sculptures in the round (Pls. XV, XX, etc.), and remain attached to the wall where they lean against it. Sometimes a strut like extension of their contour or shape (Pl. XXXIII) helps towards an increased height of their relief.

The triple belt of images as shown in this Plate has its major sculptures in the two central rows of the wall; their position, in the direction of the compass, determines their iconography. Different aspects of Viṣṇu figure in the centre of the main Bhadras in the South, West and East. In the South (Pl. III) are seen Viṣṇu on Garuḍa in the Vedikā, the lowest part of the wall proper, Viṣṇu and Lakṣmī in the first belt, and above it the Varāha-avatār in the second. The third belt has Devatās in their chariot (cf. its Āsanapaṭṭaka, etc. with that of the open, pillared, balconies of the Maṇḍapa in the extreme right of the Plate), in the Bhadras. The host of gods, in scenes of their sports (krīḍā-araṃbha; S.S. LVII. 644 f) is established in this narrow and high belt; the Aṣṭadikpālas and the other definitely identifiable gods occupy the highest offset on the respective Ratha and, as a rule, throughout the several zones; the innermost recess has invariably a Śārdūla for its subject; it is a Kṛtrimagrāsa (S.S. LVII. 777), a 'devourer made by art', its face is that of a horned lion or horned woman and often has the beak of a parrot, the proboscis of an elephant, a hog's snout or a ram's muzzle. Above the belts of images, a triple entablature is carried across the top of the wall, oversected by Siṃhakarṇas of the two Bhadras (the one a Karṇabhadra); their apex touches the level whence springs the Śikhara.

The identity of each buttress in the vertical direction is shown as much in its divided yet unbroken continuity as in the iconography of its sculptures. It is further stressed by the small Śṛṅga or turret which caps each buttress and by the particular configuration at the base, which here has been compared to a Stūpa, within the Vedikā.

To the row of small Śṛṅgas (tilaka) based on the entablature (uttara, the architrave) are added, towards the middle on each face of the Prāsāda, Uromañjarīs and also Naṣṭaśṛṅgas filling the corners (S.S. LVII. 745). Āmalasāra and small Āmalasārī crown each of the Śikharas but the finials have disappeared.

The transition from the Prāsāda to the Maṇḍapa—the place of the Antarāla and Śukanāsā—is marked in this Plate by the Karṇabhadra on the right and the carved panels above it (cf. Pl. XLIX).

The Maṇḍapa sends its Pītha with a forceful projection against the Vimāna anticipating further salients which terminate with the ends of the 'transept' in the balconies of the Maṇḍapa.

The walls of the Maṇḍapa are an exact continuation of those of the Prāsāda. But the coronation by a Śikhara of its own is not there on any buttress. Pyramidal miniature superstructures in tiers take their place, though with a looser discipline.

PLATE IV. ŚIKHARA OF THE KANDARĪYA TEMPLE

From the South West; cf. Pl. I.

The rhythmical compactness of the Śikhara and the dwindling of sculptured form into the texture of the monumental shape are brought about by the order of Uromañjarīs, four in each of the main directions, the lower clinging to the 'chest' (uras) of the higher. They are flanked by Karṇamañjarīs in parallel horizontal rows, three Karṇaśṛṅgas on the two lower and one in the third row, fill the corners from the Uromañjarīs in the East to those in the South. Intervening between Uromañjarīs and Karṇaśṛṅgas are Naṣṭaśṛṅgas (Khaṇḍarekhā) or 'hidden' small Śikharas, whose edge (koṇa) and Āmalaka are to be seen whereas the curvature of their sides is hidden and oversected by the adjacent Karṇaśṛṅgas. Four such Naṣṭaśṛṅgas belong to each of the two lower rows in each sub-quarter of the Śikhara. The one and only Karṇaśṛṅga, of considerably smaller size, of the third row sits on the corner (koṇa) of the Mūlamañjarī. It is flanked and exceeded by Naṣṭaśṛṅgas of considerable height. They terminate at the level of the second but last Uromañjarī and strengthen the theme of the Karṇas or edges of Uromañjarīs and Mūlamañjarī alike, with their horizontal divisions of Bhūmis.

All the Śṛṅgas are crowned by two Āmalakas (two 'aṇḍakas'; 'aṇḍaka'-'āmalaka'; S.S. LVII. 358) and a Kalaśa (some having disappeared); those of the bottom row are placed at the height of the apex of the Siṃhakarṇa above the Bhadra; those in the higher rows attain each to their own level and form horizontal clasps on the body of the Śikhara, in response to the stronger and unbroken bands of the Mekhalās on the walls of the Prāsāda. Each Śṛṅga is a replica of the Mūlamañjarī, the principal Śikhara, which emerges from the cluster of its acolytes at the height of the third Karṇaśṛṅga; there its corner is seen to spring upward, strong with many Bhūmis, whereas its full shape rises gradually above the Āmalaka of the highest Uromañjarī.

The Mūlamañjarī (the 'root' or central, main Śikhara) is a Latārekhā of the Saptaratha variety; its curve is steeper than that drawn by 'ṣaḍguṇa sūtra'; each of its four sides has seven facets ('pāga' in Orissan terminology) including the corner portion (koṇaka-pāga) which itself has one more minor central offset; the subordinate Śṛṅgas, alike in their 'structure', however have but five buttresses on each side (pañcaratha).

The Karṇaśṛṅgas spring each from a square base which has a broad central projection on each side; this, together with its accompanying mouldings and a broader necking in their midst, takes up the theme of the architrave (uttara) of the Vimāna. These sharply cut horizontal bands are further accentuated by similar casket-shapes (kūṭa) at the springing of every second Uromañjarī and in the lowest corner of the Mūlamañjarī. A similar underlining gives to every Bhūmi a firm and clear start above the cogged ring shape of the Āmalaka crowning the lower stratum. The contiguity of round Āmalakas and the bases with their straight lines, affords a rich interplay of shadow effects, a mellow deepening of the horizontal clasps and the integration of these several shapes into the body of the one great Śikhara, the superstructure of the Prāsāda.

The last consequences of the horizontal division of the Śikhara are drawn in the shape of parallel bands and neckings on the edges of all the Mañjarīs (cf. also

Pls. XLVI, XLV, XLVIII). These fillets and their interspaces, visible as parallel light and dark streaks, are the final abbreviations of miniature storeys or tiers of whose sum total the bulk of each Śikhara is made up. But, however manifold and intricate these horizontal themes are, on the total Śikhara (Pl. I) their effect is slight; the horizontal theme which remains in power is that of the corrugated Āmalakas punctuated by their globular Kalaśas and pointed Bījasvaras.

On the main surfaces of the offsets (ratha) of the Śṛṅgas, the tiers are overspun by the carved Gavākṣas, a tight fitting sheath, as if of lace, with the round eyelets of the windows and the scrolls of tracery surrounding them in several patterns (jāla; cf. also Pls. XLVI, LXXI).

In the totality of the Śikhara (Pl. I) these details are discerned as part only of the texture of the monument so that its surface vibrates at every moment of the day and the clear Indian nights with an ever responsive play of light and shade, a chiaroscuro of widest range, on its surface. The structure of the Śikhara however, the logic of its form, is a concert of ascending curves directed in many units each to a point of its own; they are organized and drawn towards the ultimate and only point on the tip of the finial of the Mūlamañjarī.

The nearer to the base the greater is the mass, the nearer to the final point, the less is the volume, and the greater is the cumulative energy gathered towards and united in it.

PLATE V. ANTARĀLA AND DOORWAY OF GARBHAGṚHA

Citragupta Temple, Khajuraho.

Flanked by the pillars and pilasters of its antechamber (antarāla), the doorway frames the image of Sūrya in the Garbhagṛha.

Although this doorway has none of the synthesis of parts, none of the rhythm which connects, unifies and elevates the spectacle of this iconostasis to the high level of realisation on which the image, the seat of divinity, is beheld (as for example the entrance into the sanctuary of the Lakṣmaṇa Temple, Khajuraho) it is simple in its proportions and clearly parcelled out. The main parts of the surround of the door are : the high threshold; the lower part of the jambs with the large images; the upper part of the antepagments with the compartments of small figures, the lintel and the overdoor. The opening of the door is equal in width to each of the jambs and this being equal to the height of the large figure groups at the bottom of the door, the height of the door is twice its width. In such pure proportions are also parcelled out the minor units of the compositions,—the three shrines of Sūrya—on the lintel, and their inter-spaces, etc. The various planes with their carvings between the powerful ovolo moulding of the outer surround and the flat innermost frame of the door with their changing shades redeem the all too regular lay out. The contrast moreover, of the modelled shapes which preponderate, with a linear type of carving in which dark shadows are set in flat tracery (door frame; lowermost fillet of base; pillars, etc.) adds richness but does not, in this particular instance, intensify the effectiveness of the display.

The large female figures in the middle of the Śākhās are badly damaged but their extremely bent postures show them at one with the billowing of their own waves: nothing else particularises them as river goddesses; the scroll canopies full of Devatās seated on lotus flowers are vestigial trees; under their branches, the companions of the goddesses are carved against the different Śākhās and the images of Nāgas lean on the outer frame of the doorway. The Dvārapālas are assigned to the pilasters flanking the doorway (cf. also Lakṣmaṇa Temple).

Some of the panels of the base far exceed in quality the rest of the carvings; the overdoor with its Gavākṣa-siṃhakarṇa frieze shows the flamboyant use of a well worn pattern. In the quantity of the required carvings, the sculpturally gifted craftsman also had his say in some of the reliefs, although the majority of the small panels (the image of Sūrya is about 5′ high) were not touched by the divine spark. The dull opulence (cf. also Pl. III) of general views of carved expanses of the temple however is not there actually. The fierce light of the Indian sun or the semi-darkness of the interior sum up the intricacies, the all too meticulous details, and make of them the texture of the temple walls in which each carving has its proper place. The angle moreover from which it is seen changes with the movement of the devotee. Within the temple he proceeds towards the Garbhagṛha; outside he walks around the temple; wherever he may halt or his eyes rest, it is done in the course of a viewing in motion, in which the carvings present themselves from innumerable angles, until one of them is singled out and his whole attention dwells on its front view.

PLATE VI. SŪRYA-BRAHMĀ-ŚIVA

Image on the west side, central Bhadra, second row in the triple belt of images of the Śiva temple, called Duladeo, Khajuraho, 10th century. Height below 2′.

Eight armed image; some of the arms are broken. The second but lowest pair might have held emblems of Viṣṇu so that this image of Sūrya, the Sun-god, would embrace Brahmā, the presiding divinity of the Sun, Viṣṇu, the presiding divinity of the Moon, and Śiva who presides over the Fire ('Īśānaśivagurudeva-paddhati', III, Ch. XII. 27-29). Such an image is a support of a meditation on Sadāśiva and has its place of special importance on a temple of Śiva.

Sūrya's "glowing" body is covered by a coat of mail; it has dwindled into a strip underneath the ornaments of his chest and extends to the belt. He is seated with his feet locked in Padmāsana, a long cloth covers them to the heels. This costume indicates that the consuming power of Sūrya's body is covered. In earlier images (from Mathurā, etc.), the body of Sūrya is completely shrouded in a coat of mail, high boots and other accoutrements of the dress of Northerners who had brought this particular cult to India.

In his two hands Sūrya holds full blown lotus flowers, symbols of manifestation, on the triple stalk of time; this aspect is also upheld by the Śiva-hand on the right holding a Triśūla, the trident—where past, present and future meet in one point, while serpents in the left Śiva-hand are amongst the ornaments of Śiva; here they strengthen, in the opposition of their nature to that of the Sun, the total symbolism (cf. sun-bird and serpent) of the image. The Brahmā hands hold the rosary (akṣamālā), the cycle of time and its resorption, and the Kamaṇḍalu.

But for the trident no other weapons are seen now in the hands of the image. The Viṣṇu hands might have held the disc and the club. The weapons held in the hands of the images of the gods represent portions of the unbearable power of the Sun which Viśvakarman had sliced away from it. Viśvakarman made the disc of Viṣṇu, the trident for Śiva and other weapons for these and the other gods out of the particles of Power that he took away from the Sun (cf. 'Matsya Purāṇa', XI. 27-30).

This power lies radiant in the fiercely calm face; it gives its forward sweeping curve to the chest and to the lotus-stalk whose flower discs are set on either side of the full visage. The triple furrowed pillar of the neck is part of the erect posture of the image. It is overlaid and surrounded by heavy ornaments, arms and the weapons. The balance of form in the horizontal which passes through the lotus discs and the face and correlates their shapes amidst themselves and with the vertical of the body, has all the concentration of the mind and heart of the artist; the rest shows the skill of his hand applied on the framework of established tradition.

The small mutilated image of Aruṇa, in the centre of the drapery, near the edge of the pedestal, lies in the vertical axis by which the Kīrttimukha in the crown of Sūrya is linked to the three horses carved on the pedestal, the seat of the chariot of the Sun-god.

PLATES VII—VIII. AGNI

Fire, the Guardian (dik-pāla) of the South-Eastern direction; on a Pratiratha (cf. 'Aparājitaprabhā', V. 12) in the South-East of the wall of the Kandarīya Temple, Khajuraho. The height of this and other images of the Kandarīya temple is c. 2′ 9″.

Front and profile of the face of the image of Agni; it is carved standing, with a gently swaying 'bhaṅga' of the body and holding a book and a Kamaṇḍalu in his two left hands; the lower right hand shows the boon-giving Mudrā, the upper right hand is broken.

The high crown of matted locks is not shown in the photograph, where only the root of the hair and horn-like locks are seen shading in a wide arch a low forehead, the rest of the face being encircled by the curls and terminated by the point of the beard, a tongue of fire. It rests on the chest against a pattern of jewellery similar to that of the Sūrya image though more simple and harmonising with the locks, the hair and the stern kindness of the face. The curly outline of the beard separates the face from the body and gives it the impressiveness of a mask smoothly modelled in flat curves in whose sweep the eyes without sockets, the wide brows have the strongest vibration. It spreads over the entire face which is unruffled, but changeable in expression; benevolent and irascible (Pl. VII), withdrawn and mysterious (Pl. VIII).

PLATE IX. PART OF WALL OF LAKSMAṆA TEMPLE

Khajuraho (954 A.D.); the back of a seat (āsana) such as surround the balconies (Bhadra; śālā) and run along the Ardhamaṇḍapa. (Fig. on p. 255.)

From the seat (āsana paṭṭa) in the interior rises its back projecting outward with an obtuse angle (kakṣāsana; approximate height: 2′ 4″). It is part of the Candrāvalokana, the upper and open portion of the balcony (see Pl. LI) somewhat corresponding to a bay-window. The Vedi is here the vertical portion of the wall, below the lotus petal edge; it corresponds in its position to the 'jaṅghā' of the wall (see Pl. I), *i.e.*, to its lowermost zone.

The Vedi consists here of carved posts; they rise from a slightly recessed necking (rājasenā), itself divided by uprights into panels filled with deep shadows, figures and rosettes. The pillars of the Vedi are set in couples of which one is replete with a creamy scroll which has come forth from the mouth of a Kīrttimukha placed in profile or three quarter profile in one of the lower corners of the carved panel. The other pillar has its surface divided into several sections of which the 'overbrimming vase' and foliage is uppermost; below is an 'Āmalaka ring'; then follow a Kīrttimukha, a scroll device inscribed in a circle and surrounded by scrolls, and, at the bottom, a scroll-creeper panel. These symbols of Indian and Nomadic extraction are carved, mature in every detail, in a florid relief. It would appear overcharged were it not so strongly permeated by linear rhythms accompanied by deep shadows. The reduction of the profuse modelling to a linear design is seen from some distance when the 'pillars' of the Vedi appear as part of the entire temple where they produce a white and black pattern which is furthermore strengthened by the vertical fissures between the coupled pillars and the short interstice between the capital shape and the straight edge of the adjacent pillar.

On many of these pillar-shapes, and elsewhere too (the lotus-cyma, and Pl. X), the linear pattern is worked out in its colour contrast of light and dark and the relief is left in this unfinished stage, as if on purpose.

The coping of the Vedi projects boldly over each capital shape; it recedes with a Gavākṣa-pediment, flanked by air-spirits, above each of the large Kīrttimukha-scroll-creeper-panels. Its wider projections are carved as miniature triple roofs, each (tri-chādya) crowned by an Āmalaka. The hard horizontal shadow thrown by the coping is intensified by a broader and more mellow band of shadows which cling to the rugged triple-rooflet shapes and to the lotus petal cyma above them.

The Āsana-paṭṭa with its slanting back in rail form belongs to a stone-bench (cf. Pl. LXXVI) on which the pilgrims may rest in the ambulatory and the hall of the temple. The slanting back is made of round uprights—of bamboo prototype—by twos, and alternating with broad carved posts similar in kind to those of the Vedi and rich in pattern. [A similar Vedi, having a bench with its back sloping outwards, forms the parapet of the high terrace of the Lakṣmaṇa Temple; it connects the four small shrines in the corners (Fig. on p. 255).]

The whole architecture of the Vedi and Āsana is translated into stone from a wood and bamboo construction of carved posts and beams and slender bamboo upright, airily joined. The thickness of the posts belongs to their versions in stone; the high seat of the bench is supported by heavy pillars (Pl. LI), their shapes, fully carved, emerge from it and on it rest monumental superstructures.

Images and architectural units are juxtaposed; geometrical shapes and fully modelled figures are contiguous.

The walls of the temple are effective in several respects according to the distance from where they are seen. From afar, their intricacy is absorbed by the light into the texture of the temple walls. The sculptural work is integrated in the monumental building. Seen closely, and with the attention focussed on any of its parts, that particular unit is all engrossing in its significance as symbol and visual form. Between these extreme views is the one in which the reference is seen of one unit to the next, their combination, contrast and balance in the wisdom of their plan.

PLATE X. OUTERMOST SURROUND OF DOORWAY

Part view; on the right of the Garbhagṛha, and adjacent wall; Duladeo Temple, Khajuraho.

The Śārdūla panel on the left is sunk into the antepagment (siṃhaśākhā) in the corner between the doorway and the wall of the Antarāla, at a right angle to it. The fillet of rosettes is the side of the antepagment, and borders on the wall whose scroll panel is seen in a strong artificial light. Next to it, a pilaster projects; it is set off against a lateral facet.

The compositional theme of the three main panels is the wave. It rises and falls and carries its movement to the top of every scroll, lays it down at the crest of the main wave and having completed its eddying and interlacing in varied configurations, it returns its impact to its main carrier. This is shown as a creeper's stalk pervading the whole panel and from it stem other branches which have one wave length only. They are cut flat and sharp, perpendicularly, in the stone in a pattern of light and darkness, intricate yet clear; the carving is left unfinished where further elaboration was not essential, to the effect, at the side of the entrance to the Garbhagṛha. In the surround of the door however they are clad in the shape of the Śārdūla with its rider and counterplayer who holds the creature's tail in one hand and threatens it with the weapon held in the other; the protagonists are almost equal in size. But, when the warrior brandishes the same weapon while he has mounted the animal, he has lost his stature and the animal's head is turned back, leering open mouthed towards its diminutive rider. These bodies are formed of a concatenation of waves; crossing at many points of their courses they ascend from the bottom (not shown in the reproduction) to the top of the panel and enmesh the playful fury of the recurrent combat. Three wave movements are thus interlaced; viewed from the top of the panel, the one glides from the chest-curve of the Lion to its buttocks, sweeps with its crest over the warrior and descends to the next lion's chest, rising towards its buttocks whence the play goes on as before. The second wave passes from the profile of the lion's head to the root of its tail and rising, passes from the warrior's chest to his leg thrown forward, then again engulfs the next lion and sinks from the root of its tail to the warrior's chest, supports his contracted body and once again mounts along the lion's face, etc., below. The third wave passes along the topmost lion's rounded chest and the claws of his feet, thence across the warrior's chest thrust forward, thence to his buttocks and left leg thrown back, and then down to chest and claws of the second swastika-poised mannekin, and thus onward. The waves intersect on chest and buttocks of the Lion and on the warrior's chest; within the waves the small rider is engulfed securely on the back of the Śārdūla.

The shapes of man and the Lion are modelled like skins which tightly fit an afflatus of divine energy. In Pl. X, mediaeval Indian sculpture is quick with life clear in its form.

The masters of the Duladeo Temple (Pls. XXIV-XXVIII) worked on a high level of inspiration. The word Vasala (Vāsara?) inscribed in different places on the Duladeo Temple might be the name of a leading sculptor.

PLATE XI. SURASUNDARĪ

Image on the South West wall, 2nd belt of the Kandarīya temple (height 2′ 9″), Khajuraho.

The image is that of a very young Celestial Beauty, a serving maid to the high purpose of the greater gods. Heavy featured, heavy limbed, coltishly stubborn, she holds a gourd-shaped vessel close to her body. A small figure of a man or a Gaṇa squats at her feet and sips what little drink has inadvertently flown out to him from the full vessel of her overwhelming bounty.

The figure turns towards the wall of the temple in three quarter back view, and its face is shown in profile. It forms a volume placed diagonally in space against the ground of the relief. Her elephantine shoulder is pushed forward in her slow and unconcerned movement; it is summed up by the—extremely consciously—apportioned flux of the scarf across shoulder and back. The arm is drawn back towards it so as to allow its full effect to the globe of the breast and the milder curve of the hip. The angular, half awkward, half capricious drawing back of the arm, its elbow touching the scarf, leads to the key-point of the disposition of the volume of the figure within the prism of the stone on whose socle surface her feet are firmly planted.

In this key-point, the main directions intersect of the three-dimensional composition of this carving. The one diagonal in space is laid from the hand to the chignon, and the second diagonal connects the right shoulder with the tip of the scarf and which is fitted into the outline of the figure, on the left. The rectangle formed by these two diagonals has for its one side the edge of the buttress on the right, and for the other, a parallel drawn from the end of the chignon to the left heel. This rectangular prism is but half of the whole; the lower part, from the end of the scarf down to the heels is similarly traversed by two diagonals in space, linking the one, the direction of the small person on the right, with the end of the scarf of the goddess, and the other, her left heel with the hand holding the vessel. In this way the two congruous space prisms are similarly filled by the disposition of the round volumes of the image. The compositional movement in space leads from the shoulder in the foreground on the right to the left buttock in the background, and thence, in the lower half, to the foreground in front of the arm and leg of the small person. The highest surfaces of the volumes, on the right, are anchored in the depth at the opposite side, in the middle of the height of this image, at the end of the scarf.

The second compositional movement in space connects the hand in the foreground, placed at the same height as the end of the scarf,—with the end of the chignon on top; and with the left heel of the goddess; either of these are near to the middle ground of the relief. The compositional directions link the salient points in space of the image, across the depth of the carving, and connect its various levels amongst each other. This organisation in space is caught in a lozenge-net of diagonal lines which have their two main corners in the middle line of the image drawn at the end of the scarf, and across the hand and a loop of the hip-ornament, on the right, the one at the left tip of the scarf the other in the hand. The two other corners of the central compositional lozenge coincide, the upper with the meeting point of elbow and scarf and the lower with the point where the other end of the scarf emerges just below the knee. The meeting of elbow and scarf and also the place of the knee are the critical compositional points. They play moreover their rôle in the physiognomy of the form of the image, with its acuteness of the sharp bend in the elbow of the elephantine arm, and, similar in its over-emphasis, the stretched straightness of the legs which makes them appear jointless, more poles than legs were it not for the swelling curves of the thighs.

The overstrained movement which makes joints bend at unforeseen angles or stretched out of existence, in this particular carving, is mild (see however Pls. XIII, XV, etc.); its curves are smooth; loops and clasps formed by various parts of the costume, in close adherence to the modelled body, mediate between the linear rhythms and the richer depth movements. Their interplay is steadied by oval and globular shapes such as the vessel, the face and the various fruit like shapes of the chignon, etc., which accompany head and back. All these rounded weights are strung along either side of the swaying and turning body. In its long, smooth legs is straightened out the exuberance of the upper part of the figure. To them the small person at the bottom is the final correspondence.

PLATE XII. SURASUNDARĪ

Part view. Kandarīya Temple, SE wall (second row); Khajuraho.

The image faces away from the buttress on which it leans but the inward look, the long curves of eye and brow, the chignon at the back of the head, even the long necklace lead backwards, to the wall of the temple.

The left hand is raised with Triśūla-hasta, the right holds a bowl. Its curve is taken up, aggrandised, and leads along the arm of the image to the wall of the buttress. In the bowl of this arm the goddess proffers her body and gesture. The inward look, the harking back, of the goddess are accompanied by the sculptural disposition of the carving. Watchful of her secrecy, effortless and noble, this crowned goddess carries the bowl and gesture and also her own shape, in obedience to her task. As simple as is the shape of the bowl, are her ornaments. Closely adhering to the body they define its shape and show in their own, more linear way, its amplitude. Laid on the forehead, like an ornament, is the arch of the brow. It holds in its curves the expanse of the face, shown in front view and in profile at the same time.

On another buttress wall, in the background, the image of another goddess is seen, its echo, it would seem were it not that it carries out a different function of its own and is, as an image, complete in itself, and, like its neighbour, part of the wall of the temple.

PLATE XIII. SURASUNDARĪ

Kandarīya Temple, South East, first belt. Khajuraho.

The walls at the back and behind the image act as screens which throw into full relief the sophisticated fragility of this high strung and enticing goddess.

Wreathed around the axis of this sculpture, the lower part of the body in three quarter back view is turned at the hips so that the bust is seen in almost three quarter profile, the arm is thrown back for this purpose; the lowered head, almost completely in profile view is laid across the slightly tilted vertical of the figure; the face opens up towards the right from the chalice shaped chignon. This crescendo in volume of the head in one direction, while the face is lowered and seems to withdraw into itself in the opposite direction, is repeated in the next lower section of the 'statue' where the arm is pushed back in an acute angle where the breasts are seen and the hand clings to their round contour. The shoulder joint is here in the centre of the co-ordinates of the composition (cf. the rôle of the elbow, in Pl. XI), one passes through the elbow and the shoulder joint, the other from the contact of hand and breast, to the top of the chignon; through the centre of these co-ordinates moreover passes the main vertical of the image. It is tilted forward, follows the inner outline of the right leg and passes through the outer corner of the eye. There also passes the horizontal axis of the head, at a right angle to the main vertical; it has its parallel in a line drawn from the elbow to the hip girdle, at a point below which festoons are attached to it. Parallels to the main vertical connect the right elbow and the back of the chignon, and the raised left elbow with the outline of the right hip where the girdle rests. Thus the volumes around the sculptural axis are co-ordinated in the surface of the image, especially the cones or jutting angles of the arms. These moreover are diagonally connected in space and are balanced by the co-ordinate along which the body turns round in the hip, from buttock to waist. These co-ordinates are laid diagonally across the figure and have their centre at the tip of the armlet. The movement of the figure and the placing of its volumes around its sculptural axis, are balanced according to a geometrical plan in the surface; the linear rhythm of the composition and the three dimensional spiralic disposition of its volumes around their axis are integrated in this 'statue of the temple wall'.

Raised on high legs, the hip surges into roundness, restrained by chains of jewellery. This solid effervescence, bubble of carved stone, is the basic shape of the smaller globular and the large, angular volumes which are tossed around the body-axis in the upper part of the image of this eery temptress, uncrowned, ambiguous, and straining the possibilities of mediaeval sculpture to a critical point.

PLATE XIV. SURASUNDARĪ, HOLDING A MIRROR

Viśvanātha Temple (c. 1000 A.D.), South wall (2nd belt). Khajuraho.

Steeped in the consciousness of her young, full and perishable body and swaying with the onrush of its sap, the celestial damsel looks deep into the mirror and her head droops towards its reflection on the curved surface held up and resting on her shoulder, part of her own sculptural shape. Recognition makes self-contained the group of the goddess and the mirror. The wave of her triply bent shape, rises, falls and rests on her stance. All conflicts appear resolved, all contingencies known. With a heavy heart and the smile of youth tribute is rendered to life which takes its course through her body.

At home, if somewhat tired, in its harmonious shape, this image leaves no room for the pained charm of conflicting elements of form (as Pl. XIII, etc.). Here Indian 'naturalism' has made an image of Śakti as 'natura naturans' knowing her work and accepting her shape as its result.

PLATE XV. SURASUNDARĪ, PAINTING THE SOLE OF HER FOOT WITH RED LAC

Kandarīya Temple, West wall (2nd belt). Khajuraho.

The image of this crowned goddess represents an extremely complex type of mediaeval sculpture; its emotional finesse is on the point of outgrowing sculptural form. Writhing around its axis the image soars on her left leg pillar. The other is folded up within an acute angle; it is supported by an attendant,—carrying a bag on his back—of rich plastic vitality; his flexed, bouncing figure lends weight to the group, makes it rest on the sprightly support; it is a counter-player to the leg-pillar, while it also accompanies the upward diagonal of the raised leg whose painted foot is stretched with a ballet-dancer's discipline. To this, most powerful accent in the group, the upper part of the body responds by a measured conduct of its limbs, first backwards in space towards the wall, then upward, leaning against it and sending forth ball or egg shapes and other smaller volumes each clearly set off from the other.

Power and grace of a heroic vision have shaped the lower half of the image. Its angles are sustained by curved shapes of the keenest tension. Were they blown in glass, they might easily be shattered by their own contact. But not all the images of this temple are carved with so high a tension of rarified form. The figure on the adjacent surface of the buttress, on the right, is sturdy with a weightiness balanced from the sole to the top of her crown.

PLATE XVI. SURASUNDARĪ

Part view;* Kandarīya Temple, East wall (1st belt). Khajuraho.

Mediaeval form, built with the substance of ancient Indian sculpture, is conscious of its linear energy. It compresses the pulsations of the plastic form in acute rhythms of outline and internal design.

Angles are sharp in the meeting of the many subtle curves of which is made up every limb and feature. The nose, for example, disdainful and getting scent of all things, is vibrant from its tip to the slight depression on its back; a sharp and luscious young animal's organ; thence it is led upwards in a shallow curve and straightens towards its root when the feeler brows swoop upon the total expanse of the eye in front view.

The eyes of these images are overstatements of their shape. Where the mediaeval vision prevails, completeness of their frontal view is maintained in the profile of the face; no foreshortening lessens their steady pathos.

PLATE XVII. APSARĀ

Part view, S.W. wall, innermost recess, between two buttresses;
2nd belt; H. of figure : c. 1′. Ḍuladeo Temple, Khajuraho.

The seriousness of this celestial dancer resides in a straight profile which is the key to a context of lines and volumes set against one another in wide angles. The volume of the head and the straight high crown, have their unified keen outline inclined against the square plane below it. Its rounded edge is the raised arm, bent in this sharp angle as if throwing a dice, similar in shape to the ear-ring, as part of this particular dance. Right angles dominate the face ; feathery pendants of the necklace, hair lowered into, and then brushed up from, the forehead, frame and soften the valour of this sculpture.

PLATE XVIII. ŚĀḶABHAÑJIKĀ

Bracket figure on the Ucchālaka of a pillar in the Maṇḍapa
of the Lakṣmaṇa temple; 954 A.D.; Khajuraho.

Woman and tree, in close touch and conformity of their volumes and movements, are lent different shapes and names of one rhythm whose wave ascends from the woman's left toes, magnificently places her leg, turns, curves her back and rises in one sweep, comprising arms and head, to find its way down where the

* The whole figure is reproduced in 'Surasundari', ISOA, Pl. I.

ball is to drop from her hand and the stem of the tree bends to the right. There it points to the small attendant, on the right, while the fluttering scarf rounds up her outline on the right and leads the eye to her child-attendant on the left.

Waves of movement, in the surface and in depth fill the prism of the strut which is set into the capital. They follow a similar order to those in Pl. X, but are clothed in more opulent, less fervent plastic shapes. Their roundness is more spreading, more yielding than it was in shaping the image on Pl. XIV. Creamy and luxuriant though the modelling is, it is not shaped throughout by rhythmic energy. The right outline of the figure vacillates and the drawing of the leg is weak.

The great ascending curve of the leg in the dance of the limbs is balanced by the arms held horizontally, and the weight of the canopy of the tree.

The two adjacent brackets are in the shape of Śārdūlas. Ucchālaka (S.S. LVII. 188; LXII. passim, LXIII. 57, etc.) is the extension of the shaft of the pillar above its capital and up to the second or sur-capital.

PLATE XIX. APSARĀ

Fragment. (Height c. 1′ 10″) on a thin buttress of the Antarabhitti, lower belt, South; Viśvanātha Temple, Khajuraho.

Writhing around its axis, the volume of this figure is integrated in its movement, her youth in every curve, her feline sadness in her tortuous rapture.

The knowledge of her body is so intimate that width and roundness of the lower part and the harsh length of her arm are but phases and stresses in a movement which is the nature itself of this image. She is the spirit of the dance; her sculptured hieroglyph is attached to the wall of the temple.

PLATE XX. APSARĀ

H : 2′ 1″; on the West of the Antarabhitti of the Garbhagṛha; Pārśvanātha Temple, c. 1000 A.D., Khajuraho.

The similarity of the attitudes of the figures on Pls. XVIII-XX shows the possibilities of form of one related sculptural theme. The image on Pl. XX is adjusted to a corner of the wall; two surfaces at a right angle shield the figure; on the right, where the pillars are, the central niche of a Tīrthaṅkara juts out; in the recess on the left is a Śārdūla.

The vigour of the movement of the Apsarā is the more apparent for being encased by the plain walls. No greater fitness of sculpture, walls and space can be found in Khajuraho. Mediaeval power of movement and ancient Indian 'naturalism' are amalgamated in the perfection of this sculpture.

PLATE XXI. APSARĀ

On a pilaster of the interior of the Ardha-Maṇḍapa of the Duladeo Temple, H. 2′ 3¼″, Khajuraho.

Here the movement of the celestial dancer is in full swing; evolved from the convolution around the body axis, it unfolds in front of the wall; arm, scarf and crown spread like wings while the body is part of the wall against which it leans with the oblique cross of its head and arms.

Strings of jewellery and stringy folds of garments are adjusted, by degrees, to the creeper pattern (cf. Pl. X), one step deeper, on the wall surface where the rhythm of the dance reverberates in contrasts of light and darkness.

PLATE XXII. APSARĀ

On a pilaster of the interior of the Ardha-Maṇḍapa of the Duladeo Temple, Fragment (H. c. 1′ 8½″), Khajuraho.

Ripples of movement are in the pearl chains, tress, crown and scarf of this torso of a dancer, powerful in build and impact. Deep in its volume, vibrant in its surface, in any profile, the glory of this breathing body is centred in its belly.

The wall which forms the background of these dancers (Pls. XXI-XXII) is graded in three successive levels. The images have the foremost and the middle plane for their ground; the one on Pl. XXI leans on them while that on Pl. XXII is driven forward together with them.

PLATE XXIII. FLYING DEVAS

(Vidyādharas ?); detached sculpture, now inserted in the east wall of the platform of the 19th century Pratāpeśvar Temple (H. of carving c. 10″); Khajuraho, 10th century.

Flying, fighting, these heroic celestials are martial rhythm embodied as sculpture: interlaced triangles within sword and club, face against face, body against body, the backs slashing through space, the spine a scimitar, the haunches stretched with the fierceness of a tiger's shape, their arms and weapons are thrown back each to the opposite hip. The heads are streamlined, egg-shaped, Gorgo-mouthed, the lips denude a terrific mass of teeth, the eyes bulge and nostrils tremble in this combat in mid-air, or also in the turmoil of the passionate, the subtle body of man.

(Leaves, in the upper part of the carving, above the shield of the 'swordsman' partly hide it from view).

PLATE XXIV. GAṆA

Centre of the lintel of the entrance to the Garbhagṛha, Duladeo Temple, Khajuraho. Its projection from the lintel is c. 10″.

The flying four-armed Gaṇa raises a conch shell (?) to his lips while he carries Śiva in a pillared 'chariot'. The fillet, above the head and upper hands of the Gaṇa, is the edge of the bottom of the chariot. The Gaṇa functions as a console. His image is carved against the enrichments of the lintel and below the corbel on which the image of Śiva is enthroned.

His person, a mere quantity (gaṇa) is distended with the air, which he is about to set into vibration by blowing the conch shell, heralding by sound,—which is the quality of ether (ākāśa), the first element in the order of manifestation,—that Śiva, the Lord, has come. The form-giving vibration is not only conveyed by an auditory symbol and its instrument, the conch, but radiates halo-like around the facial orb of the Gaṇa and forms his wavy hair.

The upper right hand is 'Haṃsāsya'; thumb and forefinger are joined like a Haṃsa's bill; the upper left (damaged), as if upholding the chariot, is held in Patākā (flag) pose.

PLATES XXV-XXVIII. FLYING DEVAS (VIDYĀDHARAS)

Uppermost belt of images, Duladeo Temple, South West, Khajuraho. (Height: below 1½′), Pl. XXVIII shows the original in somewhat less than actual size.

The highest of the three belts of sculptures is here the region of the Vidyādharas. The images of these wizards are carved flying singly, on the buttresses; and flying in pairs, with their consorts, in the recesses of the wall. They carry weapons (Pl. XXV) and garlands, brandish swords, play on musical instruments ('vyālamukha vīṇā', Pl. XXVII; 'veṇu', the bamboo flute, Pl. XXVIII), carry dance in their hands, flight in their legs (Pl. XXVI) and sentiment or detachment in their faces. Alike to angels they have the appearance of young boys, but they fly by a qualification of their wingless bodies; scarves accompany their movement and music. Its sound is as varied as is their form, which is of the purest mediaeval cast (Pl. XXVI), on the high level of serenity on which the images soar (Pls. XXV, XXVIII).

PLATE XXIX. CĀMUṆḌĪ

Part View. Fragment of image (Height of the fragment 2′ 5″), originally from Jaina Temple; Khajuraho Museum.

Cāmuṇḍī, Yakṣiṇī of the twenty-first Tīrthaṅkara, resembles the Hindu goddess Cāmuṇḍā, the seventh Mother (mātṛkā). In some of her images Cāmuṇḍā is represented as a dancer. Extreme emaciation, darkness in cadaverous cavities, facial hinges bared, eye-sockets as stringy as are her necklace and ribs below pendant empty breasts are the ornaments of the Mother, in her destructive form. Night and decay scream from deep hollows. A feeble halo rounds them off.

The death-body of this aspect of the goddess, its osseous mortal form, is carved with the same mastery as is the breathing subtle body of the gods eviternally sixteen years old.

PLATES XXX-XXXI. MITHUNA

Devī Jagadambā Temple; South Wall, 2nd belt (Height 2′ 6″); Khajuraho.

In this most perfect composition of its kind, the hem of the loin-cloth,—opening, slipping,—is part of the diagonal theme of raised, interlaced shapes forming waves, in depth, and squares and rectangles, in the surface, all of which begin, and are supported, on the stem of the legs, from the touching of feet, on the ground, to ever renewed contacts. In their fingers, twist of the hair or the folding of the cloth are spells and evocations, of that state of being a couple of which the entire composition is an image.

PLATE XXXII. MITHUNA, AND TWO SAKHĪS

Part view, Viśvanātha Temple, South wall; Khajuraho.

The particular 'bandha' in which the male and female body attain their union, their size and maturity (Pl. XXXIII), their physiognomical types, the kind and degree of their absorption, the form in which their group is cast, the correspondence of movements, directions and shapes of the central group and of the attendants, all these are knit into the unity of the work of art as the visible form of its ultimate meaning.

PLATE XXXIII. MITHUNA

Devī Jagadambā Temple, South wall; 2nd belt; Height 2′ 6″, Khajuraho.

PLATE XXXIV. MITHUNA

Detached fragment of small size, from Khajuraho; Private collection, Benares.

PLATE XXXV. NANDIN

At the feet of an image of a Śiva-Pratihāra; Kandarīya Temple, West wall, Khajuraho.

The small figure of the bull reclines on the pedestal, its head raised and turned towards the god whose figure towers above it. Spirals of convex and concave planes meet in sharp edges; they are the shape of the animal and convey its movement.

PLATE XXXVI. MŪSAKA

Image carved in the round; Height 1′ 1″; Length 1′ 4¾″; Width 7½″.

The mouse, the Vāhana of Gaṇeśa, is carved from a rectangular block of which the pedestal is the lower portion. Mūṣaka rests paw and face on a heap of Laḍḍu, ball shaped sweets, in a bowl; the mouse watches over the sweets, which pleases its invisible rider.

The 'statue' of the mouse, a smooth, compact volume held in convex surfaces is as much a work of mediaeval type as is the Nandin (Pl. XXXV) though it has neither its tension nor incisiveness.

PLATE XXXVII. ARDHANĀRĪŚVARA

Detached image; buff sandstone, 10th century; place of discovery unknown; private collection; Benares.

The image is 'gracefully' (lalitāsana) enthroned on an oval seat and is flanked by pillars. The hands of Śiva, the Lord (Īśvara) hold trident and rosary in Kaṭaka-hasta; Pārvatī, his beloved, holds up a mirror and raises a jar. Images of this kind are also known as those of Gaurīśvara, the right side being equivalent to Puruṣa, and the left to Prakṛti (V. Dh. III. LV. 2-5). The two halves, the male and the female, which are one in divinity, have been coalesced without effort in a homely sculpture; a miniature Nandin looks up to Śiva.

The fierce fervour and rarified economy of the form of Candella work are not in this sculpture. It is broader and less subtle, in modelling. Its four-square heaviness is the contribution of a neighbouring school of mediaeval sculpture which was given full scope on the Cedi temples of the Central Provinces.

PLATE XXXVIII. TĀRĀ

Fragment of image; buff sandstone, 11th century. Sārnāth, near Benares, Sārnāth Museum.

"May Tārā, the mistress of the Three worlds bestow happiness on you, Tārā, whose body is Dharma, whose mind is full of mercy, clarity her intellect, her eyes beauteous with friendship and love, her hands give peace."

(Buddhist inscription from Khasia; verse 3; 11-12th century; 'Epigraphia Indica', Vol. XVIII, p. 131.)

The Dhyāni-Buddha is enthroned on her diademed head; a lotus petalled halo is at the back. From her left hand in Mayūra hasta the stalk of a blue lotus flower uncoils upwards.

Different from the clear cut width of Candella sculptures (Pls. XII, XXV) like those from Khajuraho, the modelled surface of the small fragment reproduced on Pl. XXXVIII is astir with a tremulous agitation and its repercussions are in the shadows.

Rhythmic intricacy (cf. the hair as it is set off from the forehead, in Pl. XXXVIII, and in Pls. XII, XV, etc., the mode of dressing it being practically identical), is in the modelled forms and their shaded intervals. It loosens the coherence of the modelled planes and dips them into a chiaroscuro pregnant with short, scintillating accents.

The face emerges from its halo of shapes and shadows; its structure is enriched emotionally and lessened in its sculptural compactness. Shadows give a breathing tenderness to lips and nostrils and warmth to the texture of the stone.

The image of Tārā from Sārnāth is indebted to the art of the Eastern Indian school of sculpture. The Eastern Indian school is at home in Bengal and Bihar but its influence spread as far west as Sārnāth and Gorakhpur.

PLATE XXXIX. GAṆA

Detail of wall of the Śiva Temple in Pali, near Bilaspur, C.P. c. 1000 A.D.

The Gaṇa is shown emerging from the wall, to a plane higher than that of its carved surface with the Jāla network (seen on the r. and l. of the arms). His hands hold aloft a chariot. No image is enshrined in it: a lozenge shape with symmetrical scrolls is set between the lateral pillars (cf. Pl. IX, a four petalled shape). Below the Gaṇa, and beneath a 'giripatrikā' fillet, a number of animals face forward straining to draw the chariot; a frieze of Haṃsas below forms the enrichment of the next lower fillet of the wall.

Juxtaposition of modelled shapes in deep shadows, and flat surfaces, some of which are cut perpendicularly in patterns of light and darkness, combine in the monumental effectiveness of the wall.

In this architectural detail the Gaṇa is an embodiment of the progression of the wall from within the temple and of its vertical discipline as well. The horizontal moulding formed by his chest and arms and the horizontal of his hands whose touch is quick with life are part of this caryatid-hieroglyph embodiment of the function of the wall of the temple. It is given shape in the broad idiom of sculpture of the Cedi school.

PLATE XL. APSARĀ

Vaiṣṇava temple, west side; Janjgir, east of Bilaspur, C.P., Eleventh century.

The dancing Apsarā holds her anklet of tinkling bells (nūpura) which she is about to fasten on her foot; her small companion beats the drum while keeping step with her. A Gaṇa supports her pedestal (cf. the geometry of this Gaṇa-console with that of the preceding Plate).

In the recesses, to the left and right of this pier with its images, Deva-ṛṣis hold rosaries and count their beads.

Squat and angular of shape, the fulness of summarily modelled limbs is tied to their graded levels, without daring but also without hesitation.

PLATE XLI. NĀGARĀJA

Vaiṣṇava Temple, west side; Janjgir.

With sword raised high, shield close to the body and serpent's tail coiled, the image is poised on the tip of its tail and supported by the flat coil with its deep shadow in the centre. It is balanced by the circular shield with its full centre, and which is curved into depth. Thus the volume of the image is fixed, between its canopy and the pedestal. Its energies are pent up in the contracted curves of the chest; arm and head, held high, stolidly and with a crude power, are set against the plane of the dagger cutting into the depth between wall and figure, a horizontal, top-heavy accent. Cf. also the Ṛṣi, on the left; and the matted hair or the diadem as also the total shape of each face, on Pl. XL.

Ṛṣis and Apsarās at the sides of the Nāgarāja, although of the same formal structure, lack the zest and solidity of the Nāga's image.

Unused to the rarified élan and resources of the neighbouring Candella school, the sculptors of the Cedi country packed their shapes with measured power.

PLATE XLII. HAMSAKRĪḌĀ

Detail of wall of Śiva Temple, Deo Baloda, South East of Bilaspur, C.P. c. Twelfth century.

"The sport of the Haṃsas should be carved on the walls of the temple" ('Samarāṅgaṇasūtradhāra', LVII. 360). In this panel their 'goose step' resounds in an amplitude of curves; they shape the body of the birds and their feathery accompaniment; tail and scroll of drapery are boats in which they sail and swings in which they rock. The streamers flowing from their beaks are reminiscent of the sun bird's serpent, or they may be understood as "extension of the whiteness of the swans' bodies in the shape of white cloths" ('Ādipurāṇa', XXXII. 228, 'Ind. Ant.' vol. XIV. p. 105).

PLATE XLIII. NĪLAKAṆṬHEŚVARA TEMPLE

From the West; Udayapur, Gwalior; built by the Paramāra King Udayāditya (c. 1059-1087 A.D.); Red sandstone.

In plan (p. 256), the Prāsāda has in each of the main directions—the west or back of the temple being shown on Pl. XLIII—a widely projected Bhadra whose main face is parallel to the corresponding wall of the Garbhagṛha; its sides are perpendicular to it. All the other buttresses however, between the main Bhadras (śālās) are laid out within a circle which connects their indented apices. The walls of these buttresses ('karṇa'; 'pallava'; pallavikā', the latter meaning 'bud') form a right angle. When drawing a plan of this kind, the square of the Prāsāda is not subdivided into a given number of parts, but is rotated around its centre and made to stop at regular intervals. The points of the rotating square perform a circle in which the original square of the Prāsāda is inscribed.—The Bhadras or Śālās facing the main directions do not result from the rotation of the square but are planned in the usual way, parallel to the square of the Garbhagṛha. The front face of the Śālās is also circumscribed by the same circle, or it may exceed it. It is therefore said that the projection (nirgama) of these buttresses either lies within the circle or else is measured by aliquot parts of the square of the Prāsāda (S.S. LXV. 1-2). Prāsādas having this plan are classified as "Bhūmi-ja", "country-born" and are said to be "both square and circular" in plan.

Offering their two slanting surfaces to the light at a right angle, the 'bud'-like buttresses of this kind of Prāsāda are rich with many gradations of light and shade in which the images and carvings are embedded (Pls. XLIII-IV). The Pallavikās, the faceted or 'indented' apices, further dissolve the mass of the walls into sheets of light and darkness.

The buttresses, in their Jaṅghā portion, which is the wall proper of the temple, have the appearance of pillars. Of equal height however is the Vedi with its heavy mouldings, above an Adhiṣṭhāna which vehemently projects towards the ground (Fig. on p. 260). The mouldings of the base and the perpendicular Vedikā are fused in a vertical sequence of profiles. They are rigid and ponderous in every unit and require to be seen as support and receptacle of the shade which they harbour and the light which they absorb. Although in name and shape the several mouldings

* The Temple is also known as Udayeśvara Temple; ASIAR, 1923-24; p. 133; Cunningham, 'ASI. Report', X. p. 65; VII. p. 82 f; JASB. NS. vol. X. p. 241 f.

are the same as for instance on the Adhiṣṭhāna and Vedikā of the temples in Khajuraho (Figs. on pp. 259-60) by the modifications of proportion and position their effect is altogether different. In Khajuraho light and shade are disciplined by the architectural volumes (Pl. III).

A conclave of pillar shapes assembled so as to round off the temple, forming its wall, is extended in the Śikhara in the shape of concurrent beaded chains massed together and subordinated to the flat band of Latās in each of the four directions in which the Śālā of the wall has its extension. It is sealed by the Śukanāsā in the East (Pls. XLVII-IX) and by the Śukanāsikās, each having but half the height of the Śukanāsā, in the three remaining quarters.

PLATE XLIV. PART OF WALL OF THE NĪLAKAṆṬHEŚVARA TEMPLE, UDAYAPUR

The Pallavikās, the faceted apices of the triangular buttresses, are summed up at the bottom of each of the two sides by a pillared shrine projecting on a console formed of various mouldings. The shrines are replete each with an image of a Parivāra-devatā, such as Gaṇeśa—on the left of the Plate—and with his female counterpart in the adjacent shrine at a right angle, on the same buttress. The triangular pediments of the shrines touch a moulding which is a canopy, shrunk in depth, of the image in its niche, and a clasp of the pillar shape of the "buttresses".

Higher up, a broad Vājana, or fillet—having for its enrichment (alaṃkāra) a Kīrttimukha in the centre—clasps the pillar-buttress before it is to be contracted into its neck on which rest the mouldings forming its capital. From the Kīrttimukha, extending on the main facet downwards, a heavy chain is carved terminating with a small bell in relief (prāsakiṅkiṇikā; S.S. LVII, 788).

These adornments belong to the wall as pillar (jaṅghā) proper; they are not extended at a further depth of the buttress. There the recessed planes are filled by one continuous panel having an image of Śakti as Vana-devatā, below a burly creeper which carries celestials and the figures of various animals.

Between these panels, set at an angle to each other, a Pallavikā protrudes on which the themes of the wall pillar are repeated. The horizontal mouldings in their discontinuity, the commingling of statuary and architectural themes, their alternation with full length relief panels, all these are inclined towards each other on slanting planes, steeped in light and shade. From these emerge only the most powerful accents, all in the vertical direction, whether their carriers are the round columns of the shrines or the clear cut edges of the Pallavikās. Their vertical theme is continued in the superstructure (Pl. XLIII). Dominated by it, the shadows, the mellow carvings, the juxtaposition of unrelated contrasts, redeemed by their repetition, are but the undertone; they give substance and wealth to a superstructure (Pl. XLV) in which are integrated all the disparities.

PLATE XLV. ŚIKHARA (FROM S.W.) OF THE NĪLAKAṆṬHEŚVARA TEMPLE, UDAYAPUR

The wall sends up its buttresses terminated by capital-shape mouldings. They are superimposed by an heavy ornamented fillet, a deep recess and a roof shaped moulding which demarcate the height of the wall.

The Śikhara rises thence with a slight ingress, a double zone of mouldings—its motives being those of capital shapes and fillets—forms its base. The arch of the Śikhara ascends from this base, unbroken in the four quarters, where flat Latās, with their Gavākṣa lattices are flung up to the Āmalaka, exceeding bow-shaped (dhanus), the truncated body of the Śikhara. These arches, each comprised of 3 (or 5) Latās, spring from and are partly covered by, the Śukanāsā at the bottom. Between them are seven Bhūmis of five Śṛṅgas each, in every sub-quarter. The Śṛṅgas, in each course, have all their separate socles; these again resemble the capitals and consist of tiers increasing in girth from bottom to top. These socles, having the shape of capitals, are carried on faceted square shafts inserted in a square, faceted railing (vedikā)-like 'kūṭa'.

Two horizontal motives fill the subquarters between the arches of the Latās flung upward in the four direction : (1) a course of 5 Śṛṅgas and (2) a course of 5 pillars with their capitals. Each of these courses is interspaced with the corresponding number of lesser projections, Śṛṅgas, and a repetition of the inner angles of the wall, with their panels filled with scrolls, etc. on a proportionately reduced scale.

The Śikhara thus ascends, an array of Śṛṅgas, an array of pillars, progressively diminishing in size, towards the Skandha whose edge repeats the star shaped plan of the temple, 5 pointed in each of the sub-quarters. The Latās 'transcend' the shoulder-course of the Śikhara; their arches attaining to the height of the circular 'neck', the shaft of the temple, which is clasped by an Āmalaka whose corrugated rim responds in its cusps to the angles of the star-shaped temple.

The Nīlakaṇṭheśvara temple shows the themes of its perpendicular walls continued on the curvilinear Śikhara. The close correspondence of the structure and superstructure of the temple brought about by the theme of the pillar is however not particular only to the Nīlakaṇṭheśvara temple at Udayapur, Gwalior; nor to 'star shaped' Prāsādas in general. Temples with orthogonal buttresses are similarly ordered,* the composition moreover follows the same vision whether the temples belong to the Nāgara or the Vārāṭa 'style'.** Thus they are prescribed to be built in the 'Samarāṅgaṇasūtradhāra', chapters LXIII and LXIV, treating of Nāgara and Vārāṭa Prāsādas respectively. In Central India as well as in the Deccan including the Kanarese country, the shape of the pillar is an abiding theme on many temples.

This shape plays no part in the other varieties of the Nāgara temple. On Drāviḍa temples, the pillar is a theme in the composition on the walls of the temple; in the superstructure, however, the wall pillars of the Bhūmis have little effectiveness on the early temples (Mamallapuram) for they are eclipsed by the shrines of

* The temple at Ambarnātha (plan on p. 230 A) ; cf. Cousens, 'Mediaeval Temples of the Dakhan', Pl. III., or the temple at Jhodga, ib. Pls. LIII—LV.

** The pillar as one of the main motives of the wall and superstructure may be seen on the temple of Siddheśvara at Haveri ; the temple of Mahādeva in Ittagi (Cousens, 'The Chālukyan Architecture', Pls. LXXVI, CII, etc.). An enrichment, not infrequent on the walls of Cālukyan temples, consists of a series of pillars, each supporting on its capital a curvilinear Śikhara (ib. Pl. LXXXIV, 'parapet wall'; from Bankapur).

the parapet. In later temples, where the parapet of shrines is drawn to the wall and one with it, such pillars or pilasters which are inserted between the miniature chapels themselves are converted into miniature shrines by a curvilinear roof being added to their shafts (Fig. on p. 187).

PLATE XLVI. ŚUKANĀSIKĀ AND LATĀ

Part of the central offset of the Śikhara, facing west (details of Pls. XLIII and XLV); Nīlakaṇṭheśvara Temple, Udayapur.

Firm in contour and design, the prolongation of the central buttress in the Western quarter (as also in the South and North) is set against a background of deep darkness. The purity of its vertical edges and the precision of its detailed pattern are thrown into relief by the surrounding shadows, themselves replete with meticulous carvings, whose presence is more felt than seen. Similarly the intricacies of the carvings on the highest level of the Latā itself are absorbed in the 'texture' of the monument seen as a whole (Pl. XLIII).

The broad band of the Latā is carved on three levels; the lowermost protrudes its fringe made of tiers or Bhūmis; on the next higher level the fringe of tiers emerges from below a carved lace pattern cast over, while yet revealing, however so little, the stratification. The all-over pattern is bounded on the inside by a narrow and plain vertical edge whence protrudes, accompanied by a line of deepest shadow, the central face of the Śikhara. Over it too, is cast the Gavākṣa-net, veiling and linking its strata; at the edges they emerge clean cut.

The all-over pattern has its centre in the squat Gavākṣa in the middle, opening up on each alternate stratum. Vertical clasps, midway in their shape between the oval Gavākṣa and the rectangular Bhūmi, and transferring their horizontal disposition, flank the Gavākṣas and further laterally themselves are the nucleus of a different unit of Gavākṣas. These close in above the main Gavākṣa, in the middle. They end in curls, and are repeated in S shapes, doubly holed and turned, in alternating vertical rows, confronting or addorsed; the scrolls end with a bird's head whose neck encircles the dark hole of the Gavākṣa. This 'creeper' (latā) pattern however is less effective in its rhythmical, linear continuity than it is enmeshed in densely varied black dots and strokes, forming part of the multiform vesture of the Śikhara, the Padmakośa. Although mainly a pattern in white and black, it is graded in its carved surfaces; penumbras linger in its meshes; now this, now that, way following the movement of the sun.

Against this background of carved lace are set the images of the Śukanāsā; sculptures in the round along its edge, they play their short drama from Kīrttimukha to Kīrttimukha (only the group on the right is preserved); between them is extended the Gavākṣa-part of the antefix. Pointed extrados and circular intrados circumscribe its frame—as they did when the arch of manifestation, the arch of Prakṛti, conveyed by its form only the meaning which since was summed up in the Face of Glory and given exposition in the creamy plenitude of waves of carved figures and shapes.

The image enshrined in the centre of the Gavākṣa, in its dark halo, is surrounded by receding levels of wicker-work pattern, dotted dark and light. Its basis is the apex of the roof of the temple below. It has the shape of a pyramid and consists of roof-tiers (cf. Fig. c, on p. 181). A heavy abutment, a multiple band of horizontal shadows separates this lower shrine with its smaller acolytes, their images and manifold detail —Śārdūla on elephant, the broad scroll work of the arch held together by its key-form, the diminutive Kīrttimukha—from the 'Gavākṣa'.

Tracery and statuesque images and the many intermediate degrees of sculptured form are accommodated the one by the other, each a part of the total monument, in its reasoned disposition (Pl. XLIII).

PLATE XLVII. ŚUKANĀSĀ; FACING EAST

Nīlakaṇṭheśvara Temple, Udayapur.

The main Śukanāsā (cf. Pl. XLVIII), seen from the front, is a mighty blind, whose inner trefoil arch sums up the rectangular shrine and its accompanying images, in the lower part, and the image of Śiva dancing and his accompanying goddesses in the circle above. Their dancing limbs emerge from and are bathed in deep shadows; shadows underline also the foaming scrolls of the archivolt and have settled in the Makara's jaws, its issue and riders as well; their repeated images flank the extrados, whereas the figures, carved in the round, to either side of the great Siṃhamukha and the Makaras have broken away.

The extrados of the upper arch and the split and more freely drawn lower curves, emanating from the mask, and slashing upward, their flat band and oblique surface conjoined, plain graph and flame edge, cut in one more groove of line and shadow into the seething mass of modelled shapes.

Behind the shield of the Śukanāsā are set on ever receding levels the many compact, small Śṛṅgas. Their volumes too are summed up by those of the Face of Glory on the apex of the Gavākṣa.

PLATE XLVIII. ŚUKANĀSĀ, FROM S.E.

Nīlakaṇṭheśvara Temple, Udayapur.

That the Śukanāsā is a blind, is seen in this side view where its marginal convolutions extend, detached from the body of the building, and their flaps partly cover the two superimposed miniature 'shrines' carved at its back. This is peculiar also to the Śukanāsikās (Pl. XLV) but there the antefix closely adheres to the curved body of the Śikhara whereas the great Śukanāsā in the East is the 'façade', extended upwards of the Antarāla, the antechamber or porch of the Garbhagṛha. The Antarāla acts as the narrow passage from Maṇḍapa to Garbhagṛha (Fig. on

p. 256); in the ground plan it is the incision which separates, and at the same time connects, Maṇḍapa and Prāsāda. Here it has a superstructure of its own, a keel vaulted body which juts out from the Śikhara. The sides are encased in a five storeyed mansion (Pl. XLIX) in which the image of Śiva is displayed in many of its forms and flanked by attendant divinities. The two upper storeys of this celestial mansion are shown on Pl. XLVIII. The ridge of the keel shape is capped by a massive 'covered' passage which leads from the Kīrttimukha to the central offset of the Śikhara and links the mask, to the building. The chessboard pattern on the walls of the passage is overcast by shade from the canopy or cornice so that the drama enacted there, in light and shade, responds to the more substantial engagement of contesting warriors carved in high relief below the chessboard pattern. They have an ancone fillet as their base and must be imagined as the continuation of the figures carved in the round and come forth from the mouth of the Makara, out of the pouches of the Face of Glory.

The roof, in three tiers, of the mansion of the gods, on the side face of the Śukanāsā, is replete with a web of Gavākṣas of which the unit is a major Gavākṣa with the ends of the extrados curling outward on the apex, and a minor Gavākṣa inscribed in it and linked by its extended apex to that of the larger Gavākṣa. Three openings or deep holes are thus within the betel leaf shape of the major Gavākṣa, round patch of darkness in the centre, and the two halves of the remaining part of the major Gavākṣa, forming foils in the tracery of the tympanum.

The same pattern-making division resulted in the shape of the unit of the all-over tracery of the Latās of the Mūlamañjarī (Pl. XLVI); there the conduct of lines is more staid; the foils are placed horizontally,— they are balanced by the vertical 'clasps'. Here they are gathered in flamboyant bundles.

The central offset of the small Śṛṅgas consists of a series of the flamboyant Gavākṣa units superimposed in diminishing size (Pls. XLVIII, XLVI, XLIX).

The conglomeration of volumes as shown in this Plate is not ordinarily seen from the ground. It is a partial view (cf. Pl. XLIX) in which heterogeneous shapes in juxtaposition are subservient to the up-rush of the Śikhara, speeding towards the summit.

PLATE XLIX.

Side view (from the South) of the superstructure of the Antarāla; Nīlakaṇṭheśvara Temple, Udayapur.

The multiple profiles of the lowermost part of the superstructure run continuously around the entire building, from the Prāsāda on the left to the Antarāla; they are carried over on the Maṇḍapa which projects at a deep right angle. The five storeyed mansion of the gods rests, in each of the storeys, on pillars only. In plan, such a building, with its broad middle projection on each side would conform with the Prāsāda Nandighoṣa, illustrated p. 252.

PLATE L. KĪRTTIMUKHA, THE FACE OF GLORY

Nīlakaṇṭheśvara Temple, East; Udayapur (cf. Pls. XLVII, XLVIII).

The mask is set against the tracery of the middle offsets of the Śikhara. It is the 'charioter' of the Vimāna, its driving power.

The upper part of the mask is damaged.

PLATE LI. EASTERN HALF OF SOUTH ENTRANCE TO MAṆḌAPA

Nīlakaṇṭheśvara Temple, Udayapur.

The balcony which affords the entrance is the large projection (bhadra; śālā) in the middle of the Southern part of the Maṇḍapa. A similar pillared hall provides an entrance from the North while the main entrance in the East is of the same kind.

Steps lead up across the mouldings of the projecting base (Padma, etc.) with their enrichments. The Vedi proper, the main portion of the vertical walls is underlined by a dwarf railing between boldly projecting fillets (paṭṭikā; giri patrikā of the Rājasenā or Senaka), above and below, which add their dark lines of shadows to those of the base. The Vedi, a railing of square pillars, is enlivened by the images of attendant goddesses carved in high relief from the intervening slabs. The coping (āsana paṭṭaka) of the Vedi is set with knobs which are miniature roofs of conical shape; their finial emerges from a broad Āmalaka. (No such roofs have as yet been found on any buildings. They resemble the conical roofs of a Śrīkoil of the Malabar Coast although these lack the cyma profile of the cone and are without the Āmalaka. The slanting back of the seat (kakṣāsana) juts out from the vertical wall, and runs above the Vedī, from the entrance along the walls of this balcony-hall (Fig. on p. 256); it has the shape of a balustrade in which pairs of beaded uprights are set in the spaces between the carved stone-planks.

The upper portion of the balcony, called Candrāvalokana or 'beautiful look out' has its ceiling supported by squat pillars, differing in diameters. Their shafts (stambha) rise from the seat. They are round towards the top. The capitals, (bharaṇa), a series of widening rings, are round, whereas the squarish bulk of the bracket capitals (śīrṣa) restores straightness to the walls of the Candrāvalokana.

Chessboard effects of plain surfaces cut in right angles, form the ground of some further enrichments (the Gavākṣa band in the base, etc.).

PLATE LII. INTERIOR OF MAṆḌAPA AND ANTARĀLA LEADING TO THE GARBHAGṚHA

Nīlakaṇṭheśvara Temple, Udayapur.

The image of Nandin, the pillars, their carvings and corbels, the carved doorway, the intercolumnia and door openings, impregnated with light and darkness and the scent laden atmosphere are part of the compacted interior of the temple.

The two pillars of the Antarāla, placed between the pier like 'wall-pillars' (kuḍya-stambha) are shown in this Plate; also part of one of the 4 main pillars of the Maṇḍapa (on the extreme right).—The Ekamukha sheath of the Liṅga belongs to a later age.

PLATE LIII. INTERIOR OF MAṆḌAPA AND ANTARĀLA; LEFT OF ENTRANCE TO THE GARBHAGṚHA

Nīlakaṇṭheśvara Temple, Udayapur.

One of the main pillars of the Maṇḍapa, a pillar and wall-pillar of the Antarāla and the vertical surround of the entrance to the Garbhagṛha are seen in this Plate.

The hall pillars are square at the base (2′ 9″ square) and up to more than half the height of the shaft (5′ 6″); the octagonal part is 3′ 8″ high, the circular section only 1′ 3″. The transition from the square at the root to the circle on top, with an intervening octagonal section is the rule in mediaeval pillars. The change over from the static to the dynamic architectural form has its corresponding images in the chapels carved in the four directions on the lower part of the shaft and the racing circle of exultant Gaṇas in its upper part.

The bells on their chains, on each second face of the octagonal section, transfer to pillar, stone and wall, the shape and direction of the metal bells hanging from the roof of the Maṇḍapa. On the pillar, the bells hang from the mouth of the Kīrttimukha. This is how their sound is imaged. Cf. the pillars of the interior with the corresponding wall section, Pl. XLIV.

The octagonal part of the shaft of the pillars is clasped by a belt of flying figures; high triangles rise from it across the series of rings of the round portion of the pillar. Their shapes prepare the mouldings of the round capital (bharaṇa), thence issue the bracket capitals, Hīragrahaṇa (?) and Śirṣa, with their gusts of flying Gaṇas. Their carved images are the 'outcome' of the architectural potency of the brackets; they uphold the weight of the superstructure—above the pillars, as it were. It does not press down and the shafts stand, it would appear, free of it. The Gaṇas whose shapes are fitted into those of the brackets and corbels are not caryatids. They fly horizontally from the bulk of the capital into space and appear to communicate the weight above them to the space around them. The effect of the soaring bulk of corbels and bracket capitals is supported by the pillars whose base and shaft are modifications of their vertical shape; the base projects but little from the square lower part of the shaft against which are carved shrines each housing an image. Thus the base does not spread on the ground; its mouldings and carvings form the prelude to those of the shaft and capital (see also the "wall-pillar" or pilaster).

PLATE LIV. GOMEDHA AND AMBIKĀ

Tutelary Yakṣa couple. Jain image. Candpur (24° 30′ N. 78° 19′ E) near Jhansi, Twelfth Century.

Dynamic pedantry geometrises the panel of the relief by subjecting its carved volumes to a linear discipline equal in zest and rigour. Modelled continuity, though expansive in parts,—the faces in frontal view, the Yakṣa's chest, is but a ponderous residue of an once gracious and fulsome tradition. Now the volumes which had held the Breath of Life have the shape of objects, cylinder, cones, etc.

The stem of the tree in the middle with the image of the Tīrthaṅkara Nemīnātha and the symmetry of vertical parallels of the upright chest-head-crown of the two tutelary divinities, their right hands holding the citron, and 'the child'—the two sons of Ambikā—on the left, have their balance in the horizontals of the base, the left leg of the images, the left arm of the child, the width of the chests of the images and the foliage of the tree.

The diagonal themes are indicated by the right legs and partition the relief panel as rigorously as is its orthogonal order. This geometry is also applied to the shape of the single figures and is as perspicuous in the zig-zag of the body and limbs of the child as it is in its physiognomy.

The geometry of the relief panel employs for its units, conical or cylindrical shapes such as those of the heads, of the hands and citron, the limbs, stem of the tree, etc. Graded in planes they lead into the depth of the panel.

PLATE LV. PRĀTIHĀRYA

Upper part of a Jain image; Detached sculpture, near Jain temple on top of the hill, Deogarh (24° 32′ N. 78° 15′ E), Tenth century.

A celestial spirit beating the drum (divyadhvāni) which is one of the Prātihāryas or miraculous appearances carved on the slab of the image of a Tīrthaṅkara hurls himself down, succinct as a drum beat. His body soars above the drum. Serenely the face smiles and the arms pause broadly open, while the sound of the drum reverberates in the modelling of the heads of the elephants, their trunks and the volutes of plants and 'swans' as the carved music of the sphere under whose lotus canopy is the place of the main image of this slab.

PLATE LVI. LOWER PART OF THE IMAGE OF A TĪRTHANKARA

Near Jain temple on the hill, Deogarh, c. Tenth century.

On the rigidly symmetrical pedestal of this seated image rest its legs, crossed in 'padmāsana', or 'Lotus posture'. Their horizontal volumes are supported by those of the lions forming the socle. They are neatly placed beneath the horizontal plane of the seat which has a lotus carved on it, and at a right angle, an ornate cushion and the circular cloth laid over the edge of the throne. Their crisp and meticulous ornamentation sets off the smooth volumes of limbs and lion emblems of the relief. The swinging curve of the cloth, in the vertical plane, is reabsorbed into the sculptural structure of the image by the rounded weight of the cushion and the limbs that rest on it.

PART LVII. IMAGE OF A TĪRTHANKARA

Candpur, 11th-12th Century

Its iconometry, and the accidental life encrusted on the stone by fungi, constitute to-day the impressiveness of this broken image.

Calm and widely spaced, the image is competently carved but lacks any further qualification as work of art; the petals of the lotus halo are without radiance, without fragrance, but as accurate as are the finicky carvings of the round lotus cushion seat.

PLATE LVIII. NANDIN AND ŚIVA-GAṆA

Fragment of image carved in the round. Candpur, Twelfth Century.

Tinkling bells, beads and locks, arches of eyes and chains are laid on the curved planes of the body of the animal and the child that clings to it. Its arms weigh in their balance the power of the bull's recumbent shape.

The bull is Dharma ('Viṣṇudharmottara', III. XLVIII. 18).

PLATE LIX. PRETA

Detail of fragmentary image, outside the Mālāde Temple, Gyaraspur, Gwalior (23° 40′ N. 78° 7′ E.), Tenth Century.

Ghouls, marching or dancing to the side of the main image surrounded by serpents coils, are carved in superimposed rows in one of which Pretas, each carrying a weapon, show the glee of disembodied souls.

Not the gruesome emaciated skeleton as that of Cāmuṇḍī (Pl. XXIX) but a more comfortable degree of decomposition distinguishes these dancers of death as acolytes of a power beyond it. In the images of Bhūtas, Pretas, Piśācas and Vetālas (cf. 'Mānasollāsa', II, III.1. 809-11) who are in due order: "those who have been" (bhūta), ghosts of the departed; "those who have gone before" (preta) and whose obsequial rites have not been performed; filthy fiendish goblins, and spooks who occupy corpses not their own—emotions are given expression in lugubrious and ludicrous shapes which are redeemed by their rhythm.

PLATE LX. ŚĀLABHAÑJIKĀ

Fragment from Harsiddhi Temple, Candrāvatī (Jhalawar, Malwa; c. 25° N. 76° E.), Ninth Century.

Viewed against the sculptures of Khajuraho, this figure* and also other images (Pls. LXI, LXIII, LXV) belonging to temples situated at about the same latitude but further west, and as far as Kotah State in Malwa, appear stern. The high strung elegance of Candella sculpture is absent in the sculptures of the western part of central India (including Gwalior and also Malwa) as it is also from the sculptures to the east of the Candella school (Pls. XXXIX-XLII) and from the suave Eastern Indian school whose influence extended as far as Sārnāth (Pl. XXXVIII). The same components however are fused here as in the Candella school, but the modelling is never as taut and the linear tension never as acute as it is there.

PLATE LXI. HEAD OF A VIMĀNAPĀLA

From Śiva temple in Ramgarh, Kotah, Malwa, c. 1000 A.D.
Dark buff sandstone.

Four Vimānapālas, each at a cardinal point, were placed below the Āmalaka, around the Grīvā or Neck of the Temple Pillar on the Skandha, the shoulder course, of the Vedi of the Sikhara.

The names of the four Vimānapālas are Nyakṣa, Vivasvān, Mitra and Kṣattā (Vaikhānasāgama, VIII). Vivasvān and Mitra are names of the Suns, the Ādityas, —south and west of the Brahmasthāna in the Vāstupuruṣamaṇḍala—Kṣattā is Brahmā and Nyakṣa means 'whole'.

The four heads below the Āmalaka of the temple are known to-day in Rajputana (Osia, for example) under the name Brahmamukha. Brahmā is situated in the Skandha of the temple ('Agnipurāṇa', LXI, 27).

Different figures in the various temples of India fulfil the functions and hold the place of the Vimānapālas. The head on Pl. LXI is that of a Ṛṣi—the seven Ṛṣis, according to 'Nirukta', XV. 37 are the 'rays of the Sun'—its countenance however, turbaned and bearded, belongs to the people of the country and is cast in a heroic (vīra) mould.

*Cf. JISOA, vol. I. Pl. XIII.

PLATE LXII. ŚIVA TRIPURĀNTAKA-MŪRTI

One of the three main images of Śiva in the Ghanadvāra of the Bhadras at the cardinal directions; Śiva Temple in Ramgarh, Kotah, c. 1000 A.D.

Śiva is the 'Ender' (antaka) of the Three citadels (Tripura) of the Asuras. They had been built by Maya, of gold, in heaven, of silver in mid-air and of iron, on earth. At the end of their time, it is said these citadels would unite into one and should be destructible with a single arrow.

The 10 armed image of Śiva, on Pl. LXII, is shown dancing after the total and simultaneous defeat of the Titans in heaven, on earth and in the mid-region. Śiva, the universal, all filling God holds high his bow—the Vedas; Viṣṇu is his arrow. To the right of Śiva, Gaṇeśa, his small son, takes part in the dance.

Although the image—a very high relief and partly carved in the round—is badly damaged, there is triumph to be seen in the calm face and in the bow wielding arm of the dancing God, and sovereignty in his crowned head thrown back and looking upwards. This movement is echoed in the convoluted mass of Gaṇeśa, but the rest of this very high relief is sculpturally inert, without Sattva-guṇa and perturbed by the Rajo-guṇa. The dancing legs are correctly placed in the Svastika (l) and the Kuñcita pose (r) ('Kāśyapaśilpa', LXVII, 28), but fail to convey the movement of the dance.

The fragmentation of this sculpture due to its being damaged is intensified by the deep shadows of the photograph which on the other hand strengthen the power of the oblique movement of Śiva's head.

PLATE LXIII. APSARĀ

On the wall of the Śiva Temple in Ramgarh. c. 1000 A.D.

The forced, double bend of this dancing figure, playing ball, shows the image with its scanty loin cloth, loosened and slipping down, akin in its nakedness to the images of Yakṣīs of the Kuṣāṇa age. The weighty body in its movement is upheld by the horizontal profiles of the wall against which the figure leans; its main horizontal divisions, at the joints, are underlined at the height of neck and shoulders, hip and knee by the fillets of the wall; figure and wall conform in their articulation; the lateral, excessive deviation of the Apsarā from the vertical cuts across the edges of the offset at her back, relates her movement to wall surfaces further back in depth and of greater width so that the image is related to the whole buttress across which the waves of her wilfulness are staged.

PLATE LXIV. APSARĀ

Bracket figure of the roof, inside the Maṇḍapa, of the Śiva Temple in Ramgarh. c. 1000 A.D.

Jutting out from the lateral vault of the roof of the Maṇḍapa is a corbel made of a four-armed, squat Gaṇa figure. It is part and support of a strut in the shape of a dancing Apsarā and her diminutive companion of ravishing elegance, postured below her raised leg. The figure follows the architectural movement; it fits into the ribbed vault and has its highest projections where the joists pass behind its pliant shape.

The Apsarā has her body—of a rampant lioness—wreathed around her axis. It is weighted on both ends, above is her large head and below is the contracted shape of the Gaṇa. In this way it is demarcated against the thin ribs of the vault whose curves are also those of the image. The globes however of head and breasts, bosses and knobs are set across the brittle, ambiguous context, palpably, reassuringly, as halting points in a mother of pearl iridescence of light caught and absorbed by the carved surfaces of this vault. (Cf. Pl. LXIII, which illustrates a different and more compact unity of wall and figure, from the outside of the same temple.)

PLATE LXV. BRACKET-CAPITAL OF PILLAR (PART VIEW)

Maṇḍapa of Śiva Temple in Ramgarh, Kotah, c. 1000 A.D.

With the roof now missing, the flight of the Gaṇas on the capital, is in the open. But in their original context too their figures though forming part of the capital, are neither caryatids nor Kīcakas. They are shown flying across the air from within the mass of the capital, and seem to have traversed its solid shape and emerged sturdy and intent on playing their music on flute and conchshell with their whole being which is made for this purpose. Reservoirs of air, their inflated bodies and cheeks, air-padded hands, fingers and locks, guarantee perennial power blowing the conchshell and playing flute. These wind-bags, with one leg tucked under, the other thrown backward and their second pair of hands raised as they dive into space, are propelled by a gale which torments the stone, agitates the air and penetrates both; they form a 'rājasīka' image of Ākāśa, ether itself, which is present everywhere and whose quality is sound.

PLATE LXVI. GAṆA

Part of bracket-capital in the Maṇḍapa of the Śiva Temple in Ramgarh, Kotah. c. 1000 A.D.

Emerging from between capital and bracket (cf. Pl. LIII), the general attitude of these Gaṇas is a diving into space. Pl. LXVI shows the four-armed image in the process of emerging from the pillar and part of its architectural theme. Many of these figures—not shown in these plates—have the face of an animal (for example in the Duladeo temple in Khajuraho). This belongs to the Gaṇas, in Indian iconography.

PLATE LXVII. LINGODBHAVAMŪRTI

From Harasnāth, Sikar, Rajputana (27°37′ N, 75° 8′ E); second half, Tenth Century. Central Rajputana Museum, Ajmer.* This image and the other sculptures from Harasnāth are of limestone.

In the universal night a fiery pillar appeared above the waters. Other than the pillar there was no thing; it had no beginning no end. Brahmā flew into the Empyrean and failed to reach its top; Viṣṇu dived into the depth of the sea and failed to find its bottom. The two great gods thereupon submit to its greatness and become the acolytes of the Fiery Pillar. The Fiery Pillar is Śiva; he reveals himself in its splendour.

The stele is traversed in its middle by the Fiery Pillar. On the left Brahmā is seen soaring upwards; he is also seen standing, his self-appointed mission unfulfilled, an attendant divinity of the Fiery Pillar. To the right of the Pillar, Viṣṇu, blowing his conch, hurls himself downward with the same result; he becomes an acolyte of the Pillar and his standing image swings in the same rhythm as the image of Brahmā. The top of the slab, the high region traversed by the pillar, is a palpitating mass of movement and its shapes are Haṃsa-birds and celestial spirits. The vision of the flaming pillar has been given form in this image competently though not adequately; the form is sleek and slight but succeeds in translating the Fiery Pillar into the trunk of the Tree whose branches are Brahmā, Viṣṇu and the celestial host.

PLATE LXVIII. DANCE OF THE GODS IN INDRA'S HEAVEN

Part of a frieze, Harasnāth, Sikar, Rajputana, second half, Tenth century.

"Śiva, who is joy (harṣa) is worshipped on the hill (called Harṣa) by the joyous divine host, Indra and the rest, who praised him" (verse 7 of Inscr. of the year corresponding to 970 A.D.; on the top of the hill called Harṣa; 'Ep. Ind.' II. p. 125; cf. 'ASI, Western Circle', 1910, p. 53). In the frieze of the drumming and dancing gods are Indra, seated on his elephant Airāvata; a warrior holding sword and shield, and an Apsarā. The movement sways and surges to either side of a standing god who holds a long lance and seems to have ushered in before Indra the warrior so that he becomes one of the dancers.

*Photograph by a local photographer, with the permission of the authorities, Central Rajputana Museum, Ajmer.

Indra, enthroned in a posture of ease, the right hand raised in Abhaya-mudrā, grants fearlessness; his left hand holds the Vajra. Small shapes surround him, Mātali, his mahout, and companion spirits, Marut-like.

The elephant's trunk and the warrior's legs are interlaced; the warrior's is the largest movement; across the depth of the relief, he steps forwards into the line of the celestials. Their dance vibrates, to the stamping of the feet, a suave tremor free from tension.

"The architect (sūtradhāra) of this temple of Śiva (Śaṅkarabhavana) was Caṇḍaśiva, the famed son of Vīrabhadra, omniscient like Viśvakarman in the science of architecture" (śl. 43; cf. pillar inscription of the Maṇḍapa of the Purāṇa Mahādeo Temple; 'Ind. Ant.' XLII. p. 57 f).

PLATE LXIX. THE WHEEL

Part of a carved ceiling; from Harasnāth; second half,
Tenth century, Sikar Museum; Rajputana.

The movement of the wheel is in the curves of the swords and bodies of the fighter spirits active on its rim. The centre of the wheel has the shape of a lotus. The end of a scarf, a pleated shape, is seen as if rushing through its hub. Cf. Sudarśana Cakra, Pl. LXX; and 'Jaim. Up. Brāhmaṇa', I. 3. 5. about the "total escape from this revolving universe through the hole of the wheel".

Around a lotus in a circle, figures of many shapes have been shown racing in Indian sculpture; animals seen and unseen, in the days of Barhut; cf. versions from Mohenjo-Daro showing movement around a centre whence it radiates.

The style of these figures is close to that of similar fighting spirits in Khajuraho sculptures (Pl. XXIII); their ardour is of the same kind, but its carriers have less substance, than the central Indian sculptures. Delicate and with the grace of perfect manners, the sculptures from Harasnāth show any theme as their own, in a compact density of form (Pl. LXVII), its vibrant animation (Pl. LXVIII) or ceaseless whirling rhythm (Pl. LXIX).

PLATE LXX. VIṢṆU TRIVIKRAMA

In Ghanadvāra, Harihara Temple, No. 1; Osia, near Jodhpur
(26° 18′ N, 73° 1′ E), Rajputana, about 800 A.D.

Viṣṇu, with three strides covers the whole universe. Incarnated as a dwarf, Vāmana, he had asked Bali, King of the Asuras, for a boon; he wanted only as much land as to step on. This scene fills the right corner, at the bottom. Then he takes his strides across all space, a cosmic movement in which the image of Viṣṇu is a counter-part in its own right, to that of Śiva Naṭarāja. The thrust of his left leg extends to the "Face above", to Rāhu ('Viṣṇudharmottara' III. ch. LXXXV. 53-57).

The images of Śrī and Puṣṭi (destroyed) link the the image with the architectural enrichments.

The early mediaeval relief, if compared with the sculptures of the subsequent centuries, has the compact power of a 'primitive'.

PLATE LXXI. SHRINE NEAR SACIYĀ MĀTĀ TEMPLE, OSIA

Near Jodhpur, Rajputana; c. 1100 A.D.

This small Prāsāda is a model of clarity in the disposition and proportion of its architectural theme: (1) The socle, (2) the threefold horizontal division of the wall; its Vedikā, Jaṅghā and upper part, from which springs (3) the full curve of the Śikhara, repeated by its offsets in continuation of the vertical projections of the wall. The Bhūmis with their square corner Āmalakas and the large crowning Āmalaka are balanced in the architectural composition by the pediments above the 'shrine' of the Pārśvadevatā on the Bhadras, and the large pediment in lieu of the Śukanāsā over the entrance to the Prāsāda.

The Gavākṣa net of the three inner offsets of this Pañcaratha-śikhara, has its meshes assembled in a well knit pattern; its 'centre pieces' give definition to the diminishing Bhūmis, on the edges of the superstructure. Each Bhūmi is clearly demarcated while all are united in the simplicity of this monument. The curve of the superstructure appears continued in the opposite sense by the proportionate projections of the socle; convex in the Śikhara, it is seemingly concave along the edge of wall and socle; this effect is strengthened by accompanying shadows (on the left of the Prāsāda).

PLATE LXXII. DEVATĀ; BROKEN IMAGE

From the Nīlakaṇṭheśvara (Guṇeśvara) Temple, Kekind (near Merta, 26° 39′ N. 74° 2′ E.), Jodhpur, Rajputana. Tenth Century.

jewelry, and their massing together in light and shade are qualities of Rajputana
A compositional movement of assured richness is accompanied by long stretches of dull modelling. An adroit commingling of detailed shapes, drapery, girdles, sculpture which find full scope in monumental architecture and the images carved on its walls.

PLATE LXXIII. PILLAR; PART VIEW

Nīlakaṇṭheśvara Temple, Kekind. Rajputana. Tenth Century.

The brimming vase (Pūrṇa-kumbha; 'Atharva Veda', III. 12. 8; XIX. 53. 3; Kumbhalatā, 'Śilparatna', XXVIII) with scrolls and pearl garlands, Kīrttimukha-scroll devices above, and Śārdūla-scrolls on top, add their meaning, power and beauty to the square and faceted section of the pillar.

Precision and vitality are in each of the clear cut shapes from the lotus petals right at the bottom. Emphasis is given to the edges, where cascades of parallel and similar forms act as stages of one movement of outpouring from the brimming vase.

PLATE LXXIV. UPPER PART OF PILLAR

Nīlakaṇṭheśvara Temple, Kekind, Rajputana, Tenth Century.

The transition from the octagonal to the circular section of the pillar is effected with carved chains. Part of the surface of the pillar is left rough with chisel marks; the smooth ground, the colouristic carving with its black shadows, and the modelled rhythm of the ring of flying Vidyādharas are some of the possible transformations of the shape of the pillar, into the sculpture of its several parts.

The pattern of the flying legs encircles like a cord the round body of the pillar: the fillet on top of the Gaṇas is a simple shape; between these two rings are their raised swords and arms with 'ardha-sūcī' and 'patākā hastas', and the richer context of their sturdy little bodies and round heads.

PLATE LXXV. HAMSAS AND LOTUS

Part of a carved ceiling. Nīlakaṇṭheśvara Temple, Kekind, Rajputana. Tenth Century.

Luxuriant in the fulness of their shapes are the lotus plant and the birds in their triangular compartment which they fill to perfection, as parts of a monumental rhythm that swings in the circle on whose rim they rest.

PLATE LXXVI. MAṆḌAPA

Half broken; part view, Someśvara Temple, Kiradu (near Barmer, 25° 45′ N; 71° 23′ E.) Jodhpur, Rajputana, 1148 A.D.*

The slab of the bench (āsana) on which lies the full light of the sun, was originally shielded from it by the back of the seat slanting outwards.

*H. C. Ray, 'Dynastic History of Northern India', vol. II, p. 926.

Above the level of the back of the seat and up to the swinging curves of the bracket capitals all architectural shape is within carved surfaces. The figures and their composition are subordinated and belong to the architectural shape to the same extent as their meaning in each detail, forms part of the whole temple.

PLATE LXXVII. UPPER SECTION OF A PILLAR

Kiradu, Jodhpur, Rajputana. Twelfth Century.

The theme of the circular section at the top of the shaft of this pillar is made of ring and modelled shapes.

In the upper row are Kīrttimukha and Muktā-Varāla ('Samarāṅgaṇasūtradhāra', LVII. 958), the latter forming, each time, a pearly bridge between the architectural mouldings, while the deep slits and dots in the Face of Glory have their continuation and flame in the design of the carved moulding above.

The impetuous and disciplined upward rush—it has an oblique rhythm here —of the various hosts of Gaṇas or Vidyādharas in the lower row, and other similar groups (Pl. LXXIV), are amongst the minor themes of mediaeval temple sculpture in which is caught the movement in the atmosphere and the steadfast agitation in the heart of the Bhakta.

PLATE LXXVIII. "IN THE JAWS OF THE MAKARA"

Part of bracket-capital of a pillar, Kiradu, Jodhpur, Rajputana, Twelfth Century.

The rotation of the grinding upper jaw of the Makara is given shape in a sculptural 'architecture' of arches beset with teeth and spiky frills. Wedged between teeths and jaws, a warrior holds himself erect with sword drawn, ready to smite the monster's proboscis. Its flaming eye glares at him; so do the scrolls activated from wavy fin and curly necklace; their threatening shapes are ready to assail. The entire machinery of this monster Makara architecture,—though damaged,—is in full working order. The monster's eye is met by the unperturbed egg shape of the hero's head.

PLATE LXXIX. YOUTH CARRYING A QUIVER OF ARROWS

Fragment from Kiradu, Jodhpur, Rajputana, Twelfth Century.

The wide sweep of the chest, its volume coerced by a pleated scarf, the elegiac bend of head and torso, the sweet apprehension in the broad blank face, the slow

*On loan in the Victoria and Albert Museum, South Kensington, London. Photograph, Indian Section, V. and A. Museum.

caress of the curves over graded planes, and the quick rhythms of shadows belong to the complex structure of mediaeval sculpture in Rajputana.

PLATE LXXX. BHĪṢMA ON THE BED OF ARROWS

Carving on a ruined temple, Kiradu, Jodhpur, Rajputana,
Twelfth Century.

In the "Great war", Bhīṣma, the Dreadful, the self denying, devoted and wise, son of the holy Gaṅgā, was pierced by innumerable arrows from the hands of Arjuna. Mortally wounded and sinking from his chariot he was upheld from the ground by the arrows and lay as on a couch of darts. He had the power of choosing the time of his death; he waited till the sun had crossed the vernal equinox. In these fifty-eight days he delivered the discourses which are known as the Book of Calm (Śānti-parva) and the Book of Precepts (Anuśāsana-parva) of the Mahābhārata.

The deadly arrows which form Bhīṣma's death-bed appear at the same time as shafts of light, and rays,—for the weapons are made from the body of the Sūrya, the Sun.

APPENDIX

THE HUNDRED-AND-ONE TEMPLES OF THE 'VIṢṆUDHARMOTTARA'

The Hindu temple had been fully given shape between the eighth and the twelfth centuries. In its leading types are compacted many forms of buildings. Each temple is an exposition of metaphysical knowledge and at the same time a potent residue of the shapes that had gone to its making. While it is the extended universe in a likeness and the form of the way that leads beyond it, it is also the collective shape of its own history.

The residual quality of the structure has preserved many shapes of earlier temples and also of different buildings while others were by-passed or superseded. Those which became integrated were compacted, abbreviated and variously adjusted.

Neither the temples in existence nor the groups of 20, 45 or 64 varieties of Nāgara and other temples, and of 96 Drāviḍa temples of which Vāstuvidyā treats consistently, represent all the varieties of the Hindu temple. Those preceding the beginning of the present era and the many which must have been erected in the first centuries of the first millennium, are known to some extent from their representation in—Buddhist—reliefs, etc.

The 'Viṣṇudharmottara', III. chapters LXXXVI-VIII, gives a genealogical survey of the shapes of the temples at the time of its compilation, after the seventh century, at an age when the fully compacted Hindu temple emerged. The last of these chapters treats of the proportions of the general type (Sāmānya Prāsāda) of which 100 different shapes are described in chapter LXXXVI while one temple only, the Sarvatobhadra, forms the subject of chapter LXXXVII. The norm of proportionate measurement differs from those of the Nāgara temples compiled in Chart I (p. 232A), the terminology too is partly different. The hundred and one possible shapes which followed the norm, are described vividly and grouped morphologically in eight main families.

The Sāmānya Prāsāda (Ch. LXXXVIII) is divided in three equal parts, in its vertical section. They are : Jagatī (Vasudhā), the socle or platform; Kaṭi, the wall, and Mañjarī, the superstructure. Other names of the third and topmost part of the temple in the V. Dh. are : Talpa, Kūṭa, Śṛṅga, Valabhī and Śikhara. But for the last term, the various names refer to temples forming the first and the second group within the 100 temples.

The Sāmānya-Prāsāda is set up on a square of 64 parts. On this Vāstumaṇḍala the several zones of the plan of the Prāsāda are apportioned according to a module which is given by the height of the door. The width of the Garbha is 9/8ths of this, which is also the height of the Kaṭi. The Jagatī (Vasudhā) projects from the Kaṭi by half its height (9/16ths of the height of the door). The Vāstumaṇḍala is thus not divided according to the number of its parts. These give only the frame in which the plan of the Prāsāda is laid out. A considerable margin, it seems, was provided by this apportionment, for it is enjoined that the Jagatī should neither be too narrow nor too wide (verse 9).

Seven-eights of the height of the door is the height of the image. Two-thirds of it are assigned to the image proper and one-third to its pedestal. These proportions are identical to those of the 'Bṛhat Saṃhitā'. The triple division of the total height of the temple had also been incorporated in Varāhamihira's Norm. This does not imply that the V. Dh. precedes the 'Bṛhat Saṃhitā'. Its standard norm however was known to Varāhamihira. It is clothed in the 'Viṣṇudharmottara' in a great variety of shapes (cf. 'Bhaviṣya Purāṇa', I. CXXX. 18).

The height of the door, it is repeatedly stated in the V. Dh., is double its width.[1] This too is in agreement with the norms of Chart I. The height of the door however as module of the building was not generally accepted in those Śāstras. Excepting the 'Garuḍa Purāṇa', I. XLVII. 14-16, it is not included in their several norms of the 20 Temples.[2]

The correspondences of the proportions in the plan, to those of the vertical section of the temple, are also given differently. Several possible proportions of the door and the temple are indicated. The door which measures ¼ of the Garbha is said to be auspicious and also the door whose height is ¼ of the height of the Prāsāda.

Amongst extant buildings, few seem to conform with the threefold division of the height and those that do belong to two widely distant countries; the temples of Kashmir, of the eighth and ninth centuries, are relatively nearest to it; a high socle, the walls and the superstructure are the main parts of these temples, which, moreover, have four doors. Another group of temples, in Mysore, is known as Hoysala and is about three centuries later.

THE FIRST GROUP. The several groups of temple shapes built on the basis of this norm are headed, in the first group (LXXXVI. 1-14), by the temple Himavān. Its superstructure, corresponding to the Mañjarī, the 'shoot', is spoken of as Talpa or Kūṭa; its tapering shape has three storeys (bhūmikā); they are separated from each other by recesses (uccheda), wherein are placed, presumably at the quoins, square Āmalakas. Each recess has for its enrichment a garland of lions (Siṃha-mālā). The Bhūmikās have the shape of Bhadrapīthas; they have several mouldings or courses. The temple has 4 doors, steps leading up to each. The gate house (dvāraśobhā) of the temple Himavān had also a Kūṭa; Āmalakas were placed in its first recess.

If the Kūṭa has only two storeys, the temple being in other respects similar to Himavān, its name is Mālyavān.

If the Kūṭa is without any recess and ascends in an unbroken line, it is called Śṛṅga; a temple having this kind of superstructure is called Śṛṅgavān.

This first group of temples is differentiated according to its superstructure. It has three or two Bhūmis or none; in the last instance its ascent is unbroken. This tapering superstructure is called Śṛṅga, in the 'Viṣṇudharmottara'.

[1] The height of the 3 doors of the temple Triguṇa is however three times the width of each (LXXXVI. 32-33).

[2] 'Dvāramāna', the measure of the door as module of the temple, has therefore not been included in Chart I.

THE SECOND GROUP. The temples of the second group (verses 14-20) have each a Śṛṅga for their superstructure; they are like the temple Śṛṅgavān but are distinguished by having one or two Mekhalās, each. Mekhalā is a 'zone'; its particular connotation here is not given. The distance of the Mekhalā, its 'gati', from the walls of the shrine is however one-eighth of the Prāsāda (verse 24). This is considerably less than the Jagatī. The width of the Mekhalā—in ch. LXXXVII—is one-third of the stair, *i.e.*, a twenty-fourth part of the total width of the building. Mekhalā is thus a zone of varying width surrounding the Kaṭi. Two Mekhalās may mean that the Jagatī is built in two steps so that one zone surrounds the body of the temple at a lower level than the other. A Prākāra or enclosure wall may be placed as a Mekhalā (LXXXVII. 3).[3] Niṣadha and Vindhya are amongst the names of these temples and also Gṛha. The latter has one Śṛṅga and one Mekhalā.

THE THIRD GROUP. The third family of temples (verses 21-46) adheres to the triple division in the vertical. The Kaṭi retains its name and position. Instead of the Jagatī however it is now the Mekhalā which forms the lowermost third of the structure. Another substitution is, it appears, of greater significance. The Kūṭa is replaced by a Valabhī.

The first temple of this family is itself called Valabhī. Valabhī denotes a pitched roof having a ridge (pṛṣṭha). Its slopes are on its four sides—it is a hipped roof—or on two sides only. On the ridge, three Āmalasārakas are placed. Attic rooms (garbha) or dormer windows (candraśālā) are on either side of the ridge.

The temple, called Valabhī, is rectangular in plan, its length being thrice its width.

The temples of this group have each one Mekhalā, the number of their doors depending upon their lengths. The latter is not fixed; it may be as one desires. Correspondingly, one of these temples is called Yatheṣṭa, "As you like it". There are many small chambers (garbha) in its Valabhī.

Some of these temples have a door in each direction; others have three doors and, if the height of this particular temple is thrice its width, its name is 'Triguṇa'.

The description of the Valabhī temples corresponds to the well-known early relief representations in Sāñcī, etc., and also to the shape of the Bhīma Ratha in Mamallapuram. It is however not possible to ascertain whether the slope of the Valabhī of these temples was curvilinear as it is in the above reliefs, etc., or whether their slope was straight as it is in buildings of the Malabar coast.

To this group belongs, amongst others, the temple called Śikhara. It is described as having one door, its Garbha is enclosed by walls: it has no (distinct) lateral Valabhīs, all its faces are connected (saṃyukta).

The temple Kuñjara has to be noted for its destination; it was a temple and also a residential building for Turaga Brahmācārīs.

[3] Mekhalā in the 'Samarāṅgaṇasūtradhāra' denotes a moulding of the Vedibandha; and also above the Jaṅghā (LVII. 26-7; 65, etc.; XLIX. 18). Kapotālī and Mekhalā are synonyms (cf. 64 and 26, etc.). XLIX. 18, speaks of the Mekhalā between Mañjarī and Stambha, *i.e.*, between the pilasters and the superstructure. It has windows; or the Mekhalā is in the Vedibandha and is described as decorated with dormer windows (candraśālā. LVII. 688).

The temple Kuñjara, whose name is also amongst the Twenty Temples, is here described as a Valabhī structure.

The main and primary shapes of temples are represented by the first three groups, of which the first two belong together. The one shape is that of a square temple having a one-pointed or peaked roof, while the other kind of temple has a ridged roof (Valabhī). This type of temple is not listed amongst the 20 Temples of the 'Bṛhat Saṃhitā'. The 'Matsyapurāṇa' and particularly the 'Viśvakarmaprakāśa', include it under the name Valabhīcchanda amongst the Twenty Temples. The V. P. describes it as having three Śukanāsās; the V. Dh. speaks of three Āmalasārakas. This particular temple, Valabhīcchanda, is the first of the rectangular temples in the list of the 45 temples. Incorporations and adjustments of certain types by the different schools may be seen here; a transfer of names of the temples was however, it appears, resorted to only at a later phase in the formation of the various schools of architecture.

THE FOURTH GROUP. The fourth group of temples (verses 47-77) is more complex than any of those preceding it. These temples have a tapering superstructure in two storeys, like Mālyavān of the first group, but instead of being peaked, the roof is ridged.

The Valabhī of group three appears placed on top of a building of group one. These buildings are related to extant temples, such as the Nava-Devī temple in Yageśvar (Almora District), the Vaital Deul in Bhuvaneśvar, and the Telikamandir in Gwalior. The ridge may be breadthwise (āyatā) or the Valabhī is placed at a right angle (tiryak) to the façade of the building. The former type of temple is called Bhadra, and the latter, having the entrance on its narrow side, is known as Dvārapāla. The temple Gandhamādana belongs to this group, and also the temple Guhā, which is oblong in shape.

Two temples of this family moreover embody in their plan their iconographic function. These are the temples Kamala and Garuḍa.

Kamala is a Trikūṭa temple, it has three Bhūmis in its superstructure—like Himavān—and an Āmalasāraka which implies that its point is peaked; its Valabhī is not mentioned.[4] The Prāsāda Kamala has eight Garbhas and doors in the eight directions. It has one Mekhalā.

Garuḍa is a rectangular building; it has no Valabhī in the East, its entrance side, but its shape there resembles the temple Turaga. Attached to it and raised from its high Jagatī are two small lateral shrines, having ridged roofs and facing North and South. The ridge of the main building is from East to West and that of the small wings or lateral (pārśva-Prāsāda) shrines, from North to South.

The eight-fold and the triple temple have each their particular dedications.

THE FIFTH GROUP. The fifth group of temples (verses 77-81) are most particularly Liṅga temples, not only because they house a Liṅga (as the temples of the

[4] If it had a Valabhī it might have had the shape of a dome in eight sections. The three-storeyed superstructure would have been crowned by an octagonal dome and an Āmalaka above it. Cf. the temple Triviṣṭapa, S.S. LVII. 702-706 ; it has eight Garbhagṛhas and four Valabhīs.

second group also, verse 19) but because they themselves have the shape of a Liṅga. They would thus be circular shrines; one might think of the Maniyar Math in Rajgir. These shrines have from one to three Mekhalās, they have a ridged roof (Valabhī) and one of these temples, called Sarvakīṭa, has a Kūṭa and Valabhī.

THE SIXTH GROUP. The sixth family of shapes (verses 82-88) is related to the third, the group Valabhī. The temple Caturasra, whose name and description —of a different kind—are given amongst those of the Twenty Temples, is here alike to the temple Valabhī, though its shape is square (caturasra); it has no Mekhalā.

The other temples of this group are distinguished by the absence of doors and front wall; they have pillars instead; temples of this kind should have from one to three Mekhalās or none. All these temples are like assembly halls (sabhā). Temples of this type are also known from Barhut reliefs.

These particular 'hall' temples however are not the only derivatives of the third group.

The temple Caturasra too has the same lineage. Several of its varieties are enumerated. They form the connecting link with the following group.

THE SEVENTH GROUP. The seventh group (verses 89-100) is of particular interest. In it occur most of the names of the temples in common to the 'Viṣṇudharmottara' and the lists of the Twenty Temples.

The 'Viṣṇudharmottara' begins this group with the simplest type of temple, called Gṛha. It is a square, one-storeyed house (gṛha); Lakṣmī should be installed therein. The Draupadī Ratha in Mamallapuram would come near this type if its roof could be considered as one of the shapes of the Valabhī,[5] and if the triple division of the height, in Jagatī, Kaṭi and Talpa is not considered binding in this group. The latter indeed seems implied in the description of the following representatives of the seventh group of temples in the 'Viṣṇudharmottara' of which the temple "Many-storeyed" or Bahu-Bhūmika is the first. It should have as many storeys as is desired (yatheṣṭa) and is of the type of the temple Yatheṣṭa (verse 42), that is, it has a ridged roof or Valabhī.

While the number of Bhūmis is left to the discretion of the builder of the temple Bahubhūmika, it is given explicitly in the temples described subsequently. They are 12 in number and their storeys are from 12 to one respectively, Meru having 12 storeys, 6 sides (asra) and 4 doors. Its description agrees with that in the lists of the Twenty Temples. It might, however, be thought of as crowned by a Valabhī.

The names of the temples having from 11 to 1 storey only, are respectively: Śuktimān, Mandara, Pariyātra, Alaka, Vimāna, Nandana, Pañcata, Catuṣkaka, Tribhūmi, Dvibhūmi and Ekabhūmi. But for the names of Mandara, Vimāna and Nandana (see Chart II, p. 270A) where they are given in some instances the same number of storeys, the names of this series of temples are not in the lists of the Twenty Temples.

[5] Cf. the temple Kamala whose crowning dome shape might have had eight sections.

Classification of the temples according to the number of their storeys is the rule in South Indian Vāstuśāstras. There the one storeyed temple makes the beginning. In the Nāgara schools the 12 storeyed temple heads the list which, excepting in the V. Dh., is incompletely given.[6]

If a temple of this kind is circular it is called Samudra. Nandin also is a circular Prāsāda of this family. It is described as having 8 Paricchedas, which means 8 recesses in its Kūṭa, or 8 Bhūmis, each recess having Āmalakas.

Guharāja is described as long, which may mean its plan was elliptical, and like a cave in shape.[7]

Vṛṣa is a circular temple of this group with one unbroken, tapering superstructure (śṛṅga). It has two Mekhalās. Similar to Vṛṣa, but of different shape (ākāra) are the temples Haṃsa, Ghaṭa, Siṃha and Maṇḍapa; their names indicate their respective shapes of swan, pot, lion and hall. Whatever these may have been, by name, at least, the temples of the seventh group are represented in good number amongst the Twenty Temples (Chart II).

The temples of the seventh group are introduced by the temple Gṛha, the house shape, which has a ridged roof or Valabhī. Gṛha, however is also the name of another kind of temple (verse 15) whose roof is a Śṛṅga. These two prototypal temples, called 'houses' seem to have had the one a peaked roof and the other a ridged roof.

The V. Dh. does not say whether the tapering superstructures of the temples of these seven groups were rectilinear or curvilinear. Its Bhūmis were divided by recesses and Āmalakas were placed there. These temples thus would conform with Type IA or also with Type II. The Bhūmis however are nowhere described as actual storeys, or as having their shape. They are not those of Drāviḍa temples.

THE EIGHTH GROUP. The eighth group (verses 101-111) comprises temples whose Maṇḍapas are essentially part of their plan. The temple Kailāsa heads the list. It has 5 Śikharas, 4 Maṇḍapas and 4 doors. The Maṇḍapas being in the four directions, the entrances at the cardinal points, this cross shaped temple would

[6] The V. Dh. assigns 12 storeys to Mandara, whereas 10 would obviously be the correct number in that list. Mandara has 10 storeys in the Br. S., and 12 in M.P.

[7] A temple, called Guhā, belonged to the fourth group (verse 59); the temple Gṛha however is the first of the seventh group. The alternative names Guharāja (Br.S.) and Gṛharāja in the other early lists of the 20 Temples seem to go back to older classifications of which the 'Viṣṇudharmottara' has preserved some traces.

Guhā, moreover, occurs more than once in the name and constitution of the temples in the V. Dh., Suguha (verse 121); and another temple possibly called, and being Triguha (verse 122).

In the description of the temple Sarvatobhadra (LXXXVII. 10), the small corner shrines of the central Prāsāda are described as Garbhaguhas and Prāsādas. Similarly, the chapels of the rampart are the Garbhaguhas of the enclosure (Prākāra).

Guhā thus in the V. Dh. is an equivalent of Gṛha and denotes the Garbhagṛha. Its meaning as Cave is implied in this identity. It might, besides, in the V. Dh. have connoted an oblong shape.

Kuhara, which means a cavity, may denote an interior opening or also its demarcation on the outside of the temple. The inner hollow of the Śukanāsā, the round niche in which an image is carved, is a Kuhara.

have one central Śikhara and each Maṇḍapa would have a lesser Śikhara of its own. The shapes of these Śikharas are not given.[8]

A temple Trikūṭa (see the first group) however also figures in this list and the temple Saumya which has one Śṛṅga.

The main temple of the eighth group is the temple Rājarāja. It has one lower and wider Jagatī which is as high as the knee, below, and in addition to, the Jagatī proper, whose height is one-third of the Prāsāda. This is, as usual, also the height of the Kaṭi. The Śikhara is described as having a Kuhara, the 'cave' or niche of the Śukanāsā. Connected with this temple and forming one consistent plan, is its Maṇḍapa. Similar small temples are attached in the four corners to the main temple. They too, have each a Maṇḍapa. All these temples are supported by the high Jagatī; steps lead up to it.

Further combinations of shrines and Maṇḍapas have each their specific name. The variations are given by the presence or absence of Maṇḍapas in the four directions, by the presence or absence of Śikharas on the Maṇḍapas and by the number of Maṇḍapas or shrines at the bottom of the steps.

The temple Surarāṭ for example has 4 shrines in the intermediate directions and 4 Maṇḍapas in the main directions, each of these has a Śikhara; the central Prāsāda has a Mañjarī.

These combined and centrally planned temples would correspond to certain Jain temples on the one hand and to the Hoysala Temples of Mysore on the other, both of which date from c. 1100 A.D. onward. The V. Dh. appears to describe some of their ancestral plans; the height of the Jagatī, the existence of two Jagatīs, the shrines on either side of the steps, an approximation to the triple division of the height of the temple, all these belong to the temples of the Hoysalas.

Further shapes of temples are specified (verses 111-123). Following the eighth group, they do not form a particular group. The temple Sāmānya is conspicuous by its name. It has one Śikhara. Another temple is Suguha; it has a Guhā at its back. It is followed (verse 122) by the Prāsāda Triguṇa (cf. verse 33) which may be a misnomer for Triguha : it has three Guṇas (Guhās ?). Further combinations of the various constituent elements are given each their own names : a pillared Himavān is called Nandaka (verse 123), etc.

Chapter LXXXVI of the 'Viṣṇudharmottara' gives a genealogy and morphology of the temples in which the main now extant types are not included. It begins with simple shapes and their combination; certain ancient forms of buildings are recognizable.

These form the first, second and third group. There the triple division in the vertical is firmly adhered to. The door, it appears, is an ancient module, and was superseded in the temples by the main norms (Chart I) which are based on the width of the temple or on the height of the image or Liṅga. It may be surmised that the door as module had played its part in the construction of houses.

[8] The term Śikhara, denoting the superstructure, does not occur in the seven preceding groups. A temple, called Śikhara, belongs to the third group.

The transformation of house shapes into those of temples can be followed, specially in the third group. The temples are however not 'derived' from the shapes of houses; they are on the contrary employed for the purpose of the temple so that by looking at the temple man may be liberated from all his shortcomings and attain release (LXXXVII. 63).

In their elevation, the complex shapes of the fourth and the following groups show combinations of peaked roofs and ridged roofs. They form the tapering superstructure. The ridged roof (Valabhī) however is absent from the eighth group which is representative of the temples which are particularly those of the 'Viṣṇudharmottara'. A whole chapter (LXXXVII) treats of one temple which conforms with the main characteristics of the eighth group but is of greater importance even than the temple Rājarāja. It is complete in its parts and is the architectural shape of its iconography. In this respect the temples Garuḍa and Kamala preceded it genealogically.

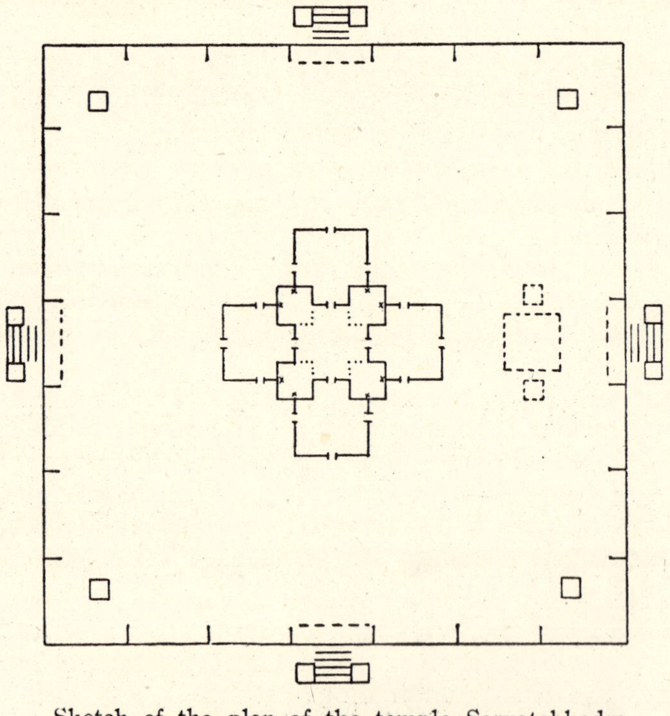

Sketch of the plan of the temple Sarvatobhadra
(V. Dh. III. LXXXVII)

SARVATOBHADRA. The temple Sarvatobhadra (proportions not given) is raised on a broad, square terrace (jagatī). It is enclosed by a rampart (prākāra) of chapels, a cloister of twenty-four Garbha-guhas (verse 42). It is approached on the four sides by stairs flanked by two small shrines. Similar in shape to these Daṃṣṭras or Devakulas are 4 chapels (devakula) in the corners of the terrace.

Each flight of steps terminates with a gate-house. Immediately behind the Eastern gate-house is a Sāmānya temple; a Garbha-Mandira, it has no Maṇḍapas but is flanked by two Himavān temples. By its position the East-West axis of the plan is given special importance. But for it the temple Sarvatobhadra and those of the eighth group are central in plan. The main temple which occupies the central position, the Sarvatobhadra temple proper, has its square Garbhagṛha surrounded in the four directions by Maṇḍapas. Each of these has four doors. In the corners of the Garbhagṛha 4 small Garbhagṛhas are inserted and correspondingly, 4 small shrines are placed in the corners between the Maṇḍapas. This cross shaped, central and radiating building is surmounted by a cluster of nine Śikharas corresponding to the four Maṇḍapas, the four small corner Prāsādas and the central Grabhagṛha. The central Śikhara is higher and dominates the eight surrounding Śikharas. The 8 Śikharas have Kuharas, or Śukanāsās in the eight directions; all the Śikharas are rich in Āmalasārakas, Jālas, Gavākṣas, (lesser) Kuharas; Cakras (wheels) and flags complete the crowning glory of this temple. Around the central shrine beautiful tanks are laid out on the terrace.

The temple Sarvatobhadra of the V. Dh. is the foremost of its "Maṇḍapa-temples". In this type of the temple, a central disposition shows welded in one plan the Garbhagṛhas and the Maṇḍapas.

The Maṇḍapa originally was a separate structure, of which twenty-seven varieties are known to the 'Viśvakarmaprākāśa (VI. 124-37) and the M. P. The Maṇḍapas have from 12 to 64 pillars, the plan of the Maṇḍapas is three sided, 8 or 16 sided or circular. By a slow process, Prāsāda and Maṇḍapa became united in the temples whose axial plan is bilaterally symmetrical (pp. 255-57). The central symmetry of several Maṇḍapas grouped around a Prāsāda or a cluster of Prāsādas had acquired several shapes which seem to represent the flower on the ancestral tree of the temples of the 'Viṣṇudharmottara'.

There are 10 descriptions at least of the Sarvatobhadra in the various Śāstras. The 'Viśvakarmaprakāśa', VI. 88-89, and the 'Matsya Purāṇa' speak of its 16 sides (asra) and the large number of Śikharas. This laconic account suggests a central projection (bhadra) on each of the four sides, which would have three sections, each less wide than the preceding. The 'Samarāṅgaṇasūtradhāra' explicitly describes the central projection having such sections (SS. LVI. 131-32. LVII. 783-86).

The 'Bṛhat Saṃhitā' LV. 27, gives the width of the square temple Sarvatobhadra as 26 Hastas. It has four doors in the four directions, a large number of Śikharas, a large number of Candraśālās and 5 storeys.[9]

The 'Samarāṅgaṇasūtradhāra' has much to say about various kinds of the Sarvatobhadra. In chapter XLIX. 107, the plan of this building has a certain affinity with the Sarvatobhadra of the V. Dh. for it includes Prāsādas in the corners (Karṇa-prāsāda) whereas the earlier texts seem to refer to one building only without the addition of subservient structures. The Sarvatobhadra of SS. XLIX, however, has no further resemblance to that of the V. Dh. It is like the other temples of that chapter, a 'hall temple' consisting of a small centre (devakoṣṭha) over four

[9] Sarvatobhadra is not only the name of several varieties of the temple in the Śāstras, it is also the first of the '4 room' buildings *i.e.*, having 4 wings (Catuśśālā-Gṛha), described in the 'Bṛhat-Saṃhitā', LII. 31, Nandyāvarta, Vardhamāna, Svastika and Rucaka, being the others. It is fit for 'kings and gods'.

parts out of the 100 parts of the square field (kṣetra) of its total extent which is occupied by three concentric Ālindas with their pillars, etc., and Prāggrivas of the façades. The Prāsādas of chapter XLIX are not exclusively temples. They form part of royal establishments where their plan is adopted to various uses which are described in chapter LI.

Sarvatobhadra, however is one of the eight temples (chapter LII) to which a Śikhara was superadded (p. 284). The Sarvatobhadra of SS. XLIX has a different structure than the temple of that name in V.P., M.P., and Br. S. In S.S. LII. it is assimilated to them, and also further assimilated to the Sarvatobhadra of the V. Dh.

The Kṣetra of 100 parts however is occupied also by other varieties of the Sarvatobhadra, in the S.S. In each of these the Garbhagṛha extends over 16 squares out of its 100 squares (LV. 23-31); certain kinds of the Sarvatobhadra are Sāndhāra temples, the width of their inner ambulatory, of their inner and outer walls being equal to the side of the square (*i.e.*, the side of the Kṣetra being 10, that of the Garbhagṛha is 4, and 1, 1 and 1 respectively, are the Bhitti, Andhakārikā and Bāhyabhitti; LVI. 123-40; LVII. 781-99; LIX. 28-40; LX. 59-66).

In this Talacchanda, however, there are slight variations in the rhythms on the Vinyāsa and Paryanta Sūtras: The Bhadra, the central projection is 6 parts out of the 10 in width, and projects only to half a part (LV. 1. c.); whereas in LVI, its width is 5, its projection 2 parts at the centre and at each side it extends over ½ part; its projection there is correspondingly less. In LVII, the pillared Bhadra is 6 parts wide and projects 1½ parts; or, there are 2 Bhadras, one in front of the other.

The variations in the plan are accompanied by variations of the vertical proportions. These are given most completely in LVII; the width of the Kṣetra being 10, the socle, Pītha, has 2½ parts; the lower part of the wall, Vedibandha, has 2¼ parts of which the mouldings, etc., are allotted: Kumbhaka 1, Masūraka ½, Antarapatraka ¼ and Mekhalā ½ part; the Jaṅghā here is assigned only 4 parts, the Śikhara 7, Grīvā ½, Āmalaka (Aṇḍaka) 1, Padmaśīrṣa (Candrikā) ½, and Kalaśa (or Kumbha with Uṣṇīṣa) 1½. The total height is more than double the width of this Sarvatobhadra temple. It has Candrāvalokanas in its Bhadras. This temple belongs to a list beginning with Meru; also the Sarvatobhadra of ch. LV, whose proportions are not completely given; but for the Jaṅghā which is assigned 5 parts, they are nearly the same, Mekhalā-Antarapatra having each ½ part.

The Sarvatobhadra of ch. LVI, belongs to the series of temples beginning with Kesarī; it stands on a Jagatī-pīṭha which is half the width of the temple high; the width of the Jagatī is twice that of the Prāsāda. The wall of this imposing structure is similarly proportioned to that of other Sarvatobhadra temples. The Jaṅghā is assigned 5 parts (as also in LV) and, above it, the Mekhalā ½ and the Antarapatra ½ part. This temple has 8 storeys (bhūmi). It can be built in 3 sizes of which the least has a width of 15 Hastas, the middle c. 27 and the largest 37 Hastas.

Second in a series, headed by 'Vimāna', is the Sarvatobhadra of ch. LIX, the height of whose shoulder course (skandha) is 20 parts, the width of the temple being 10; it has 9 Bhūmis.

In chapter LX, which treats of Nāgarakriya Prāsādas, the 3 sizes (jyeṣṭha, madhyama and kaniṣṭha) are 26, 18 and 10 Hastas respectively, and in ch. LXIII, the description is similar to that of the 'Bṛhat Saṃhitā'; 5 storeys, many Śikharas and Aṇḍakas, and Bhadraśālā are mentioned there.

Besides these, ch. LVI. 105, shortly describes another Sarvatobhadra temple, of a 'mixed' type (Miśraka Prāsāda) whereas in ch. LXI, 56-61, Sarvatobhadra is one of the 'rhythms of the floor' (talacchanda), one of the ground plans of a Drāviḍa temple, whose walls, divided into 28 parts have a Śālā of eight parts in the centre, on each of its two sides are two Kūṭas, each of three parts, and between each two projections is a recess (salilāntara) of two parts. This applies to a temple without inner ambulatory (Nirandhāra); the proportions of the Sāndhāra-talacchanda are not specified in ch. LXI.

All these temples are Sarvatobhadra, for they have not only a 'bhadra' on each of their four sides, but it has a relatively great width, or projection, or both.

The Sarvatobhadra is the one hundred and first, the temple of temples of the 'Viṣṇudharmottara'; the description of 100 temples precedes it. Sum total of the groups that had gone to its making, it is closely allied in plan to temples in Kashmir (Avantisvāmī Temple) and Mysore (Keśava T., Somnathpur).[10] The Alaṃkāras or adornments of its superstructure however, the Āmalakas, Gavākṣas, Jālas, etc., are not seen on the temples of Mysore and, excepting the Āmalaka and a modification of the Gavākṣa, they are absent from the temples of Kashmir. Where in reality the Sarvatobhadra of the 'Viṣṇudharmottara' was built and when, cannot be said as yet.

THE ICONOGRAPHY OF THE TEMPLES OF THE VIṢṆUDHARMOTTARA

The iconography of the Viṣṇu temple Sarvatobhadra is given by its plan. In the main Garbhagṛha, facing the main directions, are the four aspects of Viṣṇu; their 8 Śaktis are assigned to the Garbhagṛhas at the corners of the main Garbhagṛha. Four of the Avatārs of Viṣṇu occupy the small temples in the corners of the Jagatī. 24 gods are stationed in the cloister. Two groups of them are given: the one, headed by Garuḍa comprises the weapon-divinities or Āyudhapuruṣas of the respective forms of Viṣṇu. Ananta, Makara, and the Kaustubha Jewel are also amongst these gods. The other series of divinities does not comprise the properties and faculties of Viṣṇu but surrounds his presence with all the powers of knowledge embodied, from the Gāyatrī and the Four Vedas, to Sāṃkhya and Yoga, Pañcarātra and Pāśupata, and includes the 5 Mahābhūtas.

In the 8 small shrines below the high platform, at the side of the steps are the Pratihāras, the door keepers of Viṣṇu, or the 8 Planets are installed there or the

[10] Amongst the Cauñsaṭh Yoginī types of temples, the one in Mitavli, Gwalior, c. 11th. century (ASIAR. 1915-16, Pt. I. p. 18) consisting of 65 (!) cells in its round enclosure and a circular central temple having a Maṇḍapa, would correspond to the Sarvatobhadra more closely than the other hypæthral temples of this kind.

Guardians of the eight regions. The V. Dh. gives preference to the Pratīhāras for "they are the Dikpālas and Planets" (LXXXVII. 37). A similar identification, that of the stars and the Pada-devatās of the Vāstumaṇḍala is also given in the V. Dh. (p. 32). The gods of the Vāstumaṇḍala have their images or those of their lieutenants set up in the temple, at their proper place. The re-duction of the iconography of this Viṣṇu temple to that of the Vāstupuruṣamaṇḍala may be seen not only in the presence of the 8 Dikpālas or their substitutes but also in the number of the divinities which, counting the 4 central images as aspects of the one Viṣṇu—is 45, the number of the Vedic gods of the Vāstumaṇḍala.[11]

Any temple, however, of any shape, planned according to the Vāstumaṇḍala, incorporates in its shrines and innermost sanctuaries,—or in its walls around the one and only Garbhagṛha—the eight directions of space and their presiding principles; it is a place of manifestation of the various forms of the eightfold principle such as the Aṣṭa-mūrti of Śiva, in the temple Kamala.

Equally significant however with this reduction of a specific iconography, and its architectural plan to that of the underlying Vāstumaṇḍala, are specific shapes of temples which belong to definite divinities. The Śiva temples, housing a Liṅga (the fifth group of temples) are foremost amongst them. Nonetheless, the second group, the Śṛṅga temples, small square shrines having a peaked roof were also Liṅga shrines (verse 19), though not exclusively as they could be dedicated also to all the other gods (verse 17).

The Valabhī temples, on the other hand, had a more spacious interior, those forming the sixth group were supported by pillars, and had an open front. The temple Valabhī itself, thrice as long as it was wide, had three Āmalakas on its roof. They were made to correspond to the presence of a ternary of gods in the interior; Brahmā, Viṣṇu and Śiva, or Viṣṇu, between Sun and Moon, were thus installed. The Valabhī building, however, by its very shape, is accommodating; more than a ternary of images or also but one image can be housed there. Thus other Valabhī temples are described as housing groups of gods, the Mothers, Planets, Stars, all the 12 Suns, 11 Rudras, 8 Vasus, 8 Dikpālas, etc. The Valabhī temples were adjustments of actual houses or of halls (sabhā); they left no lasting mark on the Hindu temple.[12] Their roof however, as it were, was lifted from them and raised to the third, fourth and twelfth storey on the temples of group seven; this position the Valabhī holds to this day also on South Indian Gopuras.

A specific shape of the temple, as closely connected with the shape and name of its deity as are the Liṅga temples, is the temple Garuḍa. It resembles the bird Garuḍa having two wings: these have the shape of attached shrines; the main building of the temple forms the body of Garuḍa, the Sun-bird, who carries Sūrya, the Sun. The temple here has the shape of the Vāhana and thus is similar in its function of conveying divinity to those temples which were built in the likeness of the chariots of the gods.

The Sun temple Garuḍa houses the image of Sūrya, in the central building. It is flanked in the lateral shrines by Daṇḍa and Piṅgala or by Saturn and Yama

[11] No divinities are assigned to the Garbhamandira and its lateral Himavān shrines.
[12] Valabhī, cf. also S.S. XLIX. 132-34.

or by Keśava (Viṣṇu) and Śiva. This is its primary destination. In it however other gods too were enshrined and their 'lateral' divinities. They are : Candra the Moon, Kāma, Indra, Yama, Varuṇa and Kuvera. They are connected with and thus are substituted for Sūrya. Garuḍa himself, the Bird form and Vāhana of the Sun, has also his image enshrined as the main divinity; he is flanked by Kāśyapa and Vinatā.

Sūrya and his attendants are substituted not only by gods of the family of the Sun but by one of the three great gods, Brahmā, Śiva or Vāsudeva and their lateral divinities. Vāsudeva may be accompanied by Rudra (Śiva) and Brahmā or also by Garuḍa and Ananta or also by Garuḍa and Aruṇa, the Vāhana and the Charioteer of Sūrya.

To whichever god the temple Garuḍa is dedicated, it is a temple of Sūrya who shines in all these images. Dharma in the main temple and Artha and Kāma in its wings may also be worshipped in this temple the purpose of whose construction like that of any temple is to attain Mokṣa ('Viśvakarmaprakāśa', VI. 10).

The relation of the shape of the temples and their dedication at the age of the 'Viṣṇudharmottara',—at a date from the seventh century but prior to the 'Samarāṅgaṇasūtradhāra', are manifold. Specific shapes of the temple were dedicated to specific gods : the Śiva Liṅga temples of the fifth group and the Lakṣmī shrine Gṛha of the seventh group. Shapes specifically designed for a particular god were also used for other deities : the temple Garuḍa. House or hall shapes were used as places of image worship : the 'sabhā'-shaped temples of group three and the sixth group. The temples were laid out in conformity with the Vāstupuruṣamaṇḍala and were thus suited for dedication to one particular deity and his aspects : the Viṣṇu temple Sarvatobhadra, or to different gods and their aspects : the temple Kamala.

Several traditions are represented in the V. Dh. Some of them are also embodied in other accounts. The 20 temples of the 'Viśvakarmaprakāśa' were destined to enshrine a Liṅga (VI. 106-7). They have the same purpose in the 'Matsyapurāṇa' which however adds—from another tradition—3 further names to the 20 temples. Two of them, Valabhīcchanda and Gṛha—both of them described in the V. Dh. are temples of Gaurī, in the M.P.[13] The selfsame 20 temples in the 'Bṛhat Saṃhitā' however house an image (pratimā, LV. 16).

The V. Dh. does not, as a rule, give the dedication of those of the twenty temples which it describes.

The shapes of the 20 temples in the 'Viṣṇudharmottara' are composite and complex; they do not convey any definite dedication and were used as Śiva temples, or images were enshrined in them, according to the various needs of devotion.

Thus, concluding its chapter on the temples, the 'Garuḍa Purāṇa', I. XLVII. 35 f, sums up the position : "All these temples are different from each other in construction, shape and measurement; some have a socle, others are without it. The temples are built according to the different images. Due to different traditions

[13] The 'Viśvakarmaprakāśa' does not include these names in its enumeration but adds the description of Valabhīcchanda and Śrīvṛkṣa (VI. 90 and 106). Gṛha and Valabhīcchanda are temples of the Goddess, also in the V.Dh., either of them is dedicated to Lakṣmī ; Valabhīcchanda is also dedicated to Durgā as well as to Brahmā, Viṣṇu, Śiva, etc., etc.

('saṃskāra', in which are comprised the schools of architecture and the influences that acted on them) and on account of the differences in shape and name there exist many different Prāsādas of the Gods".[14]

THE POSITION OF THE VISṆUDHARMOTTARA IN VĀSTUŚĀSTRA

These differences constitute the wealth of the form of the temples and are its resources. Heterogeneous and many as they are the knowledge of their use, the science of architecture, has but one source. It is in God who reveals it to a Sage and who transmits it to his successor. Śiva is the fountain and origin of the science of architecture, or Brahmā or Viṣṇu. This is how Āgamas, Purāṇas and Vāstuśāstras tell of Vāstuvidyā, which, being auxiliary to the Veda, is part of the primordial Knowledge. The sequences of the preceptors and the schools which they represent lead each on the one end into a particular province and phase of temple building activity, while by the other end they converge in the primordial Knowledge and in God for whom the temples are raised on firm ground.

In the majority of the Vāstuśāstras, Śiva who has also taught the 64 arts to Garga (p. 48)—is the source whence Vāstuvidyā, the science of architecture, is revealed, as in the 'Viśvakarmaprakāśa', I. 3-4; 'Agnipurāṇa', chapters XCIX f; in the 'Mayamata', 'Kāśyapaśilpa' and 'Mānasāra', whereas it is Brahmā in the selfsame 'Viśvakarmaprakāśa', XIII, 108 f, in the 'Bṛhatsaṃhitā' and the 'Īśāna-śivagurudevapaddhati'.

Viṣṇu, in his Matsya Avatār, imparted the science to Manu. The names of its 18 preceptors (p. 141) are given in the same passage of the 'Matsyapurāṇa' (CCLII. 2 f.).[15] In Viṣṇu (Hayagrīva) the 'Hayaśīrṣapañcarātra', has its origin

[14] The margin for differences in the dedication is wider even than that for the orientation of the temples (p. 233). While the underlying principles of the latter are recognizable in most of the texts—the 'Agni Purāṇa', XXXIX. 9f. being in agreement with S.S. and Ī.P.—, the 'Viśvakarmaprakāśa', VII. 107-10, and the 'Matsya Purāṇa', CCLXX. 31-4, amongst the early sources, assign Viṣṇu Jalaśāyin to the North-East and Śrīnivāsa (Lakṣmī) to the West. Nandin however is in front of the temple, or in the East, and as these texts treat of Śiva temples exclusively, the usual position of Śiva is ceded to Viṣṇu, and his place in the West is occupied by Lakṣmī.

[15] The following names of the eighteen Preceptors are associated with extant treatises:

Atri: 'Samūrtārcanādhikaraṇa' or 'Ātreya Tantra'.

Viśvakarman: 'Viśvakarmaprakāśa'; cf. also M.S. (RASB. No. 7845); 'Vāstuprakaraṇaṃ' (Viśvabharati Library, Shantiniketan; cf. Ph. N. Bose, 'Śilpa Śāstraṃ', Punjab Oriental Series, vol. XVII; introduction). Cf also Acharya, 'Dictionary', s.v.—'Aparājitaprabhā', Ms., RASB. III. I. 63.

Maya: 'Mayamata', etc. cf Acharya, op. cit.

Nārada: 'Vāstuvidhāna', 'Nāradaśilpaśāstra' (Adyar, IX. J. 33).

Śukra: 'Śukranītisāra'.

The names moreover of the following preceptors out of the eighteen names in the 'Matsyapurāṇa' are referred to in extant Vāstuśāstras as authorities on which the respective treatises are based:

Bhṛgu: 'Hayaśīrṣapañcarātra', I. 3-4.

Atri (Ātreya): 'Agni Purāṇa'; 'Bṛhat Saṃhitā', Commentary.

and also the earlier chapters of the 'Agnipurāṇa' (XXXIX f). They begin with the words: "Hayagrīva said."

The 'Viśvakarmaprakāśa' thus represents two traditions, the one (I. 3-4), originated in Śiva and transmitted to Parāśara, Bṛhadratha, Viśvakarman and to his pupil, who compiled the V.P., and the other (XIII, 108 f), originated in Brahmā and imparted to Garga who transmitted the knowledge to Parāśara.

Within the second tradition is, in the main, Varāhamihira's summary in the 'Bṛhat Saṃhitā'. His account is based on Garga (LV. 31), but also on Manu.

To Manu, in the 'Matsyapurāṇa' the science was imparted by Viṣṇu; it is in almost complete agreement with the 'Viśvakarmaprākaśa' and, though uttered by Viṣṇu pertains exclusively to Śiva temples.

The manifold interconnections within these texts are shown as much by their statements as by the names of those to whom they are attributed.

In the 'Viṣṇudharmottara', III, chapters LXXXVI-VIII, it is Mārkaṇḍeya, who instructs King Vajra in the science of architecture.[16] Mārkaṇḍeya, according to the 'Hayaśīrṣapañcarātra' I. 1-7, had received the science from Bhṛgu to whom it had been transmitted by Maheśvara (Śiva). Maheśvara had received it from Brahmā, and Brahmā from Viṣṇu as Hayaśīrṣa.

Vasiṣṭha: Br. S. Comm.; 'Agni Purāṇa'; 'Devī Purāṇa', LXXII. 1-4.
Viśvakarman: 'Bṛhat Saṃhitā', 'Agni Purāṇa'.
Maya: 'Bṛhat Saṃhitā ; Īśānaśivagurudevapaddhati'.
Nārada: 'Agni Purāṇa'; 'Mānasāra'.
Nagnajit: 'Bṛhat Saṃhitā'; 'Citralakṣaṇa'.
Nandīśa (Nandin): Br. S. Comm.
Śukra: Br. S. Comm.; 'Nāradaśilpaśāstra'.
Bṛhaspati: Br. S. Comm.; 'Nāradaśilpaśāstra', 'Devī Purāṇa'; 'Mānasāra'.

In addition to the eighteen Preceptors of the 'Matsya Purāṇa', the 'Agni Purāṇa', XXXIX. 1-6, gives the names of 25 Tantras amongst which six of the names of the 'Matsyapurāṇa' are included as 'authors' and also the 'Hayaśīrṣapañcarātra' as 'Hayaśīrṣa-tantra'. The 25 Tantras, most of which are known as yet by their names only, appear to have belonged to Madhyadeśa (A.P. XXXIX. 6.).

Of the many preceptors and authorities whose names are not included in the "Eighteen", the following have been referred to in the present context:

Parāśara: 'Viśvakarmaprakāśa'; Br. S. Comm.; 'Manuṣyālayacandrikā'.

Mārkaṇḍeya: 'Mārkaṇḍeya-vāstuśāstra', cf. Ph. N. Bose, 'Principles of Indian Śilpaśāstra', (Punjab Oriental Series, vol. XII. p. 12). Two works by Mārkaṇḍeya are referred to in the 'Manuṣyālayacandrikā', I. 7-9.

Aparājita, a mind-born son of Viśvakarman: 'Samarāṅgaṇasūtradhāra' II. I. The 'Aparājitapṛcchā', 'Aparājitaprabhā' and the 'Aparājitasūtra' of the 'Bṛhacchilpaśāstra' bear his name. Marīci, the author of the 'Vaikhānasāgama' is referred to in the 'Nāradaśilpaśāstra'.

Further authorities referred to in the Commentary of the 'Bṛhat Saṃhitā' include Kāśyapa to whom might be traced back the prototype of the 'Kāśyapaśilpa'.

Śrī Kumāra, the author of the 'Śilparatna' may have his place in the tradition as a successor of the Preceptor Kumāra (Svāmīkārttika) of the 'Matsyapurāṇa'.

[16] In part II. ch. XXIX, Puṣkara (Śiva?) instructs Bhārgava Rāma. 'Pauṣkara' is one of the 25 Tantras of the 'Agnipurāṇa', XXXIX. It is not known to which dynasty King Vajra belonged. If the name Bṛhadratha, in the 'Viśvakarmaprakāśa' could be taken to refer to the last Maurya King of that name, the 'Viśvakarmaprakāśa' would thereby show its teaching established in Eastern India before 184 B.C.

The continuity of the tradition is given not only by the contents but frequently also by the names of the Śāstras and those who compiled them. The 'Viśvakarmaprakāśa' for example is the work of a disciple of Viśvakarmā. Originally, the name Viśvakarmā is that of the working aspect of the Supreme Principle, Brahmā being its thinking aspect. Thus Viśvakarmā is a proper name not only of a great architect, but every Sthapati is descended from Viśvakarmā. Correspondingly, the other three classes of craftsmen are born of Maya, Tvaṣṭṛ and Manu, respectively, these four archetypal workers having originated from the four faces of Viśvakarmā. ('Mānasāra', II). Thus is undone ontologically the fall of the architect and the craftsmen (those who are Vaiśyas and Śūdras, cf. 'Samarāṅgaṇasūtradhāra' VII. 14-17) as narrated in the 'Brahmavaivarta Purāṇa'.

The wealth and contingencies which time, place and the ethnical carriers have brought to the structure of the temple are comprehended in Vāstuśāstra. Their minutiae are measured against abiding principles. All the time the architect carries within him the knowledge and responsibility of his descent which is confirmed,—or of his fall—which is redeemed, by his work which implies a realisation of its origin and purpose.

॥ नारदीयं वास्तुपुरुषविधानम् ॥*

अथ अष्टमोऽध्यायः

अथातः सम्प्रवक्ष्यामि वास्तुचक्रस्य लक्षणम् ।
दशोर्ध्वरेखां १ विन्यस्य तिर्यग्रेखा दशास्तथा ॥१॥
तद्रेखान्तं त्रिशूलं च तत्सन्धौ बीजमेव च ।
कोणाग्रे दण्डरेखां च पार्श्वे...२ विनिक्षिपेत् ॥२॥
एवं कृते भवेच्चक्रं वास्तुचक्रं प्रकीर्त्तितम् ।
वास्तुचक्रे वास्तुदेवं शयानं वामभागतः ॥३॥
वामादि (पादादि) केशपर्यन्तं वामाङ्गाद्दक्षिणाङ्गतः ।
उत्तमाङ्गे त्रिकोणं स्याल्ललाटे द्विपदं तथा ॥४॥
कर्णयोः षट्पदं चैव नेत्रे द्विपदमेव च ।
चिबुकैकपदं प्रोक्तं कण्ठे त्वेकपदं तथा ॥५॥
बाहुमूले द्विरेखा स्यादुरसि सार्धषट्पदम ।
भुजस्थाने तु षट्कोणं अङ्गुल्यामृतुकोणकम् ॥६॥
कुक्षौ तु रामकोणं स्यात्कट्यां षट्कोणमेव च ।
गुदे त्रिकोणं सौर्यं स्यादण्डे रेखाद्वयं तथा ॥७॥
ऊरुदेशे चतुष्कोणं ३ जानुदेशे त्रिकोणकम् ।
जङ्घे तु भूतकोणं स्यात्पदे कोणद्वयं तथा ॥८॥
कटिश्च ४ त्रिकोणं स्यादङ्गुल्यां सप्त रेखिकाः ।
शेषास्साधंषयः कोणा अनुक्ताङ्गे नियोजिताः ॥९॥
तत्तदङ्गे वदान्यत्र ५ सावशेषेण संयुतम् ।
ऐशानं शिरोमूलं नैषस (नैर्ऋत) स्पादमूलतः ॥१०॥
नक्षत्रपादपर्यन्तं बाहुस्थानं प्रकीर्त्तितम् ।
कर्णस्थानं नगपदं:इन्द्रकोणं कटिर्भवेत् ॥११॥
अङ्गुलिनिर्देशमारभ्य ऊरुदेशावधिस्तथा ।
पुराणसंख्याकोणं स्याज्जानुदेशं द्विपञ्चकम् ॥१२॥
उत्तमाङ्गादि पादान्तं प्रत्यङ्गं कोणलक्षणम् ।
आहत्यैकाशीतिसंख्या-पदं वास्तुनरस्य च ॥१३॥
वास्तुनो लक्षणं वक्ष्ये अघोरेण सुविस्तृतम् ।
वास्तु ब्रह्मेति विलोतं ६ विराजा निर्मितं पुरा ॥१४॥
शिवविष्णुस्थलादीनां ७ वास्तु हीनं यदा भवेत् ।
देवालयस्य निर्माणे पत्तने ग्राममन्दिरे ॥१५॥
उत्सवे चाभिषेके च वास्तुकर्माचरेत्सुधीः ।
वास्तुपूजाविहीनं यद् विनाशं व्रजति ध्रुवम् ॥१६॥
शतयोजनविस्तीर्णं त्रिंशद्योजनमायतम् ।
शुद्धस्फटिकसङ्काशं चतुर्हस्तं किरीटिनम् ॥१७॥
पीताम्बरधरं देवं मुक्तामयविभूषितम् ।
भूतले न्यस्तदोर्वामं दक्षिणं जानुमूलतः ॥१८॥
चन्द्रचूडं त्रिनेत्रं च ८ प्रसन्नवदनाम्बुजम् ।
अङ्गदान्नूपुरान् हारान् वलयां शुभभूषणान् ॥१९॥
दधानं भूतलावासं सर्वालङ्कारसंयुतम् ।
पादादिकेशपर्यन्तम् ईशानादिषु योजयेत् ॥२०॥
एकाशीतिसमाख्याता देवतान्तत्र ९ निक्षिपेत् ।
पञ्चवक्त्रेण पुरुषम् आकृत्या कल्पयेद्बुधः ॥२१॥
शिल्पिना कुशलेनैव शास्त्रज्ञेन विचक्षणः ।
सम्प्रदायेन सिध्यन्ति देशिकैरुपदेशतः ॥२२॥
प्रस्तरत्रययुक्तेन मार्गेनेह १० लिखेद् बुधः ।
वृत्तं तु शिरसंस्थाने षट्कोणमुरसि स्थितम् ॥२३॥
त्रिकोणं कुक्षिरित्याहुरूर्ध्वचन्द्रं तु जान्वतः ।
पादं तु चतुरस्रं च त्वादशान्ते ११ तु बिन्दवः ॥२४॥

* See p. 11, 'Vāstuvidhāna'.

१। रेखा। २। तत्र। ३। चतुष्कोणं। ४। कट्यां च। ५। वदाम्यत्र। ६। विख्यातं। ७। स्थलादीनि। ८। तु। ९। देवतास्तत्र। १०। मार्गेणेह। ११। प्रादेशान्ते

एवं षड्वङ्ग १२ संभूतं पञ्चभूतं च संभवम् ।
मूलाधारादिषड्भेदं शब्दस्पर्शादिसंभवम् ॥२५॥
अन्यत्सर्वं भावनया कल्पितं वास्तुपूरुषे ।
एतत्सर्वं समालोक्य १३ यन्त्रं रूपं च साधयेत् ॥२६॥
स्वगुरोर्मुखतः कार्य १४ बुध्या शास्त्रेण चार्जुन ।
सम्प्रदायेन कर्त्तव्यमिदं प्रस्तारमार्गतः ॥२७॥
श्रीचक्रे कथितं देवैर्भू कैलासनगोत्तमान् १५ ।
यथाकायं यथाशास्त्रं तथैवेदं प्रकीर्त्तितम् ॥२८॥
नरप्रस्तारमिति तद्वास्तुप्रस्तारमित्यपि ।
वदन्ति सर्वलोकानि १६ यथार्थं तु रहस्यतः ॥२९॥
वैष्णवाय १७ सुगोप्तव्यं शिवमार्गविदूषकैः १८ ।
वदेच्छुद्धाय शैवाय मन्त्रं मन्त्रोद्भवे दिने ॥३०॥
क्रियाज्ञानविधानेषु चतुराय वदेद् बुधः ॥३१॥
इदं शरीरं पुरुषस्य वास्तुनः
शरीरयन्त्रं शिवकायगौरवम् ।
योगीन्द्रमुख्यैः करणं रहस्यतः
शिवागमे मुख्यफलप्रदं तत् ॥३२॥

इति नारदीये वास्तुपुरुषविधाने वास्तुचक्रपुरुषविधिर्नाम
॥ अष्टमोऽध्यायः ॥

॥ अथ दशमोऽध्यायः ॥

अथातस्सम्प्रवक्ष्यामि वास्तुचक्रस्य दैवतान् ।
प्रतिकोणं समासाद्य प्रत्यङ्गं निवसन्ति च ॥१॥
कथं स्याद्वास्तुचक्रस्य एकाशीतिपदं कृतम् ।
शिरः शिखा ललाटं च नेत्रं श्रोत्रं च नासिका ॥२॥
ताल्वे चिग्रुकश्चैव १ आस्यं च मुखमण्डलम् ।
उपकर्णं कर्णदेशं उपबाहू च बाहु च ॥३॥
उरश्च हृदयं चैव कुक्षिहस्ताङ्गुलीयकम् ॥४॥
ऊरू जानू जङ्घदेशं पादं पादाङ्गुलीयकम् ।
भ्रुवौ च अस्थिमांसं च मेदोमज्जान्त्ररक्तकम् ॥५॥
त्वत्स्नेयवो २ नवद्वारा एकाशीतिपदे स्थिताः ।
षट्कोणं श्वेतवर्णं स्याद्वसुकोणं तु शुभ्रकम् ॥६॥
चतुष्कोणं रक्तवर्णं कौसुम्भं वसुकोणकम् ।
विंशत्कोणं पीतवर्णं श्यामं षट्कोणमेव च ॥७॥
कृष्णं द्वाविंशतिश्चैव त्रिशन्नीलं तथैव च ।
अष्टकोणं पितृ (पीत) वर्णं रक्तपीतं वसुस्तथा ॥८॥
पीतनीलं तु षट्कोणं हारीतं नवमं तथा ।
एकविंशं द्वितयं विद्यात्पाटलद्वितयं तथा ॥९॥
एवं वर्णानि तत्रैव पदे चित्रमिव स्थितम् ।
एवं बुध्या समालोच्य शास्त्राण्यागमवंशजान् ॥१०॥
सर्वमालोच्य कर्त्तव्यं वास्तुपूजाविधानतः ।
देवालये नदीतीरे मण्डपे राजमन्दिरे ॥११॥
उत्सवे नूतनस्थाने नगरग्रामबन्धने ।
एतेषु पूजा कर्त्तव्या वास्तुदेवस्य पूजनम् ३ ॥१२॥
कन्यामासं समारभ्य कार्त्तिकान्तं त्रिमासके ।
पूर्वायां दिशि शीर्षं स्याच्चापादिघटमासके ॥१३॥
दक्षिणस्यां शिरो विन्द्यान्मिथुनादित्रिमासके ।
उत्तरस्यां शिरो विन्द्याच्चरवास्त्वोरिदं शिरः ॥१४॥
स्थिरवास्तोस्तु सर्वत्र ईशान्यां दिशि मूर्धतः ॥१५॥
स्थिरकार्याणि ४ सर्वत्र स्थिरवास्तुं प्रपूजयेत् ।
चरकार्येषु सर्वत्र चरवास्तुं प्रपूजयेत् ॥१६॥
स्थिरवास्तोस्त्रिपुरुषं कारयित्वा विधानतः ।
पूजयेच्छिवसामीप्यं व्रजन्त्यन्ते सदा प्रजाः ॥१७॥

॥ इति नारदीये वास्तुविधाने दशमोऽध्यायः ॥

१२। षडङ्ग। १३। समालोच्य। १४। कार्यं। १५। नगोत्तमाः। १६। सर्वलोकेषु। १७। वैष्णवात्त् १८। शिवमार्गविदूषकात्। १। चिबुकं चैव। २। त्वक्स्नायवो। ३। पूजने। ४। स्थिरकार्येषु।

॥ हयशीर्षपञ्चरात्रम् ॥*

॥ अथ त्रयोदशः पटलः ॥

श्रीभगवानुवाच :—

प्रासादं संप्रवक्ष्यामि सर्व्वसाधारणं शृणु ।
चतुरस्रीकृतं क्षेत्रं भजेत् षोडशधा पुनः ॥३१०॥
मध्ये तस्य चतुर्भिस्तु कुर्य्यादायसमन्वितम् ।
द्वादशैव तु भागादि भित्त्यर्थं परिकल्पयेत ॥३११॥
जङ्घोच्छ्रायं तु कर्त्तव्यं चतुर्भागेन चायतम् ।
जङ्घाया द्विगुणोच्छ्रायं मञ्जर्य्याः कल्पयेद् बुधः ॥३१२॥
चतुर्भागेन मञ्जर्य्याः कार्य्या सम्यक् प्रदक्षिणा ।
उन्मालानिगमं कार्य्यमुभयोः पार्श्वयोः समम् ॥३१३॥
शिखरेण समं कार्य्यं मानं जगतिविस्तरम् ।
द्विगुणैर्वापि कर्त्तव्यं यथाशोभानुरूपतः ॥३१४॥
विस्तारं मण्डपस्याग्रे गर्भं सूत्रद्वयेन तु ।
दैर्घ्यात् पादादिकं कार्य्यं मध्ये स्तम्भैर्व्विभूषितम ॥३१५॥
प्रासादगर्भमानं वा कुर्व्वन्ति मुखमण्डपम ।
एकाशीतिपदैर्व्वास्तुच्छायामण्डपमारभेत् ॥३१६॥
शक्ताद्यान् द्वारविन्यासे पदान्तस्थान् यजेत् सुरान् ।
तथा प्राकारविन्यासे यजेद्द्वात्रिंशदन्तगान् ॥३१७॥
सर्व्वसाधारणं चैव प्रासादस्य तु लक्षणम् ।
मानेन प्रतिमाया वा प्रासादमपरं शृणु ॥३१८॥
प्रतिमायाः प्रमाणेन कर्त्तव्या पिण्डिका शुभा ।
गर्भस्तु पिण्डिकार्द्धेन गर्भमानात्तु भित्तयः ॥३१९॥
भित्तिरायाममानेन १ उच्छ्रायं तु प्रकल्पयेत् ।
भित्तिच्छायं २ तद्द्विगुणं शिखरं कल्पयेद् बुधः ॥३२०॥
शिखरस्य तु तुर्य्येण भ्रमणं परिकल्पयेत् ।
शिखरस्य चतुर्थेन अग्रतो मूलमण्डपम् ॥३२१॥
अष्टमांशेन गर्भस्य रथकानां तु निर्गमः ।
परिधेर्गुणभागेन रथकांस्तत्र कल्पयेत् ॥३२२॥
तत्तृतीयेन वा कुर्य्याद्रथकानां तु निर्गमम् ।
वारत्रयं स्थापनीयं रथकत्रितये सदा ॥३२३॥
शिखरार्थं हि सूत्राणि रत्नानि विनिपातयेत् ।
कलशस्योर्ध्वतः सूत्रं तिर्य्यक्सूत्रं निपातयेत् ॥३२४॥
शिखरस्योर्ध्वभागस्थं सिंहं तत्र च कारयेत् ।
शुकनासां स्थिरीकृत्य मध्यशङ्कौ विचारयेत् ॥३२५॥
अपरे च तथा पार्श्वे तद्वत् सूत्रं निधापयेत् ।
तदूर्ध्वं तु भवेदीशकस्यमानेन सारवान् ३ ॥३२६॥
स्कन्धभग्नं न कर्त्तव्यं विकरालं तथैव च ।
ऊर्ध्वं तु वेदिकामानात् कलशं परिकल्पयेत् ॥३२७॥

* A Ms. of the 'Hayaśīrṣapañcarātra' is in the Library of the Varendra Research Society, Rajshahi. The Ms. has not been published; certain chapters however have been printed (I—XIV). Ch. XIII is copied from the printed portion of the text and follows the numeration of its verses.

१। भित्ते। २। भिरयुच्छ्रायं। ३। तदूर्ध्वं तु भवद्वेदी सकण्ठामलसारकम् ॥

विस्तारं द्विगुणं द्वारं ४ कर्त्तव्यं तु सुशोभनम् ।
जातरूपं सरे कुर्य्यात् चक्रं वा स्वरदुःस्वरैः ॥३२८॥
औडुम्बरकृतस्वर्णं दत्त्वा शाखां न्यसेद् बुधः ।
तूर्य्यमङ्गलघोषेण ब्राह्मणान् स्वस्तिवाच्य च ॥३२९॥
द्वारस्य तु चतुर्थांशे कार्य्यौ चण्डप्रचण्डकौ ।
दण्डहस्तौ तु कर्त्तव्यौ विष्वक्सेनोपमावुभौ ॥३३०॥
शाखार्द्धे न्यस्य रत्नानि न्यसेदूर्ध्वमुडुम्बरम् ।
तस्य मध्ये स्थिता देवी शङ्खलक्ष्मी सुरेश्वरी ॥३३१॥
कर्त्तव्या दिग्गजैः सा तु स्थाप्यमाना मठेन तु ५ ।
शाखोडुम्बरकैः कार्य्यौ पत्रावल्यादिभूषितौ ॥३३२॥
एकशाखं त्रिशाखं वा षट्शाखं द्वारमिष्यते ।
नवशाखं च कुर्व्वन्ति अत ऊर्ध्वं न कारयेत् ॥३३३॥
विष्णुरुद्रवरुणाद्यैः शाखां यत्नाद्विभूषयेत् ।
प्रासादस्य चतुर्भागः प्राकारस्योच्छ्रयो भवेत् ॥३३४॥
प्रासादात् पादहीनस्तु गोपुरस्योच्छ्रयो भवेत् ।
पञ्चहस्तस्य देवस्य एकहस्ता तु पीठिका ॥३३५॥
तस्मात्तु द्विगुणः प्रोक्तस्तथा गरुडमण्डपः ।
एकहस्ताद्धि कुर्व्वीत त्रिंशद्धस्तान्तमेव च ॥३३६॥
एकभूम्यादिकं कुर्य्यात् सप्तभूम्यन्तमेव च ।
वायव्यां नागनाम्ना तु विष्णवे चैकभूमिकाम् ॥३३७॥
द्विभौमिकं तथाग्नेयं माहेन्द्रं तु त्रिभौमिकम् ।
चतुर्भागं तु वारुण्यां सौरं स्यात् पञ्चभौमिकम् ॥३३८॥
सौम्यं षड्भौमिकं ज्ञेयं वैष्णवं सप्तभौमिकम् ।
गरुत्वन्तं तथा कुर्य्यादुपरिष्टाच्चतुर्दिशम् ॥३३९॥

कुर्य्याद्धि प्रतिमामानं दिक्षु चाष्टस्वरोपरि ।
महावराहमैन्द्र्यां तु नरसिंहं तु दक्षिणे ॥३४०॥
प्रतीच्यां श्रीधरं देवमुदीच्यां हयशीर्षकम् ।
आग्नेय्यां जामदग्न्यं तु नैर्ऋत्यां राममेव च ॥३४१॥
वामनं चैव वायव्यां वासुदेवमथापरे ।
पूर्व्वभूमौ तु शयनं द्वितीये चासनं भवेत् ॥३४२॥
स्थानमेवं तृतीये तु चतुर्थे यानमेव च ।
पञ्चमे योगनिद्रां तु षष्ठे योगासनं भवेत् ॥३४३॥
स्नानयोगसमायुक्तं सप्तमे परिकल्पयेत् ।
नानाकाराक्षरैर्य्यत्नात् पत्रकं वा विभूषितम् ॥३४४॥
नानाप्रकारपुष्पाद्यैर्यथाशोभं प्रकल्पयेत् ।
कनिष्ठमध्यमेष्टानां प्रासादानां यथाक्रमम् ॥३४५॥
वसुभार्गवविष्णिवन्द्रैः प्रदेया रचना बुधैः ।
द्वारस्य चाष्टमे युक्ते नवमे दशमे तथा ॥३४६॥
ललाटरेखा नैव स्यात् आयस्य शृणु सांप्रतम् ।
यावत् कुम्भैरभिप्रेतः प्रासादकर्त्तॄणानघ ! ॥३४७॥
तावद्भिरङ्गुलैरायो वसुभागेन वा भवेत् ।
एकस्तम्भो ध्वजो ज्ञेयो द्विस्तम्भा वेदिका मता ॥३४८॥
कुलभूम्यन्तरे नित्यं चतुस्तम्भं प्रकल्पयेत् ।
तोरणस्य विधानं तु कथितं तु तवानघ ! ॥३४९॥
प्रासादाग्रे यदा कार्य्या वेदिका स्तम्भसंयुता ।
वैष्णवैस्तु तदा कार्य्या वेदिका स्तम्भसंयुता ॥३५०॥

॥ इति प्रासादलक्षणपटलस्त्रयोदशः ॥१३॥

४ । विस्तारद्विगुणं द्वारं । ५ । स्नाप्यमाना घटेन तु ।

॥ कामिकागमः ॥*

॥ एकोनपञ्चाशः पटलः ॥

नागरादिप्रभेदं तु प्रवक्ष्यामि विशेषतः ।
विन्ध्यान्तं चैव कृष्णान्तं कन्यान्तं तु हिमाचलात् ॥१॥
तस्मात्तस्माक्रियाधात्रीयुक्तसत्वतमोरजाः ।
नागरं द्राविडं चैव वेसरं सार्वदेशिकम् ॥२॥
कालिङ्गं च वराटं च षड्विधं त्विह कीर्त्तितम् ।
नागरं सात्विको १ क्षेत्रे वेसरं स्यात्तमोऽधिके ॥३॥
राजसे द्राविडं चैव सर्वदेश्यं सर्वत्र सम्मतम् ।
कालिङ्गं च वराटं च ग्राह्यं सत्वरजोऽधिके ॥४॥
कुलं मसूकरं २ जङ्घा कपोतं शिखरं गलम् ।
ऊर्ध्वेन्द्वामलसारेणाष्टवर्गः कुम्भशूलयुक् ॥५॥
अन्यैः परिनिक्षिप्तं प्रोक्तवर्गाष्टकं तु यत् ।
अन्यैः प्रतीरयैः ३ कोणैरन्योन्याधिकभद्रजैः ॥६॥
त्रिभिर्वा पञ्चभिर्भागैर्नवभिर्वाथ सप्तभिः ।
साष्टधा नवभिर्नीचैर्युक्तो वा दवकस्तकैः ४ ॥७॥
स्वच्छन्दाङ्गं विचित्राङ्गं सन्तारः प्रस्तरः कियान् ।
ऊहप्रत्यूहसंयुक्तैरेजातीशांशमुण्डयुक् ५ ॥८॥
सकर्माकर्मजं यं तु मण्डनानलसारकम् ६ ।
शुकनासिकया युक्तं पार्श्वयोः प्रमुखे मुखे ॥९॥
कुण्डमण्डपसंयुक्तमङ्गप्रत्यङ्गकल्पितम् ।
यथाशक्ति यथाशोभं विधातव्यं हि नागरम् ॥१०॥
हो [दो] रभ्यन्तरस्तम्भभित्तितुल्यसमन्वितम् ।
प्रकृत्यपरजं मूर्ध्नि सोपपीठमसूरकम् ॥११॥
समस्तम्भां यत्तु सभासमपि भागभाक् ७ ।
जन्मोपपीठानुष्ठानस्तम्भप्रस्तरकन्धरैः ॥१२॥
शिखरे ८ स्तूपिकाभ्यां च षड्वर्गैस्सहितं तु यन् ।
मानसूत्राब्दहिर्निर्यात्समसूत्राङ्गभद्रकम् ॥१३॥
समस्तम्भान्तरस्योर्ध्वप्रस्तरान्तरबन्धनम् ।
मध्यकर्णमिदं गच्छेत्प्रमाणभवनान्वितम ॥१४॥
एवमादिविशिष्टाङ्गं विमानं द्राविडं मतम् ।
युक्तद्राविडविन्यासनागरक्रिययाऽन्वितम् ॥१५॥
नागरं धामिडोद्दिष्ट ९ विशेषेण विभूषितम् ।
सखण्डखण्डहर्म्यं तु कण्ठमायोभयात्मकः १० ॥१६॥
उत्तरोत्तरतो व्यूहयुक्तान्तरतलक्रिया ।
एवमादिविचित्राङ्गं विमानं नाम वेसरम् ॥१७॥
मूलादूर्ध्वोर्ध्वसन्धेयं तदुपर्यस्ततां मा(ग)तम् ।
तदुपर्युत्थितग्रीवशिखास्तूपिकयान्विता ॥१८॥
भद्रोपभद्रचित्राङ्गस्तम्भान्तरतलक्रियाम् ।
साधारणतला सप्तकाथ स्तम्भनिवेशनम् ॥१९॥
श्रोण्याकारक्रियोपेतच्छायाप्रस्तरबन्धनम् ।
एवमाद्यङ्गवैचित्र्यं वराटं धाम सम्मतम् ॥२०॥
विनां धारितयो ११ रस्य पताका बाह्यमण्डनम् ।
उत्तराधा १२ लुपारोहक्रियां धारिकयान्वितम् ॥२१॥
उन्नता वा न तस्याङ्गैः सर्वाङ्गैः परिमण्डलम् ।
चतुरश्राष्टवृत्ताभग्रीवाशिखरसौरभम् ॥२२॥

* Copied from a manuscript in the Government Sanskrit College Library, Calcutta, which is a copy of the manuscript No. D.5421 of Government Oriental Manuscripts Library, Madras.

१। सात्विके। २। मूलं मसूरकं। ३। रथैः। ४। भागसप्तकैः। ५। जंगतीशांशमुण्डयुक्। ६। कण्ठमामलसारकं। ७। समस्तम्भान्तरं यत्तु सभागमपि भागभाक्। ८। शिखरैः। ९। द्रामिडो। १०। सखण्डाऽखण्डहर्म्यं तु कण्ठपार्श्वोभयात्मकः। ११। विनाऽधारिकयो। १२। धो।

ईदृग्भूताङ्गसङ्कल्पं कालिङ्गं सद्म सम्मतम् ।
नालिकां धारिकां धारां हीरारस्या ? हि मण्डलम् ॥२३॥
कपोतशालया युक्तं ब्रह्मद्वारपताकया ।
षड्विंशाकृतियुक् सद्म सम्मतं सर्वदेशिकम् ॥२४॥
प्रत्येकं त्रिविधं प्रोक्तं द्विमित्यै १३ स्त्वधुनोच्यते ।
हस्तच्छेदपरीहार नानाकृतसमीकृतम् ॥२५॥
अथ संव्रत्स १४ मुत्पन्नैर्नागरं तत्समागतम् ।
हस्तच्छेदपरीहृत्यै १५ हित्वा समविधानवत् ॥२६॥
भद्रालङ्कारसंयुक्तं द्रामिडं चेति कीर्त्तितम् ।
लब्धमात्रा न १६ हीनं तु नातिरिक्तं सवस्त्रकम् ॥२७॥
उत्तरोत्तरनिर्युक्तं सङ्करं वेसरं मतम् ।
त्रि-पञ्च-सप्त-द्वि-चतुः-षड्भक्त्यैकतलक्रमात् ॥२८॥
नागरादिषु षड्भेदहीनं मध्यममुत्तमम् ।
साक्षाद् द्वित्रिचतुःपञ्चतलमष्टनवांशकम् ॥२९॥
कनिष्ठं मध्यमं ज्ञेयं दशांशैकादशांशकम् ।
श्रेष्ठत्रयोदशांशं तु द्वादशांशमिति स्मृतम् ॥३०॥
तथा षट्सप्तभौमं त्रिः पञ्चद्विस्सप्तभागभाक् ।
तथा चाष्टतलं प्रोक्तं नवभूमं १७ निकेतनम् ॥३१॥
सप्ता १८ दश द्विरष्टांशं नवाष्टादिदशांशकम ।
विमानं द(ण्ड) राभौमं तु द्वात्रिंशत्सप्तभागयुक् ॥३२॥
एकादशतलं द्वित्रिभागयुग्विदशांशकम् १९ ।
युग्माऽयुग्मत्रिभूम्यादि या सा त्रित्र्यंशवर्धनात् ॥३३॥
दशाद्वादशभूम्यां तु संख्या ख्याता क्रमागता ।
कनिष्ठमध्यमा श्रेष्ठा नागरादिषु पञ्चसु ॥३४॥
अविरोधेन विन्यासभाषणं सर्वदेशिकम् ।
असमं नाग २० द्राविडा चेत्समागता ॥३५॥

द्विविधं २१ भक्तयो ग्राह्या वेसरे सार्वदेशिके ।
अनन्योनाधिकर्षीणं २२ क्षीणा नागरयामिनी ॥३६॥
द्राविडे सङ्गविश्लेषे क्षेत्रभागोदितक्षणात् ।
ईषदूनाधिका वा स्युर्वेसरादिषु भक्तयः ॥३७॥
त्रिचतुःपञ्चमात्राभिः कपोतैः स्थलभिश्च यः ।
एवं भक्तिविभागस्तु गर्भगेहमथोच्यते ॥३८॥
सैकत्रिपञ्चभक्त्यंशषण्णवैकादशांशकम् ।
नागरे सैकभौमः स्यात्प्रासादस्यैकनालका ॥३९॥
श्रेष्ठमध्यमहीनस्य बहिर्दशोषेण भक्तिता ।
गर्भ त्रि षडष्ट दश त्रिचतुः पञ्चभागभाक् ॥४०॥
द्वितको २३ नागरस्योक्ता नालगेहविशालता ।
षोडशांशे तु षड्भागे गर्भसप्तदशांशके ॥४१॥
अष्टादशांशे सप्तांशास्त्रितले नागरस्य तु ।
द्राविडे त्रिचतुः पञ्चभागैर्नील २४ विशालता ॥४२॥
गर्भे नवदशांशे तु वस्वांशे २५ विंशदंशके ।
त्रिसप्ते तु नवांशं त्रितलद्रामिडे मतः ॥४३॥
त्रिपञ्चसप्तभिर्नालषडष्टदशभाजिते ।
वेसरस्यैकभौमस्य श्रेष्ठमध्याधमक्रमात् ॥४४॥
नवैकादशविश्वेन्दु चतुः पञ्च षडंशकम् ।
वेसरे द्वितलस्योक्त नालो गृह २६ विशालता ॥४५॥
द्वित्रिवेदांशके विंशत्र्यंशे नवदिगंशकः ।
वेसरं गर्भगेहं स्यात्तदन्ते तु द्विजोत्तमाः ॥४६॥
एकद्वित्रितलानां तु गर्भस्त्वेवमुदाहृतः ।
नागरोक्तं वराटे स्यात्कालिङ्गे द्रामिडोद्यतम् २७ ॥४७॥
वेसरोक्तं तु यत्सर्वं तद्योग्यं सार्वदेशिके ।
यथाक्रमं वा तद्ग्राह्यं २८ सर्वे वा सार्वदेशिके ॥४८॥

१३। द्विविध। १४। सम्पत्। १५। हस्तच्छेदपरीहारं। १६। लब्धमात्रान्नहीनं। १७। भौमं। १८। सप्त। १९। द्विदशांशकम्। २०। असमां नागरं प्राहुः। २१। द्विविधा। २२। क्षीणा। २३। द्वितले। २४। नाल। २५। वस्वंशो। २६। नालगेहविशालता। २७। द्रामिडोक्तवत्। २८। तद्ग्राह्यं।

अष्ट त्रि त्रिदश त्रिंशद् गर्भः स्यात् त्रितलादिषु ।
एतत्सर्वं च सामान्यं विशेषालङ्कृतिस्थितः २९ ॥४९॥
श्रेयः श्रेयः सुनाडीके श्रेयः श्रेयसि वा मता ३० ।
एवं गर्भगृहं प्रोक्तं भद्रस्य विधिरुच्यते ॥५०॥
सैकत्रिपञ्चपंक्त्यंशपञ्चषड्सप्तविस्तरः ।
तत्तारैरंशनिष्क्रान्तं मध्ये मूषा ३१ कनीयसी ॥५१॥
कनिष्ठे नवपञ्चांशा सप्तत्र्यशा च मध्यमे ।
त्र्यंशकैकांशके षट् स्युर्नागरादिष्वनुक्रमात् ॥५२॥
निष्क्रान्तिरासां पूर्वोक्तनीत्यैव परिकल्पितः ।
शाक्तिकन्याः ३२ कामदान्ताः पञ्चाशद्द्रामिडोचिताः ॥५३॥
वास ३३ द्विगुण उत्सेधाः ३४ कामदाख्या स्तनावरे ।
एकद्वित्रिचतुः पञ्चभागैरु ३५ द्विगुणाधिकाः ॥५४॥
अष्टांशषु विशालेषु उत्सेधः शान्तिकाधिकम् ।
वराटे चापि कालिङ्गे वेसरे नागरोक्तवत् ॥५५॥
नागरे समहस्ता स्युर्द्रामिडादिषु पूर्ववत् ।
स्वायंभुवादिलिङ्गानां पूजांशपरिणाहके ॥५६॥
पञ्चा ३६ दशांशके पञ्चभोभागेनो ३७ त्सेधं तु शान्तिकम् ।
नागर समलिङ्गान्तं नागे ३८ सप्तदशांशके ॥५७॥
नागरं पौष्टिकं नाम सप्तांशोच्चं शिवाधिकम् ।
एकोनविंशदंशात्तु नवांशं वधमानकम् ॥५८॥
जयदं नागरं तस्मादशांशोतितुङ्गकम् ।
अद्भुतं चाभिवारं च तदर्धं सर्वदेशिकम् ॥५९॥
एतन्नागरलिङ्गे तु सौधमोजः पदेन तु ।
परिणाहे विकारांशे भूतकौशिकधातुभिः ॥६०॥
हृदयं द्रामिडं प्रोक्तं शान्तिपुष्टिजयावहम् ।
तत्तदर्धांश ३९ काधिक्य हीनद्व्यन्तरमानकम् ॥६१॥
अद्भुत चाभिवारं च सर्वकामिकमुच्यते ।
नाहे तु भास्करे भागे त्रिचतुःपञ्चभागिकम् ॥६२॥
पौष्टिकं तुङ्गजयदं जयदं वेसरं मतम् ।
पूर्वोक्तविधिना ज्ञेया अद्भुताद्यास्त्रयस्त्रयः ॥६३॥
द्रामिडे वेसरे लिङ्गे समभागप्रमाणतः ।
प्रासादं योजयेद्विद्वान्यथाशास्त्रं द्विजोत्तमाः ॥६४॥
कानवेलस्य ? दैर्घ्यं यत्तद् द्विरष्टांशके कृते ।
भूतवेदगुणव्यासनाहरं ४० शान्तिकादिकम् ॥६५॥
अर्धार्धाधिकहीनं तु द्व्यक्षरं तु विशालकम् ।
अद्भुतं चाभिवारं च नागरं सार्वकामिकम् ॥६६॥
अष्टादशांशके तुङ्गे कौशिकेन्द्रियवेदकम् ४१ ।
द्रामिडं शान्तिकादि स्यादद्भुतदृढ पूर्ववत् ४२ ॥६७॥
वेसरे विंशदशे तु वसुभानुरसांशकम् ।
शान्तिकादिक्रमेण स्यादद्भुताद्यथ पूवकम् ४३ ॥६८॥
लिङ्गायामसमो व्यासः पूजांशोच्चद्वयेन वा ।
तदन्तरेऽष्टभागे तु पूर्ववत्परिकल्पयेत् ॥६९॥
विष्णुभागसमुत्सेधशषां ४४ भूगतमिष्यते ।
विष्णुभागे तु तुल्यांशो नाधिका वाऽथपीठिका ॥७०॥
निष्कम्भ ४५ त्रिगुणो व्यासोऽधस्ताद्ब्रह्मशिलां न्यसेत् ।
व्यासत्रिभाग उत्सेधश्चतुरशैक एव वा ।७१॥
यस्य लिङ्गस्य विष्कम्भश्चाष्टभागकमेव वा ।
नवभागैकभागं वा गांम्भीर्यमवटस्य तु ॥७२॥
एषां ४६ नागरलिङ्गे तु ब्रह्मणे कथिता शिला ।
गर्भकर्णस्य तुर्यांशा व्यासोक्तत्र्यंशकोदया ॥७३॥
लिङ्गव्यासाष्टभागैक तत्रा ४७ द्रामिडभूशिला ।
गर्भादघचतुर्भागा हीनविस्तारसंयुतम् ४८ ॥७४॥
तद्वत्पादांशादयापेतशिला वा वेसरे मता ।
लिङ्गपीठे शिलायामसजातीये सुसम्पदे ॥७५॥

२९ । स्थितम् अथवा स्त्विदम् । ३० ! मतम् । ३१ । भूषा । ३२ । शान्तिकाद्याः । ३३ । भाग । ३४ । उत्सेधः । ३५ । भागे तु । ३६ । पञ्च । ३७ । भागेन । ३८ । भागे । ३९ । तत्तदर्धांश । ४० । नाहकं । ४१ । तुङ्गकम् । ४२ । अद्भुताद्युक्तपूर्ववत् । ४३ । स्याद्द्भुताद्युक्तपूर्वकम् । ४४ । शेष । ४५ । विष्कम्भ । ४६ । एवं । ४७ । भागैकमात्रा । ४८ । संयुता ।

विपरीते विपत्त्यै स्यात्कर्त्तुः कारयितुस्तथा ।
अयं विभागो लिङ्गे तु नेष्यते सार्वदेशिके ॥७६॥
प्रासादेऽपि तथा लिङ्गनियमो नेष्यते बुधैः ।
एवं पीठशिलायां च नियमो नेष्यतेऽत्र तु ॥७७॥
मुख्यत्वात्सर्वलिङ्गेभ्यस्सर्वत्रापि च सम्मतम् ।
तथा प्रासाद एवं स्यात्पीठश्चापि तथैव च ॥७८॥
शान्तिदं पौष्टिजयदमद्भुतं सार्वकामिकम् ।
शान्तिकोच्चोच्छ्र्येऽष्टांशभागोच्छ्रायविनिर्मितम् ॥७९॥
विभागश्चरणोत्सेधः प्रस्तरोऽष्टांशहीनकः ।
त्रिभाग गलमित्युक्तमर्धांशं शिखरोदयम् ॥८०॥
स्तूपिकाष्टांशहीनं स्यात् द्रामिडं चैकभूमिकम् ।
नवदाशांष्टांशयुग्ममसुद्विगुण भवेत् ४९ ॥८१॥
तारोच्चप्रस्तरो भागो गलभागविनिर्मितम् ।
त्रिभागशिखरोत्सेधं शेषाण स्तूपिका भवेत् ५० ॥८२॥
द्रामिड ५१ पौष्टिकं प्रोक्तं दशांशे तु सपादकम् ।
मसूरद्विगुणः पादो भागविस्तार उच्यते ५२ ॥८३॥
भागमान गलं प्रोक्तं स्वार्थांश ५३ तु शिरा भवेत् ।
सद्म विकाजय्य ५४ द्रामिड परिकीर्त्तितम् ॥८४॥
द्वादशांशे सपादांश मसूर त्रिभागभाक् ।
द्विपादः पाद इत्युक्तः सपादः प्रस्तरोदयः ॥८५॥
एकांशं गलमित्युक्तं चतुरर्धं शिरोभवेत् ।
सपादभागस्तूप्युच्चमद्भुद [तं] द्रामिडं भवेत् ॥८६॥
त्रयोदशांशे सार्धांशमसूरं वा त्रिभागतः ।
सपादः प्रस्तरः प्रोक्त एकेन गलमिष्यते ॥८७॥
पञ्चांश शिखरं ज्ञेयं सपादा स्तूपिका भवेत् ।
सार्वकामिकसञ्ज्ञं तु द्रामिडं परिकीर्त्तितम् ॥८८॥

सभद्रं वा त्रिभद्रं वा कर्णकण्ठयुतं तु वा ।
निष्ककणकूटं वा कार्यं सनीडं वा सतोरणम् ॥८९॥
एवं लक्षणसंयुक्तं विधेयं चैकभूमिकम् ।
गर्भान्तगलवेशस्तु यदि स्यान्मरणं भवेत् ॥९०॥
नागरे सार्वदेश्ये च कालिङ्गे द्रामिडेऽपि वा ।
वराटेन प्रवेशं तु वेसरे परिकल्पयेत् ॥९१॥
विष्णुर्ब्रह्मा हरश्चेति विप्रराज्यं न वैश्यकाः ।
नागरे द्राविडे धाम्नि वेसरे त्वधिपा मताः ॥९२॥
उपानात्स्तूपिपर्यन्तं युगाश्रं नागरं भवेत् ।
कर्णात्प्रभृति वृत्तं यत्तद्वेसरं परिकीर्त्तितम् ॥९३॥
सावदेशिकधाम्ने ५५ तन्नागराद्यं प्रकीर्त्तितम् ।
चतुरश्रायश्रान्तं ५६ नागरं परिकीर्त्तितम् ॥९४॥
अष्टाश्रं च षडश्रं च तत्तदायाममेव च ।
सौद्रं ? द्रामिडमित्युक्तं प्रे वसरं ५७ परिकीर्त्तितम् ॥९५॥
वृत्तवृत्तायतं व्यस्रं वृत्तं चान्यत्प्रकथ्यते ।
द्रामिडाख्यविमानेऽपि नागरादिप्रभेदिकम् ॥९६॥
लिङ्गाद्यं कथितं पूर्वं वपुस्तत्रापि कथ्यते ।
नागरे लक्षणं पूजा नागषोडशभञ्जितम् ॥९७॥
ऊर्ध्वं षड्भूतवेदांशं त्यक्तवाथोक्ष्म ५८ कारयेत् ।
विष्ण्वंशादिमुखे ५९ सूत्रे पार्श्वयोर्द्वे च लङ्घयेत् ॥९८॥
पृष्ठे तयोर्युक्तिहीने वेदाग्निनयनान्यथ ।
सहायमध्यमे भूतवेदाग्नियनानि च ॥९९॥
ज्येष्ठषट्पञ्चवेदाग्निपादभागानधस्त्यजत् ।
त्रिभागं चकभागं च द्व्यंशं सूत्रान्तरं मतम् ॥१००॥
तदर्घं पार्श्वसूत्राग्रं तारं प्रोक्तं मुनीश्वराः ।
यन्नमानं भवेत्सूत्रगाम्भीर्यं विस्तरेण च ॥१०१॥

४९। नवदशाष्टांशयुग्ममसुद्विगुणं भवेत् । ५०। त्रिभागः शिखरोत्सेधः शेषा तु स्तूपिका भवेत् । ५१। द्रामिडं । ५२। मसूरद्विगुणो भागो पादविस्तार उच्यते । ५३। स्वार्धांशः । ५४। सद्मैतज्जयदं नाम । ५५। धाम्न्ये । ५६। चतुरश्रायताश्रं च । ५७। वेसरं । ५८। त्यक्तवाधो पद्म । ५९। भिमुखे ।

होने हि भवेदष्टयवैश्चैकोत्तमं द्विजाः ।
एवं नागरलिङ्गेषु लक्षणं द्विजसत्तमाः ॥१०२॥
द्रामिडे शिवभागे तु त्रिपञ्चांशे कृते क्रमात् ।
नवभागंदशांशेन ह्येकादशविभागकैः ॥१०३॥
हीनमध्योत्तमाख्या तु लक्षणा ६० द्धारकं भवेत् ।
सप्ताष्टनवभागेभ्यस्सूत्रे संलम्बयेत्क्रमात् ॥१०४॥
त्रिचतुर्द्व्यंशके हीने यत्स्यात्तरमसूत्रयोः ।
मध्यमे भूतवेदाग्निध्यूकंश्चापि युतिर्भवेत् ॥१०५॥
षड्भूतदैववन्ह्यंशेः श्रष्ठे पृष्ठे तयार्युतिः ।
स्वभावात्सूत्रविस्तारः पक्ष्मसूत्रं प्रकल्पयेत् ॥१०६॥
षोडशांशैश्शिवायामैस्सूत्रायामो दशांशभाक् ।
चतुर्भागं तदूर्ध्वधः पृष्ठे द्व्यंशं विहाय च ॥१०७॥
बकुलाधारमारभ्य संयुतिः पार्श्वसूत्रयोः ।
अथवाऽधस्त्र्यंशं तु त्यक्त्वोर्ध्वे रुद्रभागतः ॥१०८॥
नालायामस्समुद्दिष्टश्शेषं पूर्ववदेव हि ।
एवं द्राविडलिङ्गस्य ब्रह्मसूत्रं प्रकल्पितम् ॥१०९॥
वेसरस्यार्चनांशोच्चत्रिपञ्चांशे दशांशकः ।
नालायामस्समुद्दिष्टस्त्वष्टभार ६१ प्रभृत्यधः ॥११०॥
भूतदेवगणांशेषु सङ्गमः पक्ष ६२ सूत्रयोः ।
द्वादशांशार्चनाभागेधांशा द्व्यंशा तदूर्ध्वतः ॥१११॥
नालायामो नवांशं स्यात्सङ्गमः पूर्ववद्भवेत् ।
व्यासे द्विरष्टभागे तु भागं स्यात्सूत्रविस्तृतः ६३ ॥११२॥
तदर्धं पक्ष ६४ सूत्रं स्यादन्तरं शेषपूर्ववत् ।
एवं वेसरलिङ्गस्य ब्रह्मसूत्रमुदाहृतम् ॥११३॥
सावदेशिकलिङ्गे तु विभागोयन्न ६५ कीर्तितः ।
तथा पीठं तु पीठे स्यान्नागराद्यं विधीयते ॥११४॥
अभद्रं द्रामिडे पीठ ६६ भद्रभद्रोपभद्रकम् ।
नागरे वेसरे योगे कालिङ्गेऽपि वराटके ॥११५॥

सामान्यं पीठमुद्दिष्टं प्रतिमास्त्वधुनोच्यते ।
गर्भे धिष्ण्यमसूरे च द्वारे स्तंभे च मस्तके ॥११६॥
स्तूपिकोच्चे दशांशे तु सप्तांशे प्रतिमा खरा ।
चतुर्थ्यंशो दया हीना ६७ षड्विंशत्यन्तरोऽन्तरम् ॥११७॥
नक्षत्रसंख्यतुङ्गानि प्रतिमायां भवन्ति हि ।
नागरे त्रित्रिसंख्यानि द्रामिडे नवसंख्यया ॥११८॥
वेसराणि तथान्यानि श्रेष्ठमध्याधमक्रमात् ।
सात्विकं राजसं चैव तामसं च त्रिधा क्रमात् ॥११९॥
सात्विकं स्थानके योग्यं राजसं नृत्तरूपके ।
तामसञ्चान्यरूपे तु योजनीयं विचक्षणैः ॥१२०॥
सार्वदेशिकलिङ्गे तु विमानं नेष्यते बुधैः ।
धाम वा त्वमराणां तु नागराद्यं पुरा मतम् ॥१२१॥
ग्रामे च नगरे वापि पत्तने राजधानिके ।
खेटादौ परमेशस्य ब्रह्मस्थानेऽष्टदिक्षु वा ॥१२२॥
बहिर्वाष्टासु काष्ठासु कुड्यन्तर्वा बहिष्कृता ।
एतेषामन्तरालंर्वा प्रासादं कर्तुमारभेत् ॥१२३॥
उत्तरे नागरं कुर्याद्वायौवैशानदेशके ।
दक्षिणे द्रामिडं कुर्याद्वन्हौ वा नैरृतेऽपि वा ॥१२४॥
पूर्वस्मिन्पश्चिमे वापि वेसरं हर्म्यमाचरेत् ।
सोमपार्श्वद्वये तद्वद्यमपार्श्वद्वये तथा ॥१२५॥
इन्द्रपार्श्वद्वये तद्वा ६८ वरुणोभयतस्तथा ।
धामान्येतानि सर्वाणि द्राविडानि भवन्ति हि ॥१२६॥
सार्वदेशिकहर्म्यं चेत्सर्वत्र ६९ समाचरेत् ।
एतेषामिष्टमेकाद्यमिष्टदेशे समाचरेत् ॥१२७॥
ब्राह्मे चेदग्निकोणस्थे कोष्ठं वा स्याद्वा(दा)पणस्य च ।
नैरृतस्यैशदेशस्य सभायाश्चाविरोधतः ॥१२८॥
धामान्येतानि कार्याणि वंशसूत्रानुरोधतः ।
पार्वतीभवनं सर्वदेशे स(श)र्वोक्तवन्नयेत् ॥१२९॥

६०। लक्षणोद्धारकं। ६१। भाग। ६२। पद्मसूत्रयोः। ६३। विस्तृतिः। ६४। पद्मसुत्रं। ६५। विभागोऽयं न। ६६। द्रामिडं पीठं। ६७। चतुर्थांशोदयाद्धीना। ६८। तद्वत्। ६९। सार्वदेशिकहर्म्यं चेत्सर्वं तत्र।

वल्यङ्कारकोपेते ७० द्रामिडाकारमेव च ।
विघ्नेशस्य च मध्ये वा पूर्वोक्ते वा यथा शिवे ॥१३०॥
हस्तिपृष्ठः शिवः कार्या ७१ साधारणशिवस्तु वा ।
सेना(नी ?)भवनं कार्यं यथा शर्वस्य सम्मतम् ॥१३१॥
पूर्वोक्तदेशे कर्त्तव्यं नागरं विष्णुमन्दिरम् ।
मध्यमे व ७२ चतुर्दिक्षु नैरृतेऽन्यत्र ब्रह्मणः ॥१३२॥
वेसरं धाम कर्त्तव्यं चतुर्भद्रसमन्वितम् ।
वारुण्यां वाथ याम्याग्निमध्ये वा ग्राममध्यमे ॥१३३॥
श्रीधाम वैष्णवं कुर्याद्याम्ने नैरृतमध्यमे ।
ग्रामादिमध्यमेऽन्यत्र यथा वा ब्रह्ममन्दिरम् ॥१३४॥
तथाविधेनाग्नेय्यां सूर्यस्य शिववन्मतम् ।
अष्टदिक्ष्वष्टदेशेषु क्षेत्रेशे द्रामिडं मतः ७३ ॥१३५॥
पार्वतीभवनं यद्व त्पूर्वोक्तस्थानकं द्विजाः ।
ज्येष्ठायामयथान्वाचा ? स्वीन्द्रपावकमध्यमे ॥१३६॥
पूर्वोक्तदेशे वा कार्यं तद्वन्मौलिकृतं भवेत् ।
शास्तुर्धाम विधातव्यं यथा विघ्नेशमन्दिरम् ॥१३७॥
सोमस्य सोमदिग्भागे नैरृते वाऽथ तद्गृहम् ।
नागरं सोमवायव्ये वास्तुवैश्रवणे गृहम् ॥१३८॥
सोममन्दिरवत्कार्यं वन्हौ सोमेशमध्यमे ।
कामध्यानं यथा विष्णो मुधवन्यत्र ७४ देशतः ॥१३९॥
अनुक्तानां च सर्वेषां देवानां योषितामपि ।
प्रागुक्तानां च देवानां देवीनां सार्वदेशिकम् ॥१४०॥
अथवा कारयेद्धाम तयद्वाहनसंयुतम् ७५ ।
सार्वदेशिकसंज्ञस्य प्रासादस्य च लक्षणम् ॥१४१॥
ब्रह्मशैलस्य तद्वद्देरादिलक्षणम् ७६ ।
ततदध्ययनं सिद्धं ७७ सग्राह्यं देशिकोत्तमैः ॥१४२॥
इति श्रीकामिकाख्ये महातन्त्रे क्रियापादे नागरादिविमानभेदो
॥ नाम एकोनपञ्चाशः पटलः ॥

७० । कालिङ्गाकारकोपेतं । ७१ । शिवः कार्यः । ७२ । च ७३ । मतम् । ७४ । मध्यादन्यत्र ।
७५ । तत्तद्वाहनसंयुतम् । ७६ । ब्रह्मशैलस्य पीठस्य तत्तद्देरादिलक्षणम् । ७७ । तत्तदध्ययनात्सिद्धं ।

SOURCES

VEDA

Saṃhitā

Ṛg Veda, with Comm. of Sāyaṇa ; Bombay, 1889, 1890.
Śukla Yajurveda ; Moradabad, 1940.
Vājasaneyī Saṃhitā, with Comm. of Mahīdhara ; Calcutta, 1874.
Kāṇva Saṃhitā ; Kashi Sanskrit Series, Benares, 1915.
Mādhyandina Saṃhitā ; Kashi Sanskrit Series, Benares, 1913.
Kapiṣṭhalakaṭha Saṃhitā ; Sanskrit Book Depot, Lahore, 1932.
Maitrāyaṇīya Saṃhitā, Leipzig, 1881-1886 ; 1923.
Taittirīya Saṃhitā, with Comm. of Sāyaṇa ; Asiatic Society of Bengal, Calcutta, 1860-1899.
Taittirīya Saṃhitā, with Comm. of Bhaṭṭa Bhāskara ; Mysore Government Oriental Series, 1894-1898.
Atharva Veda, with Comm. of Sāyaṇa ; Bombay, 1895-1898.

Brāhmaṇa

Aitareya Brāhmaṇa ; Ānandāśrama Sanskrit Series, Poona, 1896.
,, ,, A.S.B., Calcutta, 1895-1906.
Śatapatha Brāhmaṇa ; Śrī Venkaṭeśvara Press, Bombay, 1942.
Taittirīya Brāhmaṇa ; A.S.S., Poona, 1898.
Jaiminīya Brāhmaṇa ; Amsterdam, 1919.
,, ,, Sarasvatīvihāra Sanskrit Series, Lahore, 1937.
Jaiminīya Upaniṣad Brāhmaṇa ; Lahore, 1921.
Tāṇḍya (Pañcaviṃśa) Brāhmaṇa ; Chowkhamba Sanskrit Series, Benares, 1941.
Ṣaḍviṃśa (Adbhuta) Brāhmaṇa ; Calcutta, 1911.

Āraṇyaka

Aitareya Āraṇyaka ; A.S.B., Calcutta, 1876.
Taittirīya Āraṇyaka : A.S.B., Calcutta, 1872.

Upaniṣad

Kauṣītakibrāhmaṇa Upaniṣad, '108 Upaniṣads', Benares, 1941.
Bṛhadāraṇyaka Upaniṣad, with Comm. of Śaṅkarācārya ; A.S.S., Poona, 1915.
Īśāvāsya Upaniṣad ; '108 Upaniṣads'.
Kaṭha Upaniṣad ; '108 Upaniṣads'.
Śvetāśvatara Upaniṣad ; '108 Upaniṣads'.
Maitrāyaṇī Upaniṣad ; '108 Upaniṣads'.
Chāndogya Upaniṣad, with Comm. of Śaṅkarācārya ; A.S.S., Poona, 1915.

Kena Upaniṣad ; '108 Upaniṣads',
Aruṇa Upaniṣad ; 'Unpublished Upaniṣads', Adyar, 1933.
Rādhā Upaniṣad ; 'Upaniṣat-kośa'.
Upaniṣat-Kośa ; Bombay, 1942.

*

Sūtra

Āśvalāyana Śrautasūtra ; A.S.B., Calcutta, 1874.
Śāṅkhāyana Śrautasūtra ; A.S.B., Calcutta, 1885-89.
Kātyāyana Śrautasūtra ; K.S.S., Benares, 1933.
Āpastamba Śrautasūtra ; A.S.B., 1882-1892.
Baudhāyana Śulvasūtra ; A.S.B., Calcutta, 1904-1923.
Āśvalāyana Gṛhyasūtra ; Trivandrum Sanskrit Series, 1915.
Kātyāyana Gṛhyasūtra ; T.S.S., Trivandrum, 1915.
Pāraskara Gṛhyasūtra ; Kashi Sanskrit Series, Benares, 1920.
Bṛhaddevatā ; H.O.S., 1904.

Vyākaraṇa

Pātañjala Mahābhāṣya ; Bombay Sanskrit Series, 1885-1906.

Nirukta

Nirukta, of Yāska ; Bhandarkar Oriental Research Institute, Poona, 1918.

Jyotiṣa

Bṛhajjātaka, of Varāhamihira ; K.S.S., Benares, 1941.
Bṛhatparāśara Horā ; Bombay, 1915.
Bṛhat Saṃhitā, of Varāhamihira, with Comm. of Utpala ; Vizianagram Series, 1895-1897.
Gaṇitasārasaṃgraha, of Mahāvīra ; Madras Govt., Oriental Series, 1912.
Siddhāntaśiromaṇi, of Bhāskarācārya ; K.S.S., Benares, 1929.

* * *

Yoga

Yogasūtra, with Comm. Maṇiprabhā ; Calcutta, 1908.
Yogavāsiṣṭha, with Comm. Tātparyaprakāśa ; N.S.P., Bombay, 1911, 1918.

Vedānta

Vedāntasūtra (Brahmasūtra Śāṅkara Bhāṣya) ; N.S.P., Bombay, 1919.
Tattvaprakāśa, of Bhojarāja, with Comm. of Śrī Kumāra ; T.S.S., 1920.
Citsukhī (Bhāṣyabhāva Prakāśikā on Brahmasūtra Śāṅkara Bhāṣya), Madras University Series, Madras, 1933.

Itihāsa

Mahābhārata ; Nirṇayasagar Press, Bombay, 1909-1919.
Rāmāyaṇa ; with Comm. Tilaka ; N.S.P., Bombay, 1909.

Purāṇa

Agnipurāṇa ; A.S.S., Poona, 1900.
Bhaviṣyapurāṇa ; S. V. Press, Bombay, 1910.
Brahmāṇḍapurāṇa ; S. V. Press, Bombay, 1911.
Brahmavaivartapurāṇa ; A.S.S., Poona, 1935.
Bṛhaddharmapurāṇa ; A.S.B., Calcutta 1888-1897.
Devīpurāṇa ; S. V. Press, Bombay.
Garuḍapurāṇa ; Calcutta, 1890.
,, , chapters I-XVI ; Benares, 1914.
Harivaṃśa ; S. V. Press, Bombay, 1911.
Kālikāpurāṇa ; S. V. Press, Bombay.
Liṅgapurāṇa ; Calcutta, 1885.
Mārkaṇḍeyapurāṇa ; A.S.B., Calcutta, 1862.
Matsyapurāṇa ; A.S.S., Poona, 1907.
Padmapurāṇa ; Calcutta, 1893, 1894.
Skandapurāṇa ; S. V. Press, Bombay, 1910.
Vāyupurāṇa ; A.S.S., Poona, 1906.
Viṣṇudharmottara ; S. V. Press, Bombay, 1912.
Viṣṇupurāṇa ; S. V. Press, Bombay, 1921.

Āgama and Tantra

Gandharva Tantra, see Tantrasāra.
Hayaśīrṣapañcarātra ; Chapters I-XIV (title page missing).
Īśānaśivagurudevapaddhati ; T.S.S., Trivandrum, 1920-1924.
Jñānārṇava Tantra ; A.S.S., Poona, 1912.
Kālottara Āgama, quoted in Īśānaśivagurudevapaddhati.
Kāmikāgama ; Ms. No. D. 5431, Government Oriental Manuscript Library, Madras.
Kiraṇāgama, quoted in Īśānaśivagurudevapaddhati.
Kaulāvalī Tantra, see Tantrasāra.
Kulārṇava Tantra ; Tantrik Texts Series, Calcutta, 1917.
Mahākapila Pañcarātra, quoted in Śāradātilaka.
Mahānirvāṇa Tantra ; T.T.S., Calcutta, 1919.
Meru Tantra ; N.S.P., Bombay, 1908.
Prāṇatoṣiṇī Tantra ; see Tantrasāra.
Puraścaryārṇava of Mahārājādhirāja Pratāpasiṃha of Nepal ; Kashmir Sanskrit Series, 1901-1904.
Samūrtārcanādhikaraṇa ; Śri Venkaṭeśvara Oriental Series, Tirupati, 1943.
Śāradātilaka ; T.T.S., Calcutta, 1933.
Tantrāloka ; Kashmir Sanskrit Series, 1918.
Tantrarāja Tantra, with Comm. Manoramā ; T.T.S., Calcutta, 1919.

Tantrasamuccaya ; T.S.S., Trivandrum, 1919-1921.
Tantrasāra ; Calcutta, 1918.
Vaikhānasāgama, of Marīci ; T.S.S., Trivandrum, 1935.
Viṣṇusaṃhitā ; T.S.S., Trivandrum, 1925.

Stotra

Devīmāhātmya ; Ananta Rāma Varma Press, Trivandrum, 1931.
Lalitā Sahasranāma ; Vanivilās Press, Śrīraṅgam, 1918.
Saundaryalaharī ; Vanivilās Press, Śrīraṅgam, 1918.

Kośa

Amarakośa ; N.S.P., Bombay.
Nanārthārṇavasaṃkṣepa, of Keśavasvāmin ; T.S.S., 1913-1924.
Vācaspatya ; Calcutta, 1873-1883.

Dharmaśāstra

Manu Smṛti ; N.S.P., Bombay.

Arthaśāstra

Kauṭilīya Arthaśāstra ; T.S.S., 1921-1924.

Kāmaśāstra

Kāmasūtra, with Comm. Jayamaṅgala ; N.S.P., Bombay.

Nītiśāstra

Śukranītisāra ; Calcutta, 1882.

Vāstuśāstra

Aparājitaprabhā, of Viśvakarman ; Ms. No. III. I. 63, Royal Asiatic Society of Bengal, Calcutta.
Bhuvanapradīpa ; Ed. N. K. Bose, 'Canons of Orissan Architecture', Calcutta, 1932.
Bṛhacchilpaśāstra ; Ed. Jayanatha Anjaria, Jyoti Press, Ahmedabad, 1939.
Kāśyapaśilpa ; A.S.S., Poona, 1926.
Mānasāra ; Ed. P. K. Acharya, 1932.
Mānasollāsa, of Bhaṭṭa Someśvara ; Govt., Oriental Series, Mysore, 1926.
Manuṣyālayacandrikā ; T.S.S., Trivandrum, 1917.
Mayamata, of Mayamuni ; T.S.S., 1919.
Paurāṇikavāstuśānti-prayoga ; Bombay, 1886.
Prayogamañjarī ; Ms. No. 21, S. 11, Adyar Library.
Prayogapārijāta ; N.S.P., Bombay, 1916.
Rūpamaṇḍana ; Ms. No. 6050, Royal Asiatic Society of Bengal, Calcutta.
Samarāṅgaṇasūtradhāra ; Gaekwad Oriental Series, Baroda, 1924, 1925.
Śilparatna ; T.S.S., Trivandrum, 1922.
Śilpaśāstra, of Nārada, (Two chapters), ed. V. Raghavan, JISOA, III ; cf. infra.

Vāstumuktāvalī ; Benares, 1916.

Vāstupuruṣavidhāna, of Nārada ; Ms. 1602, Adyar Library.

Vāsturājavallabha, of Mandana Sūtradhāra, Ms., Royal Asiatic Society of Bengal, Nos. 6045 and 705.

Vāstusaṅgraha ; Ms., R.A.S.B., Calcutta ; No. 6075.

Vāstuśāstra, of Viśvakarman, Ms. No. I.G. 89, R.A.S.B., Calcutta.

Vāstuśāstra, of Viśvakarman, Ms. No. 7854 and 6145, R.A.S.B., Calcutta.

Vāstuvidyā ; Comm. by K. Mahādeva Śāstrī ; T.S.S., Trivandrum, 1940.

Viśvakarmaprakāśa ; Ed. Matṛprasād Pandey, Benares, 1937.

Viśvakarmavidyā-prakāśa ; S.V.P., Bombay, 1895.

Kāvya

Harṣacarita, Bombay, 1917, 1918.

Naiṣadhacarita, N.S.P., Bombay, 1913.

Raghuvaṃśa ; N.S.P., Bombay, 1888.

Śaṅkara Digvijaya, of Sāyaṇa, A.S.S., Poona, 1915.

* * *

Translations : Ṛg Veda (R.T.H. Griffith, Benares ; H. H. Wilson, London) ; Taittirīya Saṃhitā (A. B. Keith, Harvard Oriental Series) ; Atharva Veda (W. D. Whitney, H.O.S. ; R. T. H. Griffith, Benares) ; Aitareya Brāhmaṇa (M. Haug, Bombay ; A. B. Keith, H.O.S.) ; Śatapatha Brāhmaṇa (J. Eggeling, Sacred Books of the East) ; Chāndogya Upaniṣad (Ganganath Jha, Poona, 1942) ; Āpastamba Śrauta Sūtra (W. Caland, Göttingen) ; Śulva Sūtras : B. B. Datta, 'The Science of the Śulba', Calcutta University Press ; 1932 ; G. Thibaut, 'On the Śulva Sūtras', JASB, 1875 ; A. Bürk, 'Āpastamba Śulva Sūtra', ZDMG, 1901 ; Gṛhya Sūtras (S.B.E.) ; Bṛhaddevatā (A. A. Macdonell, H.O.S., 1904) ; Vedāntasūtras (S.B.E. and S.B.H.) ; Bṛhat Saṃhitā (H. Kern, JRAS, 1873) ; Viṣṇu Purāṇa (H. H. Wilson, S.B.E.) ; Mahānirvāṇatantra (A. Avalon, Calcutta) ; Tantrasamuccaya (Parts of Chapters I, XII, and Ch. II ; N. V. Mallaya, 'Studies in Sanskrit Texts on Temple Architecture with Special Reference to the Tantrasamuccaya', The Annamalai University Journal, vols. IX-XII) ; 'Architecture of Mānasāra' (P. K. Acharya, Oxford University Press) ; Vāstuvidyā (Chapters I-VI ; K. R. Pisharoti, Calcutta Oriental Journal, vols. I, II) ; Bhubanapradīpa., etc. (N. K. Bose, 'Canons of Orissan Architecture', Calcutta, 1932); Nāradaśilpaśāstra ('Two Chapters on Painting in the Nārada Śilpa Śāstra', by V. Raghavan, JISOA, vol. III, p. 15-32) ; Piṅgalāmata, Ch. IV (by P. C. Bagchi, JISOA, vol. XI, pp. 9-31).

*

References to books and articles in European languages are given in the footnotes.

*

Periodical Publications :

Archaeological Survey of India, Annual Reports.

" " Annual Report, Southern Circle, for Epigraphy.

" " Progress Report, Western Circle.

" " Progress Report, Southern Circle.

Bulletin de l'École Francaise d'Extrême Orient.
Bulletin de la Commission Archéologique de l'Indochine.
Bulletin of the Deccan College Research Institute.
Cunningham, Archaeological Survey of India, Reports.
Eastern Art.
Epigraphia Indica.
Études Asiatiques.
Études Traditionelles.
Indian Antiquary.
Indian Art and Letters.
Indian Culture.
Journal Asiatique.
Journal of the American Oriental Society.
Journal of the Indian Society of Oriental Art.
Journal of the Royal Asiatic Society.
Journal of the (Royal) Asiatic Society of Bengal.
Ostasiatische Zeitschrift.
Rūpaṃ.
Speculum.
The Annamalai University Journal.
The Art Bulletin.
The Indian Historical Quarterly.
Transactions of the Royal Society of British Architects.
Wiener Beiträge zur Kunst und Kultur Asiens.

INDEX

The letters following the words indicate: A., architectural term ; G., general connotations ; L., locality ; P., Prāsāda, a shape or type of temple given in Vāstu-śāstra, and T., an extant temple.

A

Ābhāsa, P., 265, 266, 293
Abhaya (mudrā), 136, 304, 403
Ābhicāra, 265
Ābhicārika, 77
Abhigamana, 299, 303, 358
Abu, Mt., 200
Ācārya, 9, 38, 84, 136, 137, 141, 358
Adbhuta, P., 264, 265, 268, 308
Ādhāra, 139
Ādhāra-pratidhiṣṇya, 139
Ādhāra-Śakti, 111
Ādhāra-śilā, 110-113, 153, 173
Adharma, 43, 93
Adhaśchanda, A., 22, 27, 31
Adhi-saṃvatsara, 36
Adhiṣṭhāna, A., 145, 146, 162, 166, 190, 213, 221, 229, 230, 245, 246, 259, 260, 262-264, 269, 311, 390
Ādi-Viṣṇu, 234
Aditi, 34, 35, 44, 56, 90, 94, 234
Āditya, 50, 56, 89-94, 234
Ādityas, 35, 44, 48, 89, 90, 92, 94, 96, 332, 399
Ādyaṅga, A., 145, 269
Āgama, 287, 290
Agastya (Nasik), L., 291, 293
Aghora, 330
Agni (Fire-Altar), 22-27, 43, 60, 68-71, 77-79, 103-105, 108, 110, 111, 126, 139, 140, 175, 231, 350
Agni (Devatā), 20, 32-34, 45, 49, 50, 83, 91-94, 234, 374
Agni-āgāra, 183
-cayana, 15
-gṛha, 183
-kṣetra, 26, 27, 47
-śālā, 183
-śaraṇa, 183
Agni (Naigameya), 77
Ahaṅkāra, 84, 338, 341
Āhavanīya (Agni), 23-26, 28, 43, 62, 69
Ahi, 32
-Vṛtra, 94
Ahicchatra, L., 149, 168, 174, 195, 280
Ahir, 341
Aihole, L., 186, 190-192, 194, 196, 205, 214, 215, 288, 355
Durga T., 150, 170, 222, 285, 322, 327
Galagnath T., 192
Hucchimalligudi T., 222
Kont Gudi T., 194, 197, 322
Lad Khan T., 148, 150, 155, 194, 246, 284
Meguti T., 151
Nārāyaṇa T., 333
Aiśvarya, 43
Ajaṇṭā, L., 124, 170, 183, 198, 308, 318, 322, 352, 353
Ajira, 48
Ajīvika, 170
Ajñāna, 43
Ākarṣiṇī, 338
Ākāśa, 96, 163, 164, 328, 401
-liṅga, 164, 249
-maṇḍapa, A., 257
Akola, L., 158
Akṣi-mocana, A., 15
Alakā, P., 415
Alaṃkāra, A., 390, 421
Alampur, L., 205, 246, 285
Alberuni, 72
Ālinda, A., 249, 250, 282, 283, 420
Alpa-Prāsāda, A., 195, 203, 221, 261-265, 280, 293
Alpa-Vimāna, A., 263, 264, 293
Amala, G., P., 281, 354
Āmalaka, A., 111, 147, 148, 154, 155, 159, 161, 174, 176, 179, 181, 184, 187-190, 193, 194, 201, 204, 206, 215, 217, 219, 242, 243, 245, 249, 250, 263, 273, 278, 279, 280,

B

Buddha, 16, 43, 53, 189, 233, 234, 309, 334, 346
-āyatana, 148
-mandira, 148
Buddhi, 332
Buddhist, 71, 102, 113, 118, 142, 145, 168, 170, 180, 182, 183, 197, 198, 277, 278, 284, 307, 346, 354, 355, 387
Budha, 38
Buḍīrghar, A., 159, 319
Bundana, Rajputana, L., 318
Bundelkhand, 365
Burdwan, L., 198, 199
Burma, L., 169, 277
Byzantine, 311

C

Caitya, A., 114, 138, 142, 148, 168, 182, 190-192, 234, 275, 319
-Prāsāda, 148
Cakra, 31, 42, 47-49, 50, 51, 72, 221, 278, 351, 403, 419
Cakravartin, 42
Cala (āsana), 159
Calcutta, 199
Cālukya, 101, 121, 173, 186, 287, 290-292, 333
Cam, 279
Cambodia, L., 171, 279, 322
Cāmuṇḍā, 234, 341, 384
Cāmuṇḍī, 234, 384, 398
Caṇḍa, 300
Caṇḍaśiva, 403
Caṇḍāla, 235,
Candella, 333, 337, 386-388, 399
Caṇḍi (kā), 234, 275
Candimau, L., 323
Candpur, L., 166, 169, 397, 398
Candra, 56, 423
Candra-śālā, A., 158, 270A, 274, 413
Candrāvalokana, A., 375, 395, 420
Candrāvatī, L., 315, 399
Candrikā, 221, 245, 367, 420
Candrodaya, P., 281
Cara-Vāstu, A., 63, 90
Carakī, 32, 95,
Caraṇa, A., 258, 268, 356
Caru, P., 281
Caruka, P., 278
Cattara Revadi Ovajja, 143
Caturaśra, A., P., 262, 263, 270A, 272, 274, 278, 415
-koṣṭha, A., 278
Caturbhuja T., Khajuraho, 365
Caturmukha, P., 281, 283
Catuṣkaka, P., 415
Catuṣkikā, A., 217, 255, 259, 366
Catuṣkoṇa, A., 270A., 272
Catuśśālā-gṛha, A., 419
Catvāla, 26
Catvara, 41
Cauñsath Yoginī T., 198, 421
Cedi, 386, 388
Ceylon, 193, 278
Chādya, A., 145, 283, 367, 369
Chāgāsura, 77, 81
Chamba, L., 102
Chandas, 8, 11, 48, 80, 132, 140
Chandaściti, 140
Chanda-Vimāna, A., 265, 266, 293
Chandol, L., 173
Chapri, L., 173
Chatri, A., 43
Chaumukh T., Ranpur, 200
Chebrolu, L., 123
Cheda, A., 272
Chezarla, L., (Kapoteśvara T.), 142, 322
Chimæra, 335
Chinthe, 368
Chitor, L., 143, 348
Cidambaram, L., 163, 164
Cidānanda, 341
Cit, 360
Citi, A., 26, 140, 145-149
Citra, P., 278
Citragupta T., see Khajuraho
Citrakūṭa, P., 281
Citraśālā, A., 274
Cola, 121, 151-153, 166, 195, 196, 202, 203, 352, 356
Comorin, Cape, 287, 288
Conjeeveram (Kāñcī), L., 123, 166, 184, 356
Cūḍā, A., 245
Cūla (ka), A., 221, 245, 276
Cuttack, L., 254
Cyavana, 35, 36
Cyclopean, 121, 125

D

H

Kailāsanātha T., see Elura
Kakara-koṣṭhaka, A., 188
Kakṣāṇa, A., 375, 495
Kalā, 47, 53, 137, 141, 245, 317, 349
-jñāna, 48
Kalabau, 158
Kalaśa, A., 112, 148, 213, 245, 246, 248, 249, 263, 270, 273, 274, 278, 279, 349, 350, 355, 359, 366, 372, 420
Kāla, 44, 74, 242, 324-326, 328, 330
-Makara, A., 324, 329
-mūrti, 242
-puruṣa, 72
Kāleśvar T., Ter, 101
Kali Yuga, 13
Kālī, 234
Kālī T., Khajuraho, 365
Kaliṅga, L., A., 262, 287, 290, 292
Kāliṅga, A., 262, 287, 290, 293
Kalna, L., 198, 199
Kalpa, 11, 36, 51, 141
-druma, 13
-sūtra, 11
Kalugumalai, L., Vettuvankovil, 114, 168
Kalyāṇa Maṇḍapa, A., 336
Kamala, P., 413, 418, 422
Kāma, 92, 347, 423
Kāmarūpa, L., 215
Kambaduru, L., 150, 152
Kampa, A., 258, 260
Kāmya (Agni), 24
Kanarese Districts, Deccan, 101, 166, 188, 192, 194, 196, 197, 200, 214, 288, 291, 292, 391
Kāñcī, L., 3 ; see also Kāñcīpuram
Kāñcīpuram, 155, 173, 203
Kandabhitti, A., 249, 254, 366
Kandarīya T., see Khajuraho
Kangra, L., 168
Kaṇika, A., 260
Kaniṣka, 344
Kaniṣṭha, A., 243, 421
Kaṇṭha, A., 158, 180, 190, 221, 232A, 242, 243, 245, 262-264, 267, 268, 277, 280, 287, 359
Kapālinī Devī T., see Bhuvaneśvar
Kapi, 38
Kapota, A., 191, 242, 246, 260, 269, 274, 282, 290, 321, 369
Kapotālī, A., 246, 248, 319, 413
Kapota-pālī, A., 238
Kapotapālikā, A., 168
Kapoteśvara T., Chezarla, 113, 142, 170, 182, 322
Kāraka, 9, 107, 134, 142
Kara-nyāsa, 305
Karjah, L., 172
Karli, L., 191, 203, 278, 352, 353
Karma-vidhi, 23
Karṇa (diagonal), 268
Karṇa, A., 247-249, 252, 348, 389
-bhadra, A., 370
-kūṭa, A., 267
-mañjarī, 249, 371
-śikhara, A., 249
-śṛṅga, A., 371
Karpara(ī), A., 367
Kartṛ, 9, 156
Kārttikeya, 234
Karuṇa (rasa), 308
Karuśa, L., Mahādevī T., 158
Kaseru, L., 288
Kāśi (Benares), 3
Kasia, L., 387
Kāśīnātha T., Paṭṭadakal, 324, 327
Kaśmīra (Kashmir), 158, 193, 200, 220, 262, 274, 277, 412, 421
Kāśmīra, A., 262
Kāśya, A., 262
Kāśyapa, 89, 92, 94, 113, 139, 238, 287, 325, 330, 331, 423, 425
Kaṭaka (hasta), 386
Kathiawar, L., 155, 158, 172, 191-193, 200, 220, 272
Kaṭi, A., 232A, 238, 411, 413, 415, 417
Kaṭima, A., 101
Kātyāyana, 28
Kātyāyanī, 234
Kaurava, A., 262
Kausala, A., 262
Kauśika, A., 262
Kaustubha, 421
Kauṭilya, 140
Kekind, L., 334, 404, 405
Kerala, L., A., 5, 102, 152, 292, 293
Kesarī, G., P., 336
Keśava, 423
Keśava T., Somanathpur, 421

O

P

Vāstoṣpati, 12, 35, 45, 77, 81, 83, 85
Vastu, 21, 37, 94
Vāstu, A., 21, 22, 36-39, 45, 50, 62, 63, 68, 74, 76, 81, 83, 94, 330, 331
-bali, A., 81
-bhavana, A., 68
-Brahmā, A., 68
-Cāmuṇḍī, 234
-daitya, A., 88
-deva, A., 82
-devatā A., 91, 140
-homa, A., 74, 80, 84
-maṇḍala, A., 27, 29, 31-33, 35, 37, 41, 46, 49, 57, 58, 62, 63, 94, 127, 150, 152, 165, 201, 232, 233, 237, 261, 411, 422
-nāga, A., 85, 90, 287
Vāstupa, 35, 36, 76, 81
Vāstupuruṣa, A., 29, 33-35, 38, 45-47, 49, 50, 53, 62, 63, 66, 67, 73, 95-97, 111, 117, 287, 288, 358-361
Vāstupuruṣa-maṇḍala, A., 6, 11, 16, 17, 22, 25, 32-34, 38, 48, 63, 78, 95, 102, 119, 127, 147, 180, 228, 235, 312, 357, 399, 423
Vāstu-rākṣasa, A., 82
-śānti, A., 74, 80
-Śāstra, A., 10, 142, 145, 154, 214, 227, 261, 262, 270, 275, 286, 288, 289, 292-294, 354, 416, 424, 426
-Vidyā, A., 141, 424
Vastvādhāra, A., 145
Vasu(s), 34, 41, 83, 90-92, 94, 422
Vāsudeva, 84, 234, 423
Vasudhā, A., 411
Vasudhādhara, P., 281
Vāsuki, 94
Vasundharā, 82
Vātāyana, A., 52
Vāvāṭa P., 290, 291
Vāyasa, 38
Vāyu, G., A., 33, 34, 50-52, 71, 92, 97, 234
Veda, 10, 91, 358, 421, 424
Vedāṅga, 11, 141
Vedha, 232
Vedi(ī), G., A., 17, 22-25, 40, 72, 133, 145-147, 174, 211, 239, 243, 245, 269, 323, 334, 349, 359, 366, 374, 389, 395, 399
-bandha, 238, 245, 246, 248, 251, 263, 413, 420
Vedic, 35, 49, 61, 80, 94, 95, 103, 105, 110, 113, 133, 140, 143, 150, 152, 153, 157, 205, 206, 232, 279, 288, 306, 360
Vedikā, A., 133, 145-147, 162, 230, 246, 269, 276, 302, 369, 389, 390, 391, 404
-bandha, A., 268, 269
Veṇu, A., G., 350, 384
-bhadra, P., 275
-kośa, A., 175, 208, 245, 348, 351
-kośa-antara, A., 349
-randhra, A., 173
Vesara, A., 154, 234, 251, 262, 286, 287, 291-293, 295
Vetāla, 398
Vettuvan-kovil, see Kalugumalai
Vibhava, P., 275
Vibhu, P., 281
Vibudha-āgāra, 138
Vicitra, P., 275
Vidarbha, L., 286
Vidarbharāṭ, 291
Vidārī, 32, 95
Vidhātā, 94
Vidyā, 11, 141
-dvāra, A., 317
-kalā, 317
Vidyādhara, 114, 247, 306, 343-345, 405, 406
Vighneśa, 234
Vihāra, A., 138, 197, 353
Vijaya, P., 101, 275, 278, 281
-bhadra, P., 229, 250
Vijayālaya Colīśvara, T., Narttamalai, 257
Vijayanagar, L., 192
Vikalpa, P., 266, 293
Vikṛti, 298
Vimala Sah, 200
Vimāna, A., 6, 52, 77, 131-133, 139, 141, 147, 155, 176, 178, 180, 183, 184, 196, 202, 203, 229, 230, 243, 270, 275, 277-281, 284, 287-289, 291-293, 344, 348, 350, 352, 359, 369, 371, 395, 415
Vimānacchanda, P., 270A, 271
Vimāna-pāla, A., 356, 399
-vatthu, 133
Vimuktakoṇa, P., 281
Vīṇā, 384
Vinatā, 423
Vināyaka, 275

Y

Z

PLATES

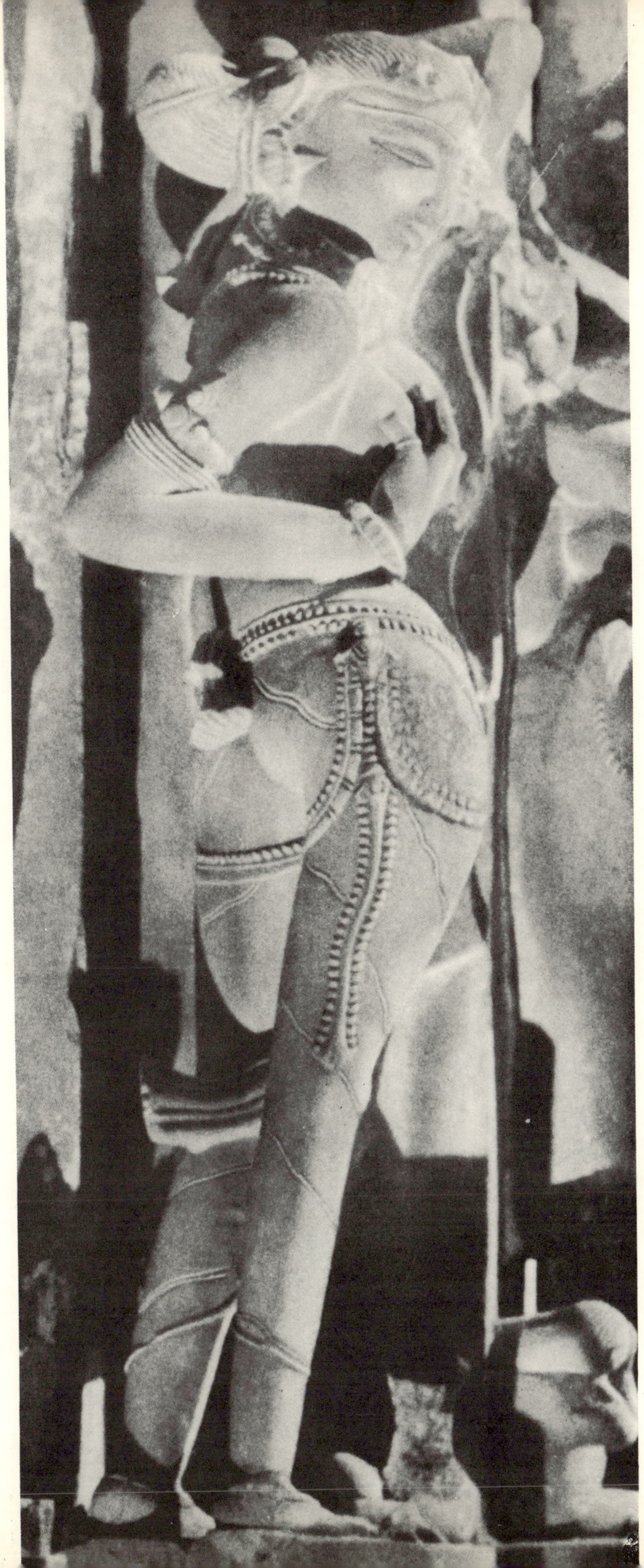

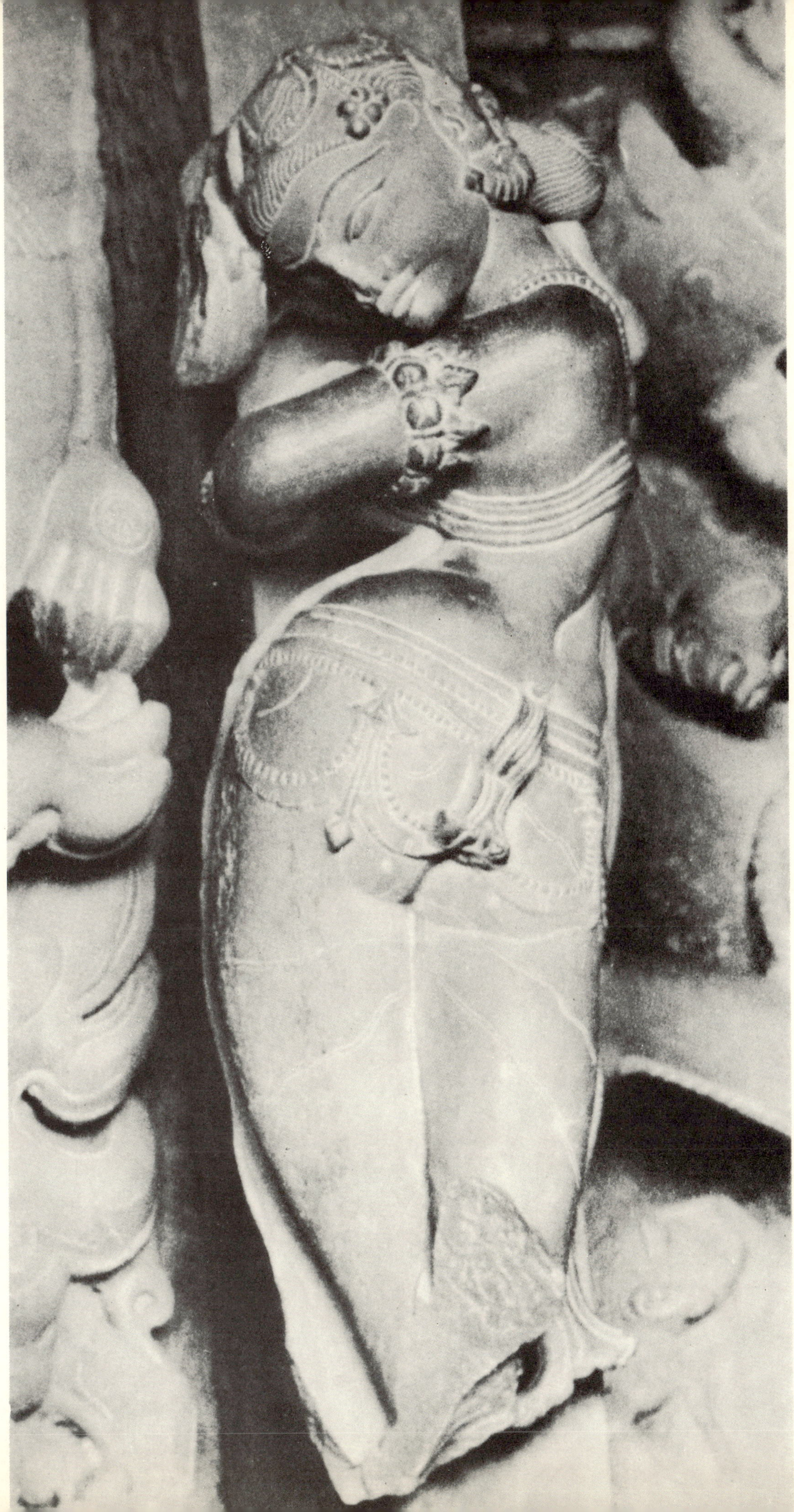

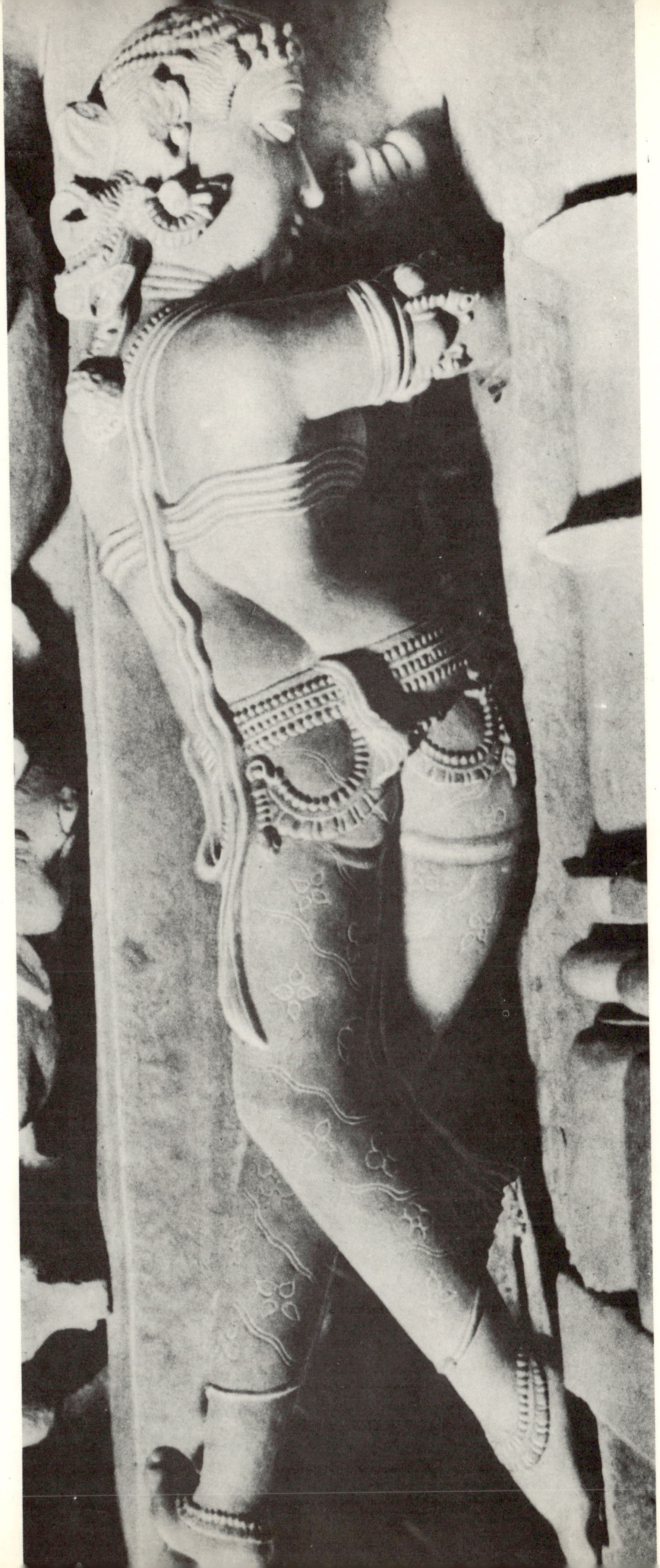

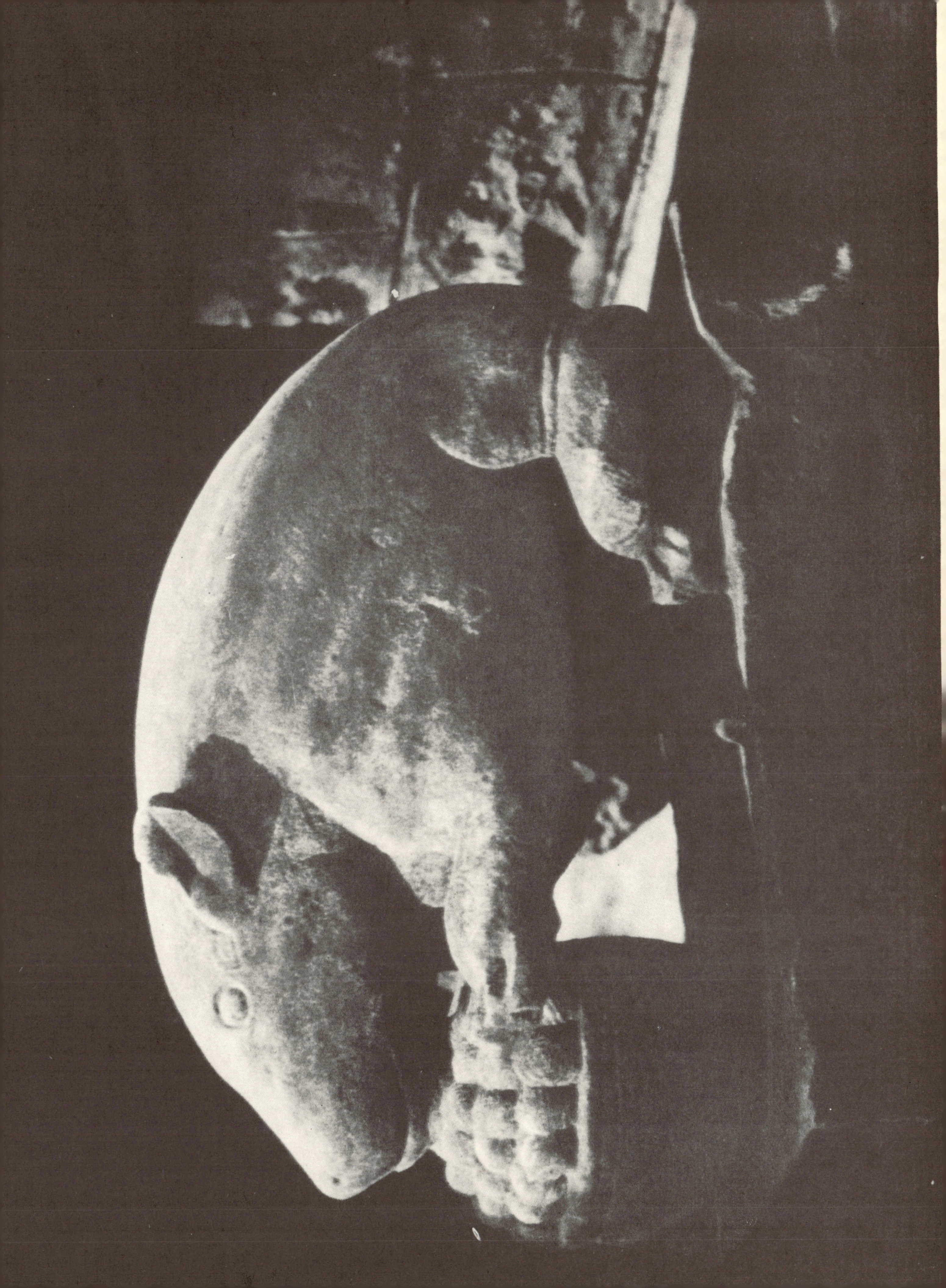

LV

LXXV

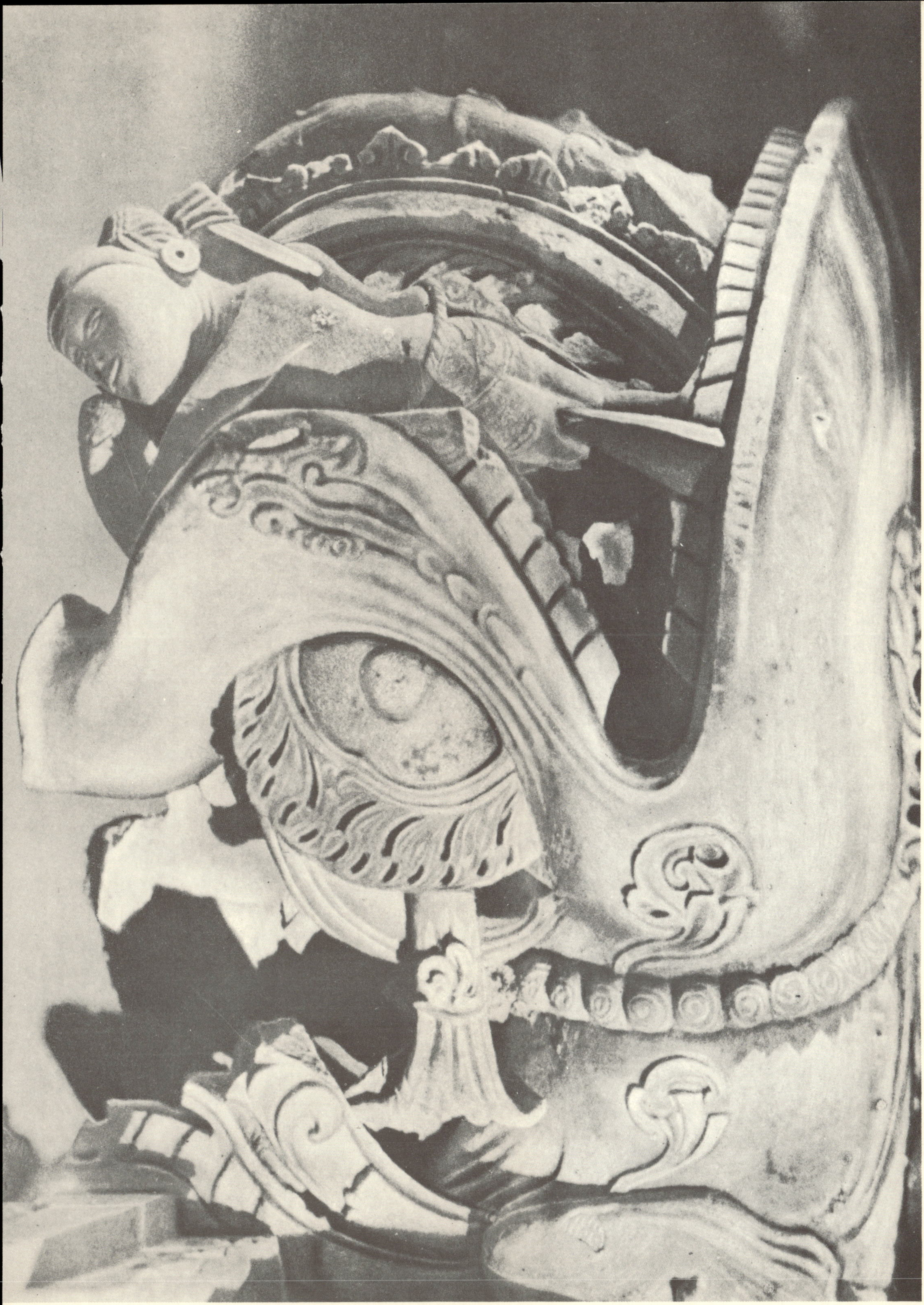